PULP METHODISM:

The Lives & Literature of Silas, Joseph & Salome Hocking, Three Cornish Novelists

by

Alan M. Kent

Pulp Methodism:
The Lives & Literature
of Silas, Joseph & Salome Hocking,
Three Cornish Novelists

Alan M. Kent

with a Foreword by John C.C. Probert

First published in 2002 by
Cornish Hillside Publications
St Austell, Cornwall PL25 4DW

© Alan M. Kent 2002
© John C.C. Probert 2002

ISBN 1 900 147 24 6 Paperback
ISBN 1 900 147 25 4 Cloth bound

Design and cover by
The Design Field, Truro, Cornwall TR12 2XN

Printed and bound by
Short Run Press Ltd, Exeter, Devon EX2 7LW

Dr Alan M. Kent, M.Phil., M.Ed. was born in St Austell and grew up in the china clay mining region of mid-Cornwall. He was educated at St Stephen-in-Brannel and the Universities of Cardiff and Exeter. In addition to being a poet, novelist and dramatist, he has several academic publications to his name. Recent works include *Wives, Mothers and Sisters: Feminism, Literature and Women Writers of Cornwall* (1998), *Voices from West Barbary: An Anthology of Anglo-Cornish Poetry 1549-1928* (2000) and *The Literature of Cornwall: Continuity, Identity, Difference 1000-2000* (2000). In 1998 he was winner of the Charles Lee Literary Competition and in 1999 winner of a Euroscript award. He has also co-edited *Looking at the Mermaid: A Reader in Cornish Literature 900-1900* (2000) and *Inside Merlin's Cave: A Cornish Arthurian Reader 1000-2000* (2000). His work has also featured in *Cornish Studies, Peripheral Visions* and *Celtic Geographies*.

John C.C. Probert was born in Redruth and gained his degree mainly in Theology. He is the Methodist District Archivist for Cornwall and the author of numerous works on Cornish Methodism including *The Sociology of Cornish Methodism* (1971), *Worship and Devotion of Cornish Methodism* (1978) and *Primitive Methodism in Cornwall: A History and Sociology* (n.d.). He is a regular contributor to *The Journal of the Cornish Methodist Historical Association*.

*To Ken Phillipps, Leonard W. Harman
and Michael E. Thorne
– three Hocking scholars*

Contents

Page 6
Acknowledgements

Page 7
Foreword

Page 9
Preface

Page 11
Introduction: The Heritage of Quintrel Quethiock

Chapter 1 – Page 31
Terras, Trelion, and Tin:
The Creation of a Written World, 1850-1878

Chapter 2 – Page 57
Who wants to be a Million-Selling novelist?:
Silas Kitto Hocking, 1850-1935

Chapter 3 – Page 97
Cornish and Christian Venturer: Joseph Hocking, 1860-1937

Chapter 4 – Page 127
Romancing Idealism: Salome Fifield Hocking,1859-1927

Chapter 5 – Page 143
From 'Pot Boiler Methodys' to 'Revolution':
The Literature of the Hockings, 1878-1937

Chapter 6 – Page 195
Friends, Relatives and Revivals: The Hocking Legacy, 1850-2001

Page 211
Conclusion: Pulp Methodism, Lost or Found?:
Old 'Ockings', New Readings 1937-2001

Page 221
Bibliography

Page 237
Index

Acknowledgements

In normal circumstances it is hard enough to research, assemble and tell the story of one writer's life. Pieces of the puzzle often remain scattered across the globe, with contradictions, frustrations and silences. To complete three literary jigsaws is not an easy task, and though there are a few tiny pieces missing, I hope I have completed three interesting pictures here. There are numerous friends, family and colleagues whom I need to thank for their help in the solution of these puzzles and, therefore, the preparation of this book.

Among these are Amy Hale, Charles Thomas, Tim Saunders, Cedric J. Appleby, Andrew C. Symons, Peter Faulkner, Roger F.S. Thorne, Brian Murdoch, John Hurst, John Rowe, Anne Dalton, James Whetter, Pat Phillipps, Courtney V. Smale, Joy Thacker, Dick and Carol Smythe, Arthur Bullock, Terry and Molly Richards, Mallvina Truscott, John Yeo, Una Dickinson, Michael Dorey, Justin Brooke, Ed Prynne, Peter Brooke, Peter Milln, Neil Kennedy, Alan Sanders, Barbara Luke, Ruth Clemo, Paul Faux, Mary Hacker, Morley Barbery, Clive Boutle, John Sansom, Melissa Hardie, David J. Keep, Michael Spinks, Derek R. Williams, Colin Brewer, Roger Winslade, Rosemary Thurlow, Les and Gill Goldman, Ben Luxon, Susie Crofut, Russell Webber, Steven Curgenven, Joan Shaw, the late Thomas Shaw and Paul Laity, and many people of St Stephen-in-Brannel.

To James Howell of the Burnley Express and David McGillivray and Graham Melville of the British Film Institute I owe much thanks, and also to Angela Broome and H.L. Douch of the Courtney Library, the Royal Institution of Cornwall, Terry Knight, Kim Cooper, Neil Williams and Joanne Hillman of the Cornish Studies Library, Cornwall Centre, Redruth, the staff at Truro and St Austell Libraries, the Morrab Library, Penzance, the Diocesan House, Truro, the Cornwall Family History Society, the Probate Registry, Bodmin, the Cornish Methodist Historical Association, the Cornwall Records Office, Truro, the Liverpool Empire Theatre, the Southport Reference Library and the John Rylands Library, Manchester. For genealogical research on the Hocking and Clemo families, I am much indebted to Paul Brewer.

I owe a special debt of gratitude to three people: the late Kenneth Phillipps who first encouraged me to read the novels of the Hockings, and two Hocking scholars – Leonard W. Harman and Michael E. Thorne. I hope that all three would look upon this work with favourable eyes. My thanks to John C.C. Probert for his guidance on Methodist social history and his illuminating foreword, and finally to my publisher – Charles Thurlow, who obtained the Harman manuscript and has been enormously helpful and patient throughout my writing of this book.

Dr Alan M. Kent, Lanbrebois / Probus, Kernow / Cornwall

Foreword

The three volume *Penguin Companion to Literature* has no entries for Silas, Joseph or Salome Hocking, though the two brothers merit a joint entry in the *Dictionary of National Biography*. There is a very good reason for this, for though they did not write 'great' literature (hence the word pulp in this book's title) they were of national importance. Silas, with *Her Benny*, was the first novelist ever to sell one million copies of one title. Works read on this scale had a big effect on the way their readers looked at life, at religion and may even have had an effect on the way they voted. Popular writing has influence both consciously and unconsciously. If you don't believe me, go into your nearest superstore and ask yourself why the girl on the tannoy always sounds as if she were the star of a soap opera.

This is not a bad parallel because the Hockings' novels fit into this genre. What is so different is that they are religious and are products of a relatively recent age which was vastly different. In attempting to write a best seller today, one cannot think of a much worse handicap than religion and Methodism into the bargain! In understanding them we need to know their place in Methodism which they also mirror. It must be stressed that Methodism is not a unity but a very broad Church. Denomination, period, social make up and whether one is referring to city, town or rural Methodism are but some of the factors making for its differences. The Wesleyans as a denomination were nearest to the Church of England, from which they sprang. The United Methodist Free Churches, to which the Hockings belonged, was a union of two groups who had seceded from the Wesleyans at two different periods. As a Church they had greater lay participation and more democracy.

With this democratic radicalism there often went more radical social views and we see this in Silas's later more sympathetic views on divorce, and the fact that Joseph and Salome were both cremated. Silas was in some ways more radical than the rest of the denomination for we learn in his *My Book of Memory* that he would not use the term Reverend. However, the Hockings were very different from the modern type of Bible Belt evangelist, who are so partial to condemning people to Hell and we also see a wider vision with Silas's social caring when ministering in Liverpool.

All that remains for me is to give a warm commendation to this book. Dr Kent not only gives us a most interesting, and well researched account of the Hocking novelists' lives but adds much local Cornish background detail, and we learn amongst other things, of their father's connection with the Terras Mine. In assessing the novels he notes how Joseph's themes changed with time. One has to remember that the spate of anti-Catholic novels come against a background of the Anglo-Catholic Revival in the Church of England. Though it partially revived the Anglicans, a price was paid in the worsening of Methodist and Anglican relations. These were generally good in Cornwall before the Oxford Movement, but this resulted in a polarisation with the Anglicans going theologically higher and the Methodists lower, and with John Henry Newman converting to Rome, they became more inflamed. The First World War marked a later turning point.

Finally he hints that the Hockings lived on to a time when their fiction was due to be pulped. They had a mighty long run for their money. It is difficult to believe that today's popular equivalents will last anywhere as near as long. Unfortunately, when one is married to one age, one becomes a widow to the next. If the books had something more of the eternal about them, they would have survived, but that is the nature of popular fiction.

But enough from me. Read on, and enjoy this most interesting book.

John C.C. Probert

Preface

Leaving the neon void of the Mersey Tunnel, I entered the city of Liverpool, head filled with old Beatles' songs, and one or two poems by Roger McGough. It was a crystal-clear spring afternoon on the 30th April 1994, and as I drove past Saturday afternoon shoppers, the Royal Liver Building, and the Anglican Cathedral on the distant horizon, it felt a good distance away from the parish of St Stephen-in-Brannel, and the china clay familiarity of mid-Cornwall. Just across from me were the now quiet docks, undergoing renovation and renewal. I had to wonder how many ships had once sailed across the globe from those basins. It must have been an incredible place to have lived one hundred years ago.

Passing the concrete, steel and glass of St John's Shopping Centre, then Lime Street train station, my destination suddenly came into view. The grand building of the Empire theatre itself was bedecked in scaffolding and, like many other structures in the city, was having its stonework cleansed after a century or so of dirt and grime, but the huge posters and billboards across its frontage confirmed that this was the place. By now, a matinee performance had ended and the audience were just leaving, clutching programmes, animated and smiling. Later, it was my turn to watch events unfold upon the stage of the vast Empire theatre.

What was I watching?

The performance was Anne Dalton's adaptation of a novel still very famous in Liverpool, simply titled *Her Benny*. Indeed, for many years, the novel was standard reading in Liverpool's primary and secondary schools. At the end of the show, the musical received rapturous applause. The audience was thrilled. At this point, at the zenith of the journey I had undertaken, an irony sank in, that here in Liverpool, the name of *Her Benny's* author, the Cornish-born novelist, Silas Kitto Hocking, was still respected, still part of the city's history and conscience. Five hundred miles away in Cornwall, relatively few knew of this tremendous success a century on, from its first publication and reception.

Personally, that performance was the start of many years of research, and as I left the theatre that night, driving past the docks, re-entering the Mersey Tunnel, I knew that I had to re-dress the imbalance. Direction and a future in Liverpool were assured. The M5 and A30 taking me westwards told me that Silas Kitto, and, as I soon discovered, his brother Joseph, and sister Salome, would no longer be lost to Cornwall.

APOLLO LEISURE & BCC PRESENT
Anne Dalton's AWARD WINNING

HER BENNY

Smash hit musical for all the family under the direction of Christopher G. Sandford

RETURNS BY POPULAR DEMAND

DAILY POST
"HER BENNY musical hits the right note..... Show looks a tour triumph..."

Southport Visitor
"HER BENNY..... was simply one of the best theatre productions ever staged..... and those who missed it, missed a real treat."

THE GUARDIAN
"It looks like an effective co-production between that upstart Lionel Bart, and the silver-tongued Andrew Lloyd-Webber."

Lancashire Life
"'Triumphant' hardly does it justice. Cheers whistles and wave after wave of wild, excited applause rattled off the rafters of this vast theatre."

EMPIRE THEATRE, LIME STREET, LIVERPOOL L1 1JE
TUESDAY 26th APRIL TILL SATURDAY 7th MAY 1994
AT 7.30pm
MATINEES THURSDAY, FRIDAY & SATURDAY AT 2.00pm (1st WEEK)
WEDNESDAY & SATURDAY AT 2.00pm (2nd WEEK)

Tickets from £5.00 to £12.50. Concessions available

BOX OFFICE
051 709 1555

GROUP BOOKINGS
051 709 6699

Advertising leaflet for *Her Benny*, 1994

Introduction:
The Heritage of Quintrel Quethiock

> *"But I was puzzled greatly. Quethiock was not a common name, and I had never heard of another man being christened Quintrel. Who then would be likely to assume the cognomen that was given to me because my mother owned a tract of land of that name in an obscure parish in Cornwall?"*
>
> From Joseph Hocking, In the Sweat of Thy Brow, 1920[1]

This book is an introductory account of the life and work of three Anglo-Cornish writers – Silas Kitto Hocking, Joseph Hocking and Salome Hocking Fifield. To most of the community of present-day Cornwall, let alone the wider population of these islands, their names now mean nothing. Despite this contemporary ignominy their novels, books and essays were once consumed and read by millions of people, forming a particular genre that I term 'pulp Methodism', perhaps the most popularly purchased texts in English-speaking territories. In addition to documenting the lives of these writers, this book also aims to consider why the Hockings were a unique phenomenon, why their work became so popular, and why it finally fell out of favour. In so doing, we shall cross the many boundaries between biography, family history, other writers and activists, the religious and literary history of these islands, and more specifically, the Hockings' origins in Cornwall.

Cornwall, it sometimes seems, is remarkably blinkered when it comes to documenting its literary history. It runs an annual arts and literary festival in Fowey devoted to the legacy of Daphne du Maurier,[2] and will go to great lengths to try to save a two-up, two-down clay-worker's cottage at Goonamarris, once occupied by the Anglo-Cornish poet Jack Clemo.[3] Despite the massive importance of the *Poldark* historical romance series, and its resultant and on-going economic impact on tourism, it is still often judged as inauthentic and popular – pulp fiction for the non-Cornish.[4] Cornwall has just about managed to gather enough enthusiasm to celebrate the life and work of one of its finest nineteenth-century poets – John Harris.[5] It still needs to properly present to the contemporary world one of the finest medieval dramas ever conceived – *Ordinalia* – on the scale of York, Chester and Oberammergau. It is only very lately, despite being honoured as a Nobel Laureate and the winner of the Booker Prize, that William Golding – a Cornishman born in Mount Wise in Newquay – has been truly celebrated as a great Cornish writer.[6]

And where in all of this celebration, this creation of a 'national' literary past – are three writers, three writers who few even consider, let alone choose to buy one of their dusty hardback books from some second-hand bookshop? The Hockings collectively put Cornwall on the mental map of more readers in Britain and America in the late nineteenth and early twentieth-century than any other writers during that phase. And yet, Cornwall lets these literary giants sleep, not knowing what lies beneath. This book dares to wake these giants, seeking a long-needed redress of this imbalance.

If the Hockings still have a reputation in Cornwall and elsewhere, it is probably amongst an elderly population who once received their novels – re-packaged and re-marketed – as Sunday School prizes at Chapel Anniversaries and Tea-treats in the early and middle decades of the twentieth century.[7] There, they could, in new, cheaply made editions, read about the further adventures of 'ultra'-Cornish heroes such as Quintrel Quethiock – a name familiar, but his actions drawn from further back in Cornish and British history. So, who were the Hockings? Fortunately, their work is gradually beginning to be better known. John A. Vickers' recent *Dictionary of Methodism in Britain and Ireland* carries the following entry on the Hocking family:

> *James and Elizabeth Hocking of St Stephen-in-Brannel, Cornwall had two sons who entered the UMFC ministry, Silas Kitto Hocking (1850-1935; e.m. 1869) had a popular ministry in Southport 1888-96 before devoting himself to writing and Liberal politics, resigning from the ministry in 1906. He wrote nearly 100 novels and his second book Her Benny sold well-over one million copies. He wrote his autobiography My Book of Memory (1923). His brother Joseph Hocking (1860-1937); e.m. 1884) also wrote nearly 100 novels, in which Cornwall, an idealised Methodism, war, jingoism and papistical infiltration of England (e.g. in The Scarlet Woman) were prominent themes. In 1909 the Catholic Truth Society published a collection of pamphlets entitled A Brace of Bigots (Dr Horton and Mr Joseph Hocking). Hocking and R.F. Horton replied the next year with Shall Rome Reconquer England? His daughter Anne Hocking was also a prolific novelist. Salome Hocking (d.1927), sister to Silas and Joseph and married to the London publisher, A.C. Fifield, was the author of about ten novels similar to those of her bothers, some of them published by the UMFC and WM Book Rooms.*[8]

Initial studies of the Hockings have been completed. Over his life, the bibliophile Leonard Harman assembled an enormous collection of Hocking novels and completed a preliminary survey of their life and work.[9] Harman was an amateur scholar, however, and the manuscript he kindly passed to myself and my publisher, was a selection of jottings and observations he had recorded over the years. Sadly, much of the material was unreferenced and many of the photographs contained within it were photocopies of original documents. A second fuller study was completed by Roger Thorne, based on the knowledge and research his father Michael had completed.[10] Though brief in its biographical detail, the booklet was the first study of the Hockings to be assembled. It is not perfect, and a few more titles have since come to light, but Thorne's work is a very helpful starting point.

Finally, there are those studies and interviews of the Hockings which were completed in the post-war period, usually for local newspapers and magazines in Cornwall, in particular, by scholars such as H.M. Creswell Payne and K.C. Phillipps,[11] who were able to recall first-hand, their experiences of meeting the Hockings and reading their texts in their early context prior to the Second World War. It is however, Harman, Thorne, Payne and Phillipps, who we might label the first generation of Hocking scholars, and this work is much indebted to their efforts. For my own part, in two recent volumes,[12] I have tried to draw attention to the work of Silas Kitto, Joseph and Salome and promote them as core contenders in any surveys of Anglo-Cornish literature.

Building on these early studies, there are, therefore, a number of methods of deconstructing and analysing the life and work of the Hockings, and I would like to allude to these next. This early scholarship, useful as it was, was too keen on showing apparently how unfashionable and formulaic the novels had become. The debate was constructed in a modernist context, where it was easy to criticise the works for their pulp qualities. The novels were read outside of their original context and compared to more canonized texts, sniggering at plotlines and illustrations, and looked upon as quirky footnotes in the story of British literary studies.

It would be fair to say that this was no different than much other literary scholarship being completed on popular texts during the post-war phase, but since then radical change in British, European and indeed global society had meant both a re-evaluation of literary studies, in particular to a canon once only described as 'English',[13] as well as our response to popular literatures of both the past and present. The growth in the field of Cultural Studies, in general, has been a positive one, facilitating new fields of study unheard of a few decades ago.[14]

Post-Modernism and Cultural studies has therefore given a favourable response to that judged Popular.[15] After all many of our high cultural symbols – started life as ones much more popular and throwaway.[16] As Bennett notes:

> There are many good reasons for studying Popular fiction. The best though, is that it matters. In the many and varied forms in which they are circulated, popular fictions saturate the rhythms of everyday life both in the past and present. In so doing, they have helped generations to define their sense of themselves, shaping their desires, fantasies, imagined pasts and projected futures.[17]

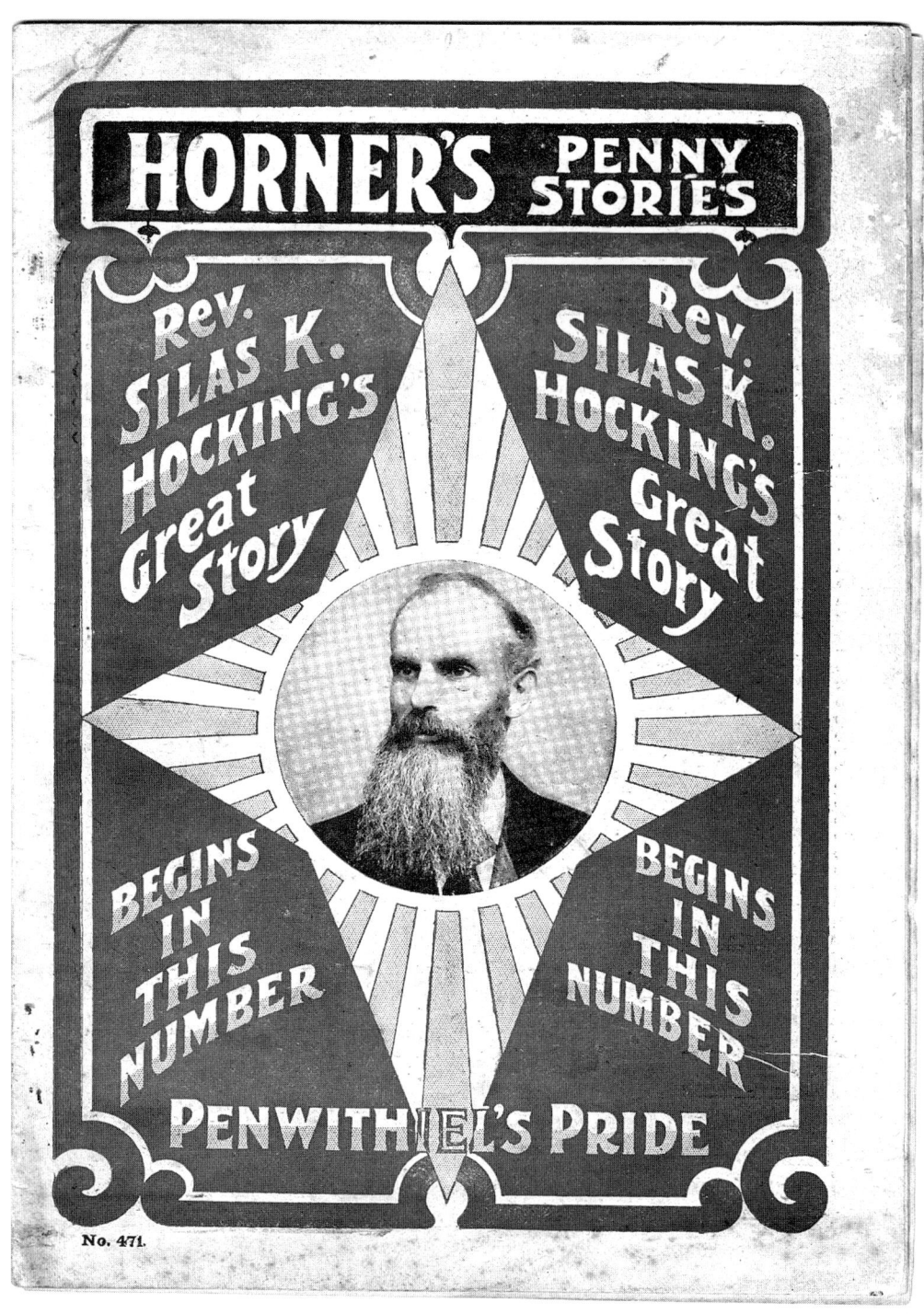

Horner's Penny Stories, No 471 published sometime in 1902. Original size 184mm by 267mm. Penwithiel's Pride was published in book form as *A Bonnie Saxon* in 1903

Yet, popular culture is still much maligned and misunderstood by many observers. Another definition is therefore helpful. One way of considering the identity of the field of canonized Literature is, to realise that it is dependent on a 'significant other' a popular or 'paraliterature'. The implication is that we, as readers and scholars, will not want to go there, in the same way that many observers have been unwilling to move away from the apparent hegemony of dominant literatures. This said, the uninitiated may still assume that the study of such a paraliterature – away from the imagined hegemony of dominant literatures (like the emergence of a genuine Anglo-Cornish literature[18]) involves a process of familiarisation with a number of 'second-rate' novelists, devoting time to peripheral works. The approach here is clearly not sympathetic to this view. What is important is to show the connections between the literary artefact and the social context in which it moves and has its being.[19] This is a much more productive mechanism for reading these texts, since we are dealing, with 'ethical fiction'. The Hockings' books never existed in a vacuum. Rather they were circulated in a specific, cultural and historical context, to put people on the 'straight and narrow'.

Cultural and Popular Literary Studies allow us the mechanisms to appreciate the Hockings' work. As novelists, the Hockings' writing, in part, was shaped by Weekly and Monthly magazines and periodicals. The form in Britain, had been established as far back as the *Gentleman's Magazine* of 1731, but the nineteenth century brought an unprecedented number to the public's attention. Most people know that Charles Dickens wrote several of his novels for serialisation in such magazines.[20] He developed the popular characters and plot-lines according to public interest and enthusiasm, even if this meant killing off some characters early on, or in some cases introducing new heroes or heroines mid-way through. Interestingly, these magazines and periodicals, have over time, been readily associated with Dickens, but less so with other writers. The fact was that increases in literacy in Britain,[21] brought about increased demand for inexpensive publications. Dickens was one part of a massive publishing programme across Britain. In the later half of the century, Weeklies became popular vehicles for developing writers.

The religious institutions were not far behind, with their own Christian-themed publications having enormous circulations around Britain. Technically, they were easy to produce and distribute, and they introduced the cliff-hanger to audiences, as readers impatiently awaited the next instalment. The clichéd picture of these is of the patriarch of the household reading the narrative aloud to the gripped family, and while this pattern of consumption occurred, no doubt there was much individual consumption too. The origins of pulp Methodism lie here. *Horner's Penny Stories* is one of the best examples.[22]

Relatively few publications of this kind have survived in Cornwall, but the Cornu-English 'get one over on they up-the-line' verse narratives and stories of Tregellas, Forfar and others were proving immensely popular. Comic in tone, they showed publishers and writers the potential for sales in an industrialised Cornwall.[23] Cornwall itself of course, had been established outside of Cornwall as a romantic and inspirational landscape as far back at the Napoleonic Wars, when the picturesque had to be found in these islands rather than on the continent.[24] This, coupled with a supposed heritage of smuggling, wrecking, sea-faring and Arthuriana made Cornwall the site of numerous fictions and melodramas in the nineteenth-century, despite what I have described elsewhere, as their 'extraordinary artificiality' in their telling of Cornish experience.[25] The developing religious tracts also relied heavily upon locations such as Cornwall, which put characters to moral tests, pushing their spiritual limits on windy clifftops, in dark caves, or down deep mineshafts.[26] Cornwall's industrial climate also provided for readers elsewhere who were tasting their own experiences of rapid industrialisation. Unscrupulous mine bosses, exploited labourers (chapel-going of course) and beautiful heroines formed a kind of narrative empathetic to events outside of Cornwall. The imagined state of Cornwall mattered a great deal, for it was endemic of the wider imagining of Britain.

The wider imagining further increased when the stories emerged in novels proper. The Hockings formed the staple diet of the reading of many British working-class homes, once a level of cultural literacy had been achieved towards the end of the nineteenth century. These Proletarian intellectuals were not always expected to think for themselves by an autodidactic establishment, yet many circumvented their expected future by self-education. Jonathan Rose in his impressive survey of the intellectual life of the British Working Classes, has detailed the relationship told by C. H. Rolph (b.1901), between his father – a London policeman, and his subscription to a so-called 'best books' list, published by the adult educator and Member of Parliament, Sir John Lubbock:

> If you already knew your way around the literary canon, it is easy to sneer at Lubbock's list; but it was enormously popular among readers like Rolph's father, who was eager to make up for an education that had been denied him, and was not ashamed to ask for a roadmap. Without it, he would never have gone beyond the authors popular in his family circle: Edgar Wallace, Silas and Joseph Hocking, Stanley Weyman, Anthony Hope, W.J. Locke, Jeffery Farnd, Emma Worboise, Mrs. Henry Wood, and Mrs Humphry Ward.[27]

Although the Hockings did not meet with Lubbock's approval, evidence from Rolph proves their popularity. He comments how (with reference to all the above authors) 'their books went through our household like a benignly infectious plague'.[28] In Rolph we are only considering one household, so it is easy to imagine the popularity of such authors across the rest of Britain, as well as the working classes' preference for Hockings over 'best books'.

I hope so far to have introduced the reader to the 'pulp', or popular aspects of this volume. I now turn to Methodism itself. To understand the history of Methodism, we have to step back into history. The Protestant break with the Roman church of the sixteenth century is reflected in both the theory and practice of Protestant worship. One issue is the status of the officiating clergy: Protestants felt that Christians needed no human intermediary – no living priest, or dead saint – to gain access to God. Protestants also eliminated celibacy and put a greater emphasis on laymen being preachers and leaders of worship, at the same time, departing from Rome in the interpretation of sacramental rituals. Rejecting priestly mediation, Protestants looked for signs of the direct activity of the Holy Spirit, as well as dismissing imagery.[29] Modernity in the form of the Enlightenment also assisted with this reform, as human reasoning was claimed to have a central role. It gave particular privilege to reason in proposals for the regulation of public and spiritual life. At the same time, theories of human nature were implicit, if not explicit, in political rhetoric and journalistic comment. People were able to discuss the nature and purpose of government and the proper training of rulers and administrators.

As Davies, and Rack detail, in the late 1720s John Wesley (1703-91), then an Anglican undergraduate at Oxford, collected fellow students in a circle others nicknamed the Methodists for their methodical and enlightened approach to Bible study and church attendance.[30] The group included John's brother, Charles (1707-88) and George Whitefield (1714-70). After a visit to a Moravian Pietist community, and three days after his brother Charles's conversion experience, John Wesley felt his own heart 'strangely warmed'.[31] Wesley began to preach to public gatherings, often of miners and workers, outside the established churches. In the fifty-three years until his death, he preached over 40,000 sermons, averaging fifteen a week, and travelled 200,000 miles, mainly on horseback. At first he had hoped his movement would tap Reformation spirituality and revitalize the Church of England from within, but Wesley oversaw its organization as an independent denomination.[32] Importantly, for our account here, it is only after Wesley's death that the Revival and social influence of Methodism begins properly.

The rules of the society and devotional groups suggest that the ideal Methodist was to be led from seeking for salvation to conversion, then to the cultivation of a holy life, and finally to the experience of Christian Perfection.[33] However, despite his own classic conversion experience, Wesley was no typical evangelist. Instead, he became wary of seeing justification by faith as sufficient in itself for salvation. This, for Martin Luther, was the very essence of salvation, but for Wesley, it was rather the means to a greater end. "Perfection" could be achieved through disciplined piety, but might be given in a moment in response to faith in Christ. He thus emphasised the importance of creating good works and constant dependence on divine grace.

Having broadly defined the history and main aims of Methodism, we might also consider the parallel concept of nonconformity. The word is now applied generally to all dissenters with Protestant sympathies, though more properly means the refusal to conform to the doctrines, policy or discipline of any Established Church. As Munsun details, the term was first used in the seventeenth century, of those who, while first agreeing with the doctrines of the Church of England, refused to conform, especially in matters of ceremony.[34] Methodism's origins are different, and Wesley would certainly not have accepted the term,[35] but in the nineteenth century, the term nonconformist conscience was applied to both. This conscience has ramifications, however, since many nonconfomists were prejudiced against all forms of fiction because it was 'untrue'. Such thought greatly impacted on both the Hockings' writing and readers' reception of their 'pulp Methodism'.

I am not a scholar of Methodism, and the above comments greatly simplify the complexities of Methodist thought. Neither does this book purport to be a history of Cornish Methodism. There are, however, a number of useful texts which give a full and critical history of the particularly Cornish take on Methodism. To some extent, much of the best-known scholarship on Methodism in Cornwall, seemed to emerge in the 1960s. This decade witnessed the publication of the standard works, including John Pearce's *The Wesleys in Cornwall* (1964), Charles Thomas' *Methodism and Self-Improvement in Nineteenth-Century Cornwall* (1965), Thomas Shaw's *The Bible Christians* (1965) and *A History of Cornish Methodism* (1967), followed in 1971 with John C. C. Probert's influential *The Sociology of Cornish Methodism*.[36] These studies were paralleling a post-war decline in chapel attendance, and on a wider scale, as Sinfield, and Brown show, a more secular and existentialist Britain.[37] In Cornwall, Methodism was relinquishing its social control, and becoming marginalised.

Earlier studies had been made however, when Methodism was at the height of its power. Peter Prescott's 1871 book, *The Case of Cornish Methodism Considered; The Missing Lynch-Pin,* comes to mind, as does Lawrence Maker's popular *Cob and Moorstone: The Curious History of some Cornish Methodist Churches,* published in 1935,[38] yet they tended to set up an agenda of individualistic studies of specific churches and chapels.[39] It took Pearce, Thomas, Shaw and Probert to begin to assess the full picture, showing how Methodism appealed to the lower middle class,[40] and how people were effectively encouraged to join the 'club' and share views, and more recently other Cornish historians started to relate these assessments to a wider reassessment of Cornish history, society and literature at home,[41] and abroad.[42]

One of the most important studies, following in the footsteps of Probert's work was Bernard Semmel's *The Methodist Revolution* (1974).[43] Semmel paralleled Probert's work in Cornwall, which was the most radical reassessment of Methodism for a number of years. He was at pains to show how wrong it was that most liberal, secular-minded historians viewed Methodism as a regressive, repressive force,[44] largely responsible for the fact that a violent counterpart to the French Revolution never occurred in Britain. Semmel demonstrated how Methodist doctrine, had been presented in a highly unfavourable light, generally accompanied by the view that Wesley and his associates were unsystematic theologicals, hopelessly confused and intellectually inadequate. To some extent, even some of the Cornish-based scholarship had taken this line.[45] Semmel, however, saw Methodism as a revolutionary force – both in spiritual and social terms – with an essentially liberal and progressive ideology, confirming and helping to advance the movement of Britain from a traditional to a modern society.

Probert, and Semmel, therefore, assisted in shaping a thorough reassessment of Methodism, which understood its pan-European radicalism, rather than that which was insular and 'conservative'. This latter position has been a difficult monolith for Methodist scholarship to remove, but the methodological position argued here will hopefully witness its further removal. The Hockings themselves would have had much sympathy with the positions taken by Probert, and Semmel; they understood Methodism within European theology and never viewed it anything other than as a radical, reforming force.

On-going research into Methodism in Cornwall is carried on by the Cornish Methodist Historical Association,[46] who regularly publish a journal containing the latest research in the field. For the uninitiated, Susan Pellowe's *A Wesley Family Book of Days* (1994) forms a very readable contemporary introduction to Methodist culture in Cornwall,[47] as does Thomas Shaw's *A Methodist Guide to Cornwall* (1991).[48] The republication of John Rowe's 1953 work *Cornwall in the Age of the Industrial Revolution* in 1993, facilitated the inclusion of two new chapters examining Methodism in Cornwall,[49] and this, alongside David Luker's 1987 thesis, *Cornish Methodism, Revivalism, and Popular Belief, c.1780-1870*, are presently the best scholarship available. Another recent work on Methodism in the Cornish context is Jeremy Lake, Jo Cox and Eric Berry's *Diversity and Vitality: The Methodist and Nonconformist Chapels of Cornwall* (2001) which although primarily an archaeological survey of the buildings, contains some history as well, including an assessment of Cornwall as 'a stronghold of Methodism', the battle for control amongst various factions, and a section on the distinctive nature of Methodism in the territory.[50] Thomas and Mattingly meanwhile, provide a useful picture of the complexities of Methodism within the overall context of Christianity within Cornwall:

> *Methodism started as an Anglican reform movement but after Wesley's death in 1791, broke away. John Wesley's first visits to Cornwall in 1743-6 coincided with the Jacobite scare and rebellion which tried to restore Catholicism in Britain. Wesley's long hair and ability to draw crowds led local J.P.s to arrest him, but after 1746, he became a regular and revered visitor to Cornwall. Like the Anglican church in the mid-17th century, Methodism was prone to splits and divisions, often on class lines. This accounts for the many different types of Methodist chapels found in any Cornish parish today. The Bible Christians, founded by William Bryant of Luxulyan with a simpler style of worship were one such splinter group.*[51]

This summarises much change and development. Undoubtedly, Wesley's initial arrest arose more from his preaching and barging into parishes than any real Jacobite connection. What however, should also be addressed at this point is a re-examination of Methodism's apparent 'union' with mining and fishing culture in Cornwall, as a cosy, symbiotic relationship. This myth is perpetrated by many scholars, and is an all too simple a view of the real nuances and complexities of Methodist culture.[52] Neither is it good enough anymore to present a picture of a somehow unified Cornish spiritual culture, rooted in Methodism in particular, as an example of Cornish ethnicity. It is important to say from outset that the two do not always merge: for instance, throughout history it has been possible to be both Cornish and Jewish, Cornish and Pagan, Cornish and Roman Catholic.[53] The Hockings may well have wished for an ideologically Methodist Cornwall (as paradoxically do many scholars and writers now), but they were aware (albeit critically) of non-heterogeneous religious beliefs in operation.

All of this said, it is, I believe, difficult for some contemporary readers to understand just how radical, progressive and innovative the Hockings were for their time period. There is no doubt, as this book will show, that for Silas and Joseph at least, their radicalism both in the Methodist ministry, and then their subsequent rebellion against the shackles of the Ministry itself, caused an enormous amount of anxiety for those in control of the Methodist Church. For them, the Hockings were dangerous men and women: they were nonconformists writing fiction. The subtext throughout this book is a revolt against the very faith that had shaped and nourished them as children, resulting at the end with some revolutionary views. It happened because both Silas and Joseph knew there needed to be new, perhaps more entertaining methods, of spiritually educating the public. Their moral fictions – their 'pulp Methodisms' – were as of as much concern to the late Victorian Methodist church, as many youth cultural activities are now.[54] They took an incredible chance, but it was one that they fundamentally believed in. Their rebellion was of the highest order. Salome too, although not, rebelling in the Methodist church in the same way; ideologically was committed to some of the most progressive and innovative ways of living that could be imagined. Her idealism was ahead of its time, and brought with it associated accusations of immorality. Her Socialist views were another matter altogether, showing a form of radicalism which even her brothers could not support. As Treve Crago has shown, Socialism was not popular in Cornwall, until a brief 'flirtation' at the end of the First World War.[55]

Yet, as the history of Christianity in Cornwall, and elsewhere has shown (not to mention other beliefs), it is the rebel that often causes the greatest change, the most spiritual development and, at the end of the day, the most followers. One only has to look at the life of Jesus Christ as an example, although there are others from every religion on the planet. Rebellion and radicalism are actually more intimately tied to religion than we imagine.[56] In their own minds these writers saw both the Reformation and evangelical Christianity as part of that rebellion. Put another way, the nonconformist conscience is given not only its utterance here, but finds its full-blown, powerful voice in Silas Kitto, Joseph and Salome Hocking. The Hockings were all products, in both the spiritual *and* material sense, of the Enlightenment, as we have seen above, yet they were also a reaction within it. Paradoxically, in some ways they were actually nearer Romanticism; issues which were to be played out in all their fictions, whether set in Liverpool or Cornwall, on the plains of Lincolnshire or America, or in the trenches of the First World War.

These issues are important when it comes to our consideration of Cornish Methodism. To the uninitiated outsider, and even to some inside Cornwall, the phenomenon of Cornish Methodism, as deconstructed by Semmel, and Probert, may seem safely internalised and ethnically associated. We need to constantly step back from this however, and reassert Methodism's wider place within the effects of the Reformation and the Enlightenment across Europe. That way, the dependable narrative that is Cornish Methodism becomes, not only reflective of changes and developments here, but wider European shifts in philosophy, religion and literature over the time. The signifiers of that history – from John and Charles Wesley themselves – to other notables like William Flamank, Samuel Drew, 'Foolish Dick' Hampton, Catherine Bryant, Billy Bray, Dr George Smith, Mark Guy Pearse[57] – are markers on a line of progressive radicalism and revolt against what they viewed as outmoded beliefs and unsustainable practice. William Carvosso of Mousehole is part of this heritage,[58] as was the Hockings, and their later inheritor and relative Jack Clemo. The seemingly conservative markings of Methodism of my and probably many other people's own childhood – tea-treats, temperance, Gwennap Pit, anniversaries, Sunday School, preachers and sermons –

were once intended as both progressive symbols of nonconformity and an alternate social life, so where – with declining numbers, closing chapels and even proposed unions with the Anglican church – did it all go wrong?

In many ways, it went wrong in exactly the same way the Hockings' books went wrong: there was a cultural shift against all the different strands of the tradition. The initial radicalism and revolt became the *status quo,* and was then attacked not only from other religious movements, many evangelical in nature, but also by a world which no longer saw the need for the Christian belief of prior generations, instead moving to atheism or materialism, as well as the search for other alternative spiritual paths.[59] The Hockings knew their revolt had become the establishment: in many ways, this is why their later novels become weaker, more polarised, because they were trying to fight back from the corner they had been forced into. They had survived many attacks, but could not have predicted the questioning and doubts surrounding Christianity that occurred in Britain after the First World War. Like Methodism itself, it was inevitably unsustainable. For a number of years there had been various social shifts and changes which had eaten away at its roots. Jack Clemo was later to put his finger on it when he comments that eventually 'they were rendered impotent as creators and interpreters by the very wholesomeness of their mental texture'.[60] Maybe this not only applies to the Hockings' pulp writings, but to Methodists themselves.

We have dealt so far, with two methods of understanding the work of the Hockings: both within Popular Culture and also within Methodism as a reaction to wider European Enlightenment. There is a third model as well, locating the Christian rebel within the context of a long line of worthies in British Literature, who battled against organised religion. We might begin with John Bunyan, author of *The Pilgrim's Progess* (1678) who was gaoled for twelve years for preaching without a license.[61] The Brontë sisters rebelled in the parsonage at Haworth, Emily in particular, author of *Wuthering Heights* (1847) being the most vehement,[62] while the Powys brothers, – Llewelyn, Theodore Francis, and John Cowper (author of *A Glastonbury Romance* (1932)[63]) rebelled against the moral conventions of Montacute vicarage. Likewise, Jack Clemo, alluded to at the start of this Introduction, and interestingly, as a relation of the Hockings (considered later in this volume), was to rebel against his mid-Cornwall chapel community, arguing for both the reality of the supernatural invasion through Christ, and other uncompromising unorthodoxy in both *Confession of a Rebel* (1949) and *The Invading Gospel: A Return to Faith* (1958).[64] In 1969 Clemo himself was to comment on how the Hockings fitted this continuum of Christian rebellion:

Some of the finest imaginative writing of the past century has been produced through the revolt of sensitive minds against the close pressure of organised religion. Personal insight has outgrown the formula, or the current "climate of opinion" has befogged it, and the resulting quest for another medium of faith had involved literary self-expression in a variety of moods and forms. Sometimes the explosion of creative life has come from an individual in solitude; here and there several members of the same family have defied the authority of tradition and written out their protective heresies. And where the revolt had been most intense the new vision had drawn to itself the aesthetic tone and idiom of the landscape amid which it was evolved, and fused with the deepest strata of racial inheritance.[65]

Though understanding the Hockings fitted into this wider scheme, Clemo was not one to be overpraising. There were, in his view, problems with the Hockings entering such a tradition:

Only when they had established themselves as representatives of the "Nonconformist conscience" did they entertain their readers with novels of adventure and romance in Cornwall. In considering them as Cornish writers, therefore, we have to notice certain inhibitions that may have resulted from the early struggle which made the associations of their childhood distasteful to them when they had escaped to a higher social level.[66]

One can understand Clemo's position and even sympathise with it, and yet he was not entirely correct. Firstly, the "Nonconformist conscience" survived into the 'novels of adventure and romance in Cornwall'. Secondly, as this book will show, the distaste of their childhood, may well have been governed by factors, other than their social progression. We might then qualify Clemo's observation by understanding that all the Hockings were to defy 'the authority of tradition' and wrote 'their protective heresies' in a time when it was particularly difficult to do.

Some other observations are pertinent here. Clemo's 'deepest strata of racial inheritance' might be recast in contemporary cultural studies as *identity*. To the Hockings that identity was clearly Cornish, and it was certainly Celtic. That they were Cornish is unmistakable. From the characterisation of figures such as Quintrel Quethiock, to narrative and Cornu-English speech, to ideology and history, it is clear the Hockings wrote from a fully Cornish perspective. Even the novels of Liverpool, Manchester and other urban centres present a curiously 'Corni-cised' view of the world. More contentious to the reader is how the Hockings considered themselves as Celtic. As Hale and Payton, and Pittock explain, defining Celtic is always a difficult task to begin with,[67] and yet despite the fact that the Celtic Revival in Cornwall, was only just emerging at the same time the Hockings were writing,[68] they intrinsically viewed themselves as Celtic.[69] Perhaps, as we shall see, this was down to the early narratives told to them by their mother, or maybe the Hockings were aware of the wider reinvention of Cornwall. Whatever the background conjecture, Silas Kitto, Joseph and Salome all regularly stop their narratives to debate issues of Celticity. Within their early fiction, it tended to be romanticised and 'twilight' rather than nationalistic and revivalist,[70] but as the Revival in Cornwall gained ground over time, aspects of the latter were incorporated.[71]

Interestingly, this view of identity provides some considerable difficulties. For one thing, those interested in subjects Celtic have tended to either look upon its heritage as Catholic, or more recently Pagan. Ireland and Brittany are particularly good examples of the former, whereas Cornwall and England are noted for the latter.[72] Celtic is not always readily associated with Protestant culture, a misnomer most readily seen in the contemporary context concerned with Northern Ireland.[73] While it might not seem apparent, there are many in Northern Ireland, who are in beliefs, Protestant, yet consider themselves Celtic – directly offsetting the usual alignment of Catholicism with Celtic, and then Celtic nationalism and Irish republicanism.[74] The association of Protestantism with Celtic will have important repercussions in the work of the Hockings; since as writers they genuinely viewed Protestantism as the natural and correct path for Celtic peoples to follow.[75] Silas in general, but Joseph in particular, provides difficulties for his anti-Catholic stance in our more ecumenical era.

Indeed, this has some correlation with the critique of the modern Cornish Revival which has suggested that the alignment of the Revivalists with the Medieval period, Catholicism, Brittany and even Mystery Play culture was antithetical to the general population of Cornwall who, by this time, were, in Payton and Deacon's words, a 'radical Liberal, Methodist, rugby-watching working-class'.[76] To add to this complexity, there are those, within Cornwall today, who believe that mythically, Methodism greatly contributed to the destruction of 'original' Cornish culture, sidelining the Cornish language and traditional leisure activities. This view is not sustainable however. In reality, Methodism came after much of the loss of the Cornish language, and leisure activities like wrestling and hurling were already on the wane, strange new preachers providing a counter-attraction.[77] Wrecking and smuggling were far less controlled by internalised Methodism than by successive government crackdowns.[78] Others believe that if the Revival had more readily aligned itself with Methodism, the 'recovery' of Cornish culture would have been far speedier.[79]

My hope here is that I have given some basis to help the reader gain both perspective upon, and close insight into, the world of the Hockings. In the chapters that follow, this book does not try to be a fully academic work. It is not. It is a biography: in effect a story. In completing such a work, I had a different agenda. I was assessing people, their lives and achievements. One forms a personal relationship with the subject – in a way that it would be impossible to do with a poem, a play or a novel. However much one wishes to be balanced and unbiased, one cannot be, for one makes judgements. Time too, is a nefarious friend. Had I really known the Hockings, I daresay this book would be very different. Sometimes, I think I would have disliked them very much. Silas Kitto was a deeply jealous man who sometimes shot himself in the foot; Joseph was intolerant, sometimes smugly virtuous, and often destructive because of this; Salome was perhaps over-sentimental and naïve. At other times, they say and write things that are so quintessentially Cornish and capture Cornish identity so well, that I am captivated. To use a Cornu-English expression, when they 'make bold', they become three of the most interesting figures of recent Cornish history.

I suppose like most people, they have different faces for different audiences, constantly changing and evolving, according to experience and need. What I can say is that I have tried to tell as comprehensive, and as a honest a story of their lives as possible. I mentioned at the start that this book is an introductory account. I would like to re-emphasise that here. Scholars following me will discover more information that I, for some reason, could not obtain. They will tell it differently. I hope this is so – for more detailed studies, in particular, of the literature of Silas Kitto and Joseph, are needed. I also hope that this volume will at least raise the Hockings' collective heads above the parapet of literary studies, this time properly assessed, and that their work can now fit into on-going research within the field of Cornish Studies. Fortunately, it seems after a long period of neglect, Cornwall is now being more readily studied within Celtic Studies,[80] as well as in literary studies, shaped by observers such as Trezise, Westland, Hurst and Saunders.[81] My one final hope is that their achievement may be more readily asserted and celebrated by Cornwall itself. At a time when a Combined University of Cornwall will soon open,[82] it is fitting that we note not only Arthur, An Gof, Trelawny, Trevithick, Davy and Jenner, but those others, perhaps even the creators of such tongue-twisters as Quintrel Quethiock – who have shaped our collective past, and are so crucial a part of our future heritage.

Notes

1. Joseph Hocking (1920) *In the Sweat of Thy Brow*, London: Hodder and Stoughton, p.8.
2. See Graham Busby and Zoë Hambly 'Literary Tourism and the Daphne du Maurier Festival' in Philip Payton (ed.) (2000) *Cornish Studies: Eight*, Exeter: University of Exeter Press, pp.197-212.
3. An attempt by the Goonvean China Clay company to demolish Jack Clemo's cottage in 2000 resulted in a public outcry. The cottage was saved and it is hoped will be relocated at Wheal Martyn China Clay Museum in the near future.
4. See observations in Alan M. Kent (2000) *The Literature of Cornwall: Continuity, Identity, Difference 1000-2000*, Bristol: Redcliffe, pp. 246-8.
5. There is a John Harris Society, who celebrate a John Harris Day around the 14th October every year (Harris was born on 14th October 1820). See *John Harris Society Newsletter*, No.5 (1999). For Harris' poetry, see Alan M. Kent (ed.) (2000) *Voices from West Barbary: An Anthology of Anglo-Cornish Poetry 1549-1928*, London: Francis Boutle, pp.125-144. See also Paul Newman (1994) *The Meads of Love: The Life and Poetry of John Harris*. Redruth: Dyllansow Truran. Interestingly, despite Harris's commitment to Methodism, none of the Hocking siblings make reference to or note of his work.
6. 'Town to honour its literary son' in *Cornish Guardian*, 26th July (2001), p.3.
7. Numerous correspondents to the author remember consuming the Hockings novels in this way. Probert notes that in Dowran, a now ruined chapel once in the St. Just circuit, that in the chapel's circulating library, Joseph Hockings' novels were once very popular. See J.C.C. Probert, 'Dowran Chapel' in *Journal of the Cornish Methodist Historical Association*, No. 5 (1995), pp.115-20.
8. John A. Vickers (ed.) (2000) *A Dictionary of Methodism in Britain and Ireland*, London: Epworth Press, p.160. This is an extremely useful publication.
9. See Harman MS.
10. See Roger F.S. Thorne (2000 [1978]) *Hocking: Or the Tales of Two Brothers. A Catalogue of the Works of the Hockings (Joseph, Silas and Salome) in the collection of the late Michael E. Thorne*. Exeter: Heatherdene.
11. See H. M. Creswell Payne (1958), 'Cornish Methodism in Fiction' in *Old Cornwall*, Vol.5; K.C. Phillipps, 'A Calling Sacrificed to Writing Novels'. In: *Western Morning News*, July (1976).
12. See Alan M. Kent (1998) *Wives, Mothers and Sisters: Feminism, Literature and Women Writers of Cornwall*. Penzance: The Jamieson Library,. pp.16-23, (2000) op.cit., pp.160-4.
13. Ibid., pp.12-13.
14. See for example, Simon During (ed.) (1993) *The Cultural Studies Reader*, London and New York: Routledge and Christopher Pawling (ed.) (1984) *Popular Fiction and Social Change*, London: Macmillan.
15. See the overview given by contributors in G. Douglas Atkins and Laura Morrow (eds.) (1989) *Contemporary Literary Theory*, London and Boston: Macmillan. Much of the best contemporary scholarship on Popular Fiction is discussed in *Diegesis: Journal of the Association of Research in Popular Fictions*.
16. See the position adopted in Christopher Hampton (1990) *The Ideology of the Text*, Milton Keynes: Open University Press.
17. Tony Bennett (ed.) (1990) *Popular Fiction: Technology, Ideology, Production, Reading*, London and New York, Routledge, p. ix.
18. A position I outline in Kent (2000) op.cit.
19. For background to this, see Louis James (1963) *Fiction for the Working Man 1830-50*, Oxford: Oxford University Press, Martha Vicinus (1974) *The Industrial Muse: A Study of British Working Class Literature*, London: Croom Helm. See also P. McCann (1977) *Popular Education and Serialization in the Nineteenth Century*, London: Methuen.
20. Peter Ackroyd (1991 [1990]) *Dickens*, London: Minerva, p.191, pp. 229-30, and pp.994-5.
21. See David Crystal (1995) *The Cambridge Encyclopedia of the English Language*. Cambridge: Cambridge University Press, pp.77-91.
22. *Horner's Penny Stories*, published by W.B. Horner, Carmelite Temple E.C.
23. See examples in Kent (ed.) (2000) op.cit., pp.85-9 and pp. 121-4.

24. See Ella Westland 'The Passionate Periphery: Cornwall and Romantic Fiction' in Ian A. Bell (ed.) (1995) *Peripheral Visions: Images of Nationhood in Contemporary British Fiction,* Cardiff: University of Wales Press, pp.153-72.
25. See Kent (2000) op.cit., p.130.
26. Ibid., pp.137-8.
27. Jonathan Rose (2001) *The Intellectual Life of the British Working Classes,* New Haven and London: Yale University Press, pp.128-9.
28. Ibid., p.129.
29. The Church of England during this phase was both 'Catholic' and 'Protestant', and some higher elements would have accepted a priestly element. Methodism, although Protestant, did look on its Ministers as different. However, laymen could not conduct the Holy Communion service in the Wesleyan Methodist Church. Bernard Walke is an example of the priestly, high church end of the Church of England in Cornwall. See Bernard Walke (1982 [1935]) *Twenty Years at St Hilary,* London: Anthony Mott. Silas and Joseph are non-priestly examples in Methodism
30. Rupert E. Davies ([1985 1963]) *Methodism,* London: Epworth Press, pp.38-55. Davies is a useful introduction. For more detail, see Henry D. Rack (1989) *Reasonable Enthusiast: John Wesley and the Rise of Methodism,* London: Epworth Press.
31. Ibid., p.51.
32. John Wesley was not always consistent in his theology. Popularly, it is said that 'he was like a man who faced one way and rode another'.
33. This means the accepting of God in one's life until one is perfect. For a useful account of Methodist theology, see Thomas A. Langford (1998) *Methodist Theology,* Peterborough: Epworth Press.
34. James Munson (1991) *The Nonconformists: In Search of a Lost Culture.* London: SPCK.
35. The Wesleyans would not have accepted the term nonconformity, being closer to the Church of England.
36. John Pearce (1964) *The Wesleys in Cornwall,* Truro: D. Bradford Barton; Charles Thomas (1965) *Methodism and Self-Improvement in Nineteenth-Century Cornwall,* Cornwall: Cornish Methodist Historical Association; Thomas Shaw (1965) *The Bible Christians.* London: Epworth Press, (1967) *A History of Cornish Methodism.* Truro: D. Bradford Barton, John C. C. Probert (1971) *The Sociology of Cornish Methodism.* Truro: Cornwall Methodist Historical Association. For a less academic, but intimate portrait of Methodism in Cornwall, see D.M. Thomas (1983) *Selected Poems,* Harmondsworth: Penguin, pp.49-52, and K.C. Phillipps (1994) *Catching Cornwall in Flight,* St Austell: Cornish Hillside Publications.
37. See Alan Sinfield 'Varieties of Religion' in Alan Sinfield (ed.) (1983) Society and Literature 1945-1970, London: Methuen, pp.87-117; Callum G. Brown (2001) *The Death of Christian Britain: Understanding Secularisation 1800-2000,* London and New York; Routledge.
38. Peter Prescott (1871) *The Case of Cornish Methodism Considered; The Missing Lynch-Pin,* London: A. Osbourne; Lawrence Maker (1935) *Cob and Moorstone: The Curious History of some Cornish Methodist Churches,* London: Epworth Press
39. For example, H. Spencer Toy (1964) *The Methodist Church at Launceston,* Launceston: Wesley Methodist Church; Thomas Shaw (1978) *Methodism at Fraddon 1819-1977,* Fraddon: Fraddon Methodist Chapel. There are numerous other examples.
40. Methodism did not always appeal to the working classes or upper classes, though there are exceptions.
41. See Philip Payton (1992) *The Making of Modern Cornwall: Historical Experience and the Persistence of 'Difference',* Redruth: Dyllansow Truran, pp.87-90; John Hurst 'Mine, Moor and Chapel: The Poetry of John Harris' in Ella Westland (ed.) (1997) *Cornwall: The Cultural Construction of Place,* Penzance: The Patten Press and the Institute of Cornish Studies, pp.40-52; Peter Isaac (2000) *A History of Evangelical Christianity in Cornwall.* Cornwall: Peter Isaac. For a useful contextualisation, see Charles Thomas, "Let... us praise one another a bit': The Writing of Cornish Methodist History' in *Journal of the Cornish Methodist Historical Association,* No.5 (2001), pp.158-170.
42. Gage McKinney (1997) *A High and Holy Place: A Mining Camp Church at New Almaden,* New Almaden, California: Pine Press. For an earlier analysis of Cornish Methodism in Mexico, see A.C. Todd (2000 [1977] *The Search for Silver: Cornish Miners in Mexico 1824-1947,* St Austell: Cornish Hillside Publications, pp.158-9.

43. Bernard Semmel (1974) *The Methodist Revolution,* London: Heinemann.
44. A view reinforced in F.E. Halliday (1959) *A History of Cornwall,* London: Duckworth, p.278.
45. A problematical view found in Frank Warnes 'The Christian Church in Cornwall' in Myrna Combellack-Harris (ed.) (1989) *Cornish Studies for Cornish Schools,* Redruth: Institute of Cornish Studies, pp.1-4. Much of this position seems to derive from the fact that Methodism rarely touched philosophical issues.
46. See *Journal of the Cornish Methodist Historical Association.*
47. Susan Pellowe (ed.) (1994) *A Wesley Family Book of Days.* Aurora, Illinois: Renard Publications.
48. Thomas Shaw (1991) *A Methodist Guide to Cornwall,* London: Methodist Publishing House.
48. See 'The Beginning of Religious Change' and 'Religion and the People after Wesley' in John Rowe (1993 [1953]) *Cornwall in the Age of the Industrial Revolution,* St Austell: Cornish Hillside Publications, pp.67.1- 67.40 and pp. 261.1 - 261.48.
49. David Luker (1987) *Cornish Methodism, Revivalism, and Popular Belief, c.1780-1870,* Ph.D., Oxford: University of Oxford.
50. Jeremy Lake, Jo Cox and Eric Berry (2001) *Diversity and Vitality: The Methodist and Nonconformist Chapels of Cornwall,* Truro: Cornwall Archaeological Unit, pp. 1-7, pp.16-17 and pp.20-35. This is a well-illustrated volume, although there are several textual inaccuracies.
51. Charles Thomas and Joanna Mattingly (2000) *The History of Christianity in Cornwall AD 500 - 2000.* Truro: Royal Institution of Cornwall, pp.30-31. Such was the fear in Cornwall over Jacobitism, that they were suspicious of all strangers including scholars like Edward Lhuyd (1660-1709). See Kent (2000) op.cit., pp.81-2.
52. Any survey of obituaries of Cornish newspapers of the nineteenth century will demonstrate that many Mining Cap'ns were Anglican, or are silent about church attendance. Often Methodism did well in isolated fishing villages, but this was often more to do with the nature of the area, rather than the industry itself. Sennen's chapel, for example, is not in the cove.
53. See Keith Pearce and Helen Fry (eds.) (2000) *The Lost Jews of Cornwall.* Bristol: Redcliffe; 'Ritual Evocations in Cornish' in *Meyn Mamvro,* No.44, p.23; Horace Keast (1983) *The Catholic Revival in Cornwall,* Cornwall: Catholic Advisory Council for Cornwall. See also the overview given in Nicholas Orme (ed.) (1991) *Unity and Variety: A History of the Church in Devon and Cornwall.* Exeter: University of Exeter Press.
54. Shakespeare's plays were the targets of much early Methodism.
55. Treve Crago "Play the Games as Men Play It': Women in Politics during the Era of the 'Cornish Proto-Alignment' 1918-1922' in Philip Payton (ed.) (2000) *Cornish Studies: Eight,* Exeter: University of Exeter Press, pp.147-160.
56. John Wesley was an early opponent of slavery. The Bible Christians had female preachers.
57. See Shaw (1967) op.cit., pp. 17-22, pp.24-5, pp.55-58, pp.55-58, pp.88-89, pp.111-2, pp. 115-6 and pp. 127-9.
58. William Carvosso (1835) *The Efficacy of Faith in the Atonement of Christ:* A Memoir, London: Wesleyan Conference Office.
59. See Sinfield (1983) op.cit.; Brown (2001) op.cit.
60. Jack Clemo 'The Hocking Brothers' in *Cornish Review,* Spring (1969), p.37.
61. See Roger Sharrock (ed.) (1987) *John Bunyan: The Pilgrim's Progess,* Harmondsworth: Penguin.
62. See David Daiches (ed.) (1965 [1847]) *Emily Brontë Wuthering Heights,* Harmondsworth: Penguin. For the Brontë's Cornish connections and Elizabeth Branwell, see Kerrow Hill (1994) *The Brontë Sisters and Sir Humphry Davy: A Sharing of Visions,* Penzance: The Jamieson Library. Brontë's father was an Irish clergyman whose background was Methodist, but who himself was firmly Anglican.
63. See John Cowper Powys (1999 [1932]) *A Glastonbury Romance,* Harmondsworth: Penguin.
64. Jack Clemo (1949) *Confession of a Rebel.* London: Chatto and Windus, (1986 [1958] *The Invading Gospel: A Return to Faith,* Basingstoke: Marshall Pickering
65. Clemo (1969) op.cit., p.36.
66. Ibid., p.37.
67. See Amy Hale and Philip Payton (eds.) (2000) *New Directions in Celtic Studies,* Exeter: University of Exeter Press, pp.1-14; Murray G.H. Pittock (1999) *Celtic Image and the British Image,* Manchester and New York: Manchester University Press, pp.1-19.

68. See Kent (2000) op.cit., pp.147-94.
69. In many of the novels, the Hockings siblings will pause and reflect on issues of Celticity.
70. See, for example, Silas Kitto Hocking (1903) *A Bonnie Saxon,* London: Frederick Warne and Company, p.66. In general, it is Silas Kitto who is more sentimentally Celtic and Joseph who is more nationalistic.
71. See Joseph Hocking (1929) *The Sign of the Triangle,* London: Ward, Lock and Company, p.38.
72. See Nigel Pennick (1996) *Celtic Sacred Landscapes,* London: Thames and Hudson. For Ireland, see pp.185-91; for Brittany, see pp.213-16. For Cornwall, see pp.208-11; for England, see pp.204-8. An interesting insight into Cornish Methodism as Catholic is given in Thomas Shaw (1970) *The Pastoral Crook: The State of Religion in the Diocese of Exeter in the Mid-Nineteenth Century,* Cornwall: The Cornish Methodist Historical Association. For an examination of the 'pattern repeating itself' see Thomas Shaw (1962) *Saint Petroc and John Wesley, Apostles in Cornwall: An Examination of the Celtic Background of Cornish Methodism,* Cornwall: Cornish Methodist Historical Association.
73. The following pubications offer insight here. See Peter Brooke (1994) *Ulster Presbyterianism,* Belfast: Athol Books; Desmond Bowen (1990) *The Protestant Crusade in Ireland,* Dublin: Gill and Macmillan.
74. There is an increasingly popular theory amongst Ulster Protestants that the Loyalist population is descended from Brittonic-speaking Picts expelled from Ulster by the Gaels, and who returned at the time of the Plantations. See Ian Adamson (1974) *Cruthin: The Ancient Kindred,* Belfast: Pretani Press. An interesting figure is the Welsh scholar William Salesbury. Salesbury was born in the first quarter of the sixteenth century and he wrote and printed the first Welsh-English dictionary. He provided a Welsh version of the Scriptures to enable Welsh people to turn to Protestantism. See R. Brinley Jones (1994) *William Salesbury,* Cardiff: University of Wales Press.
75. See observations in Michael Hechter (1975) *Internal Colonialism: The Celtic Fringe in British National Development, 1536-1966,* London: Routledge and Kegan Paul, p.77, and in Derek Hirst, 'The English Republic and the Meaning of Britain' in Brendan Bradshaw and John Morrill (eds.) (1996) *The British Problem c.1534-1707: State Formation in the Atlantic Archipelago,* Basingstoke: Macmillan, pp. 192-219. See also, useful exploration in S.J. Connolly (ed.) (1999) *Kingdoms United? Great Britain and Ireland Since 1500: Integration and Diversity,* Dublin: Four Courts Press.
76. See Bernard Deacon and Philip Payton, 'Re-inventing Cornwall: Cultural Change on the European Periphery' in Philip Payton (ed.) (1993) *Cornish Studies: One,* Exeter: University of Exeter Press, pp.72-3. Rugby may be a misnomer here. Much of Cornwall was soccer country before rugby.
77. See Kent (2000) op.cit., pp.90-91.
78. Ibid.
79. A view similar to Deacon and Payton (1993) op.cit; and touched upon by Kent (2000), pp.278-84.
80. See Hale and Payton (eds.) (2000), op.cit.
81. Simon Trezise (2000) *The West Country as a Literary Invention: Putting Fiction in its Place,* Exeter: University of Exeter Press; Westland (ed.) (1997) op.cit.; John Hurst, 'Literature in Cornwall' in Philip Payton (ed.) (1993) *Cornwall Since the War: The Contemporary History of a European Region,* Redruth: Dyllansow Truran and the Institute of Cornish Studies, pp.291-308; Tim Saunders (ed.) (1999) *The Wheel: An Anthology of Modern Poetry in Cornish 1850-1980,* London: Francis Boutle.
82. See George Hoare and Alan Stanhope (1999) *Towards a University in Cornwall: Developments in Higher Education - an update,* Camborne: Cornwall College; Combined Universities in Cornwall (2001) *Pathways to Success: Higher Education Opportunities in Cornwall,* Penryn: Combined Universities in Cornwall.

Chapter One

Terras, Trelion, and Tin: The Creation of a Written World

"When I began to write, fiction was deliberately barred out of many homes, like theatre-going. My father was distressed, that I, a minister, should write 'stories'..."

Silas Kitto Hocking, *The Cornish Guardian*, 18th June, 1926[1]

Silas Kitto Hocking's father may have been distressed that he should choose a literary career, but perhaps his father was unaware that the mid-Cornwall parish of St Stephen-in-Brannel has produced a continuum of writing stretching back from the turn of the third millennium to the Medieval period. Just opposite the present gravestones of the Hocking family stands the church, where possibly around the year 1380, the clerk of the medieval parish sat and wrote a charter relating to land in the area, a concord 'whereby Thomas Leghe of Resogoe [Resugga] and Margery, his wife, conveyed to Nicholas, son of John de Menleder, land in Menleder [Meledor], with reversion to the grantors'.[2]

Some years later, when the charter was no longer needed, the fragment was picked up – possibly by a proud father – who, on the back of it, composed in the Cornish language, still the *lingua populi*, what appears to be a wedding speech, congratulating the married couple and giving them down-to-earth, pithy advice for a successful future together. That tiny speech, now known, after it was discovered by the Cornish language scholar Henry Jenner (1848-1934), as the *Charter Endorsement* (quite insignificant compared to the other epic mystery dramas performed all over Cornwall[3]) turns out, some six hundred years later, to be the earliest surviving example of a piece of prose writing in Cornish.[4] Its message is one that still has relevance today; possibly even similar words and advice in English were spoken by Silas Kitto and Joseph Hocking when they performed marriage ceremonies during their careers as ministers, as this brief extract shows:

Hy a vyz gwreg ty da   [She will be a good wife
zyz ze synsy   for you to have,
pur wyr a lauara   I'm telling you,
ha govyn worty   O ask her!][5]

If ever then, there is a pedigree for a parish generating outstanding literature in Cornwall, then St Stephen-in-Brannel has it. More recently, it was the home of perhaps one of the most significant and visionary writers of the twentieth century – Jack Clemo – whose poetry and fiction continue to arouse world-wide interest and research.[6] Clemo, who became both deaf and blind during his life, was a realist novelist of the china-clay landscape inside and surrounding the parish, as well as a poet who projected a complex individual Christian belief (formed from a union of Methodism, Calvinism and Catholicism) onto the surrounding landscape and people of Cornwall, and elsewhere in Britain and Europe.[7] In short, he is one of the most significant writers to have emerged, not just in Cornwall, but on a world-wide scale.

To these two literary events, we may of course, now begin to add Silas Kitto, Joseph and Salome Hocking. The same parish which so influenced the author of the *Charter Endorsement* and Jack Clemo, shaped the Hockings' written world in the same way, and although, like many Cornish people over time, all three of them eventually left their home, it was to have an indelible stamp on their work. In short, the parish not only created the Hockings as novelists, but also formed much of the metaphorical, political and spiritual basis of their texts. Some literary critics are of the opinion that we should be sceptical about too neatly linking the background and life stories of writers with their work.[8] After all, novelists do not just retell their own experiences. That said, within contemporary literary studies, there is now a wider sympathy for what is generally known as 'cultural materialist' criticism, which does link the technological, political, economic, social and religious conditions that the author operated in, with the text's moment of production.[9] Put another way, this view suggests that although an author might want to write within an 'ivory tower', it is impossible to do so, for the surrounding culture of the time will still influence the way the literature is written. When in this book, we come to review the Hockings' lives and literature, this consideration should always be present, for it is impossible to gain a true reading of their work otherwise.

Their particular brand of 'pulp Methodism' was created in the parish of St Stephen-in-Brannel – or more fully, at least, to begin with, in the village of St Stephen-in-Brannel itself, and two nearby hamlets – Terras and Trelion. St Stephen-in-Brannel lies in mid-Cornwall, situated between the Fal Valley to the south, and the expanse of the modern china-clay extractive industry to the north. The village now having a population of over two and a half thousand depends greatly upon that industry, but in fact, again has a much more ancient history. The forest of Bernal is recorded in the Domesday Book of 1086. At that time it was held by 'Brictmar' and had 'land for 20 ploughs' and '10 slaves'. There were '12 villagers and 18 smallholders, 20 unbroken mares, 2 cattle and 150 sheep'.[10] According to the authority on the parish – T.J. Olver, however, the land was originally given 'by the Conqueror to his half brother, Robert of Mortain, with most of the rest of Cornwall'.[11] After the Conquest, or as, some scholars increasingly call the 'Breton return',[12] the lands passed to the crown during the reign of Henry III (1216-72), Henry being the brother of, and giving land to Richard, Earl of Cornwall.[13]

The manorial name is more difficult to assess. Some observers believe it to mean 'corn ground'[14] – which is likely, given the agricultural basis of the manor, and *bern* can mean 'a heap, a stack or a rick', fitting the corn-themed derivation. However, *bern* can also mean mount and may refer to the Beacon, which lies directly above the village, between it and Foxhole. Weatherhill argues for *bron-el* 'place of hills'.[15] Either way, the word *Bernal* was corrupted early on. The manorial parish surrounding the village is once thought to have extended southwards, towards the coast at Caerhayes, but has, over time, shrunk back towards the centre of the territory.

Two notable families had control of this manor. At Court (near Gwindra), once lay the ancient manor house of the Tanner family. As Olver details, the Earl had a liaison with a Norman Lady – one Joan de Valletort, of Trematon Castle, near Saltash, and he gave the early residence at Court to their son, Sir Walter de Cornubia. The bloodline continued in the parish until the early 1700s, 'eventually to the Hendours about 1340, the Tregarthans of Gorran Haven in 1442, and then to the Tanner family who originated in Cullumpton, Devon in about 1520'.[16] The Tanner family patronised the church, alongside St Michaels at Caerhayes and St Dennis for some 450 years.

When this Royal bloodline fell to the Tanners, the last occupants of the manor were able to claim this lineage. The heiresses were all minors, who were placed under the wardship of Sir William Trevanion of Caerhayes and Sir Piers Edgcumbe. Legitimacy of Royal ancestry could be claimed through their maternal grandmother, one Elizabeth Courtenay of Boconnoc, who had descended from Elizabeth Plantagenet, daughter of Edward I. This Boconnoc connection is important. As Olver argues:

> Between 1716 and 1720, the Pitts of Boconnoc, the family which produced the two Prime Ministers purchased the manor and property. They had bought Boconnoc in 1713 when Thomas Pitt retired from the governship of Madras and sold a very large diamond which he had acquired in India to the Regent of France for an immense sum... The Pitts were lords of the manor until 1864, but the male line had died out by reason of a fatal duel by the second Lord Camelford fifty years before. Ann, Lady Grenville, had then inherited from her brother and on her death left the Cornish estates to her husband's nephew, the Hon. George Fortescue, in whose family it had remained.[17]

Olver's account provides some important background here, since the

Fortescues would later have devastating effects on the lives of the Hocking family. The old manor house at Court, is thought to have been destroyed during the War of Five Peoples (the 'English' Civil War), yet the Tanners of the parish had power for several generations afterwards, forming part of the local Cornish squirarchy (a social group who would become the predominant villains in many of their novels).

Additionally, at Meledor, there was once a property belonging to the landed Melledor family. The title then descended onto the Rosogan family: Alice, daughter of John Melledor, married John Rosogan. By 1509, John Rosogan was one of the leading owners of tin-works and blowing-houses in Cornwall. He probably had many interests in the tin-streaming already at work in the Fal Valley and on Hensbarrow Downs. That year, during the reign of Henry VII, pardons for offences in the Stannary Courts included, among Cornish gentry so pardoned, 'John Rosogan of Meledore'.[18] In 1510 a mansion, begun by John Melledor was completed by Rosogan.

By way of interest, John Rosogan's grandson then moved to Polglaze in St Erme and became one of the leaders in the 1549 Prayer Book Rebellion, which under Humphry Arundell rose against the New Prayer Book and the conversion of the Cornish service into English.[19] Rebellion, it seems, is part of the heritage of the parish. By 1612 however, one Nicholas Rosogan sold Meledor Mansion to the Bevill family; John Bevill being the one-time High Sheriff of Cornwall from 1575-1579.

One hundred years later the mansion was sold to Philip Hawkins, and by 1838, it was held by C.H.J. Hawkins of Trewithen, Probus,[20] but by the middle of the nineteenth century, had already fallen into disrepair. Since then, the rear of the property has been rebuilt, although its Breton-looking chimney, mullioned windows, gargoyle, porch and granite facade remain in place. The property was certainly one that the Hockings knew, and would have perhaps first ignited their interest in religious turmoil and rebellion, as well as the romance of the past.

The church at St Stephen-in-Brannel was dedicated in 1261, although according to Padel, the Church of *Santus Stephanus* existed around 1166.[21] In 1291 he argues it was known as the church of *Sanctus Stephanus* in Brannel, then *St Stevyns* in 1478 and *Eglostephen* in 1578,[22] the latter perhaps proving that Cornish was still spoken in the parish until this relatively late date. St Stephen was the first martyr who was stoned to death in Jerusalem – a popular dedication in Cornwall. According to Behenna and Caddy, 'an earlier Celtic church... is thought to have stood in a nearby valley at Gwindra'.[23] This may be the reasoning for the suggestion Padel makes of an alternative name for the churchtown – *Eglosshellans* – probably meaning the 'church of Helans', a lost Celtic dedication.[24]

The present granite-built church is characterised by its fine, pinnacled tower and early Norman font, carved with trees and grotesques, one of them like a dragon. Olver argues that the crowned heads represent 'Earl Richard as King of the Romans, and his Queen, Sanchia of Provence... and King Henry III and his Queen Eleanor of Provence'.[25] The porch holds a sundial, purportedly in memory of William I and his Queen Matilda. To the south is an impressive stained glass window depicting life in the parish. In the churchyard is the noted Crying Stone, where, like many other churches in Cornwall, the news of the week was delivered after the Sunday morning service. When Methodism reached Cornwall, however, an early thatched Methodist chapel was erected near the eastern gates of the church, but this has not survived; the only memory of this early chapel being the short row of cottages know as Chapel Terrace.[26] A new chapel was completed in 1870, which formed the location of much of the Hocking siblings' worship and the background to their texts.

As well as its manorial and ecclesiastical history, the village has a record of interesting archaeological finds – all of which must have formed a backdrop to the Hockings' interest in history. To the south of the village, lies Resugga Castle, a horseshoe-shaped, iron-age hillfort, lying above Trenowth Woods. It would have been the residence of the warrior chieftains in the 4th-1st centuries BC and forms part of the pattern of these style of hillforts found all over Cornwall. Weatherhill comments that unusually 'the entrance, on the north-west, is approached by a sunken track through an isolated length of rampart which was either a protective outwork or the remains of an annexe'.[27] The fort has commanding views of the parish as well as the Fal itself, making it a near-perfect defensive point.

Close to Resugga, at Trenowth, a tin-bronze and brass collar was found, dug up in tin streaming in 1793. The Cornish antiquarian William C. Borlase describes it as 'a collar, or other ornament, of brass, once gilt and jewelled...' found at 'Trenoweth, Broad Moor, St Stephen in Branwell'.[28] The archaeologist Megaw has completed a detailed study of the collar, which is now kept in the British Museum, arguing that its manufactured decoration of 'formalised palmettes constructed by branching comma motifs, the centre of each element being picked out with the glass inlays' is distinctively Cornish.[29] He dates the find to around the 1st century AD. Finds have also been found at tin-streaming works near Gwindra. These included two pieces of gold (perhaps part of a twisted fibula). These are later – belonging to the medieval period. Alongside these were found a quarter noble of Edward III and a coin of Henry II.[30]

The other more recent historical event which has affected the parish was the discovery in the 1760s, of deposits of high quality china clay, or kaolin, by the Quaker chemist from Plymouth, William Cookworthy.[31] He had stayed with one Richard Yelland at Carloggas and opened pits there and at Rescrowsa, putting into place the beginnings of an industry which would have a dramatic effect on not only the economy of mid-Cornwall, but also upon the landscape of the whole region. Some two centuries later, the industry is still flourishing, as Thurlow demonstrates, with some of the largest open-cast quarries in western Europe, producing up to three millions tonnes of kaolin per year, with enough resources to last well into the twenty-first century.[32] Of course, in the Hockings' youth the industry was still in its infancy. In the twenty-first century, they would find their home landscape much altered from the way they knew it.

Our story proper, however, starts in the early part of the nineteenth century, not long after the first clay works of the parish were opened. The young Hockings were to begin their lives just down the hill from St Stephen-in-Brannel church, in the tiny hamlet of Terras. To the south lay Trenowth Woods and Resugga, to the north the old Tudor manor house at Meledor. There lived one Thomas Hocking, who worked as a blacksmith, probably serving the local tin mining industry, as well as the surrounding manor and emergent china clay mining industry. His blacksmith's shop is thought to have been at the rear of the present-day Automobilia museum, in prior times a Woollen Mill, then a Cash and Carry store.

His wife's name was Mary Parkin and she and Thomas Hocking had a son, born in 1816, who they named James Hocking. James Hocking inherited much of the mystery and history of the parish described above, becoming known locally and popularly as 'Jimmy Hocky'. Young James

Hocking family cottage in the late nineteenth century. The house still stands but the windows and roof have been altered

took a wife in 1844 by the name of Elizabeth Kitto (more often recorded as 'Eliza') who was born in the coastal village of St Mawes in 1822, but who may have had maritime connections with the upper end of the Fal (Penvose Quay was only two miles below Tregony[33]), and possibly, as we shall see, with the parish of Gwennap. Eliza, according to later commentators, including her own daughter Salome, her son Joseph and her grand-daughter Anne, reputedly had both Spanish and Gypsy blood in her. Whether or not this is true, it was a myth sometimes applied to the Cornish, and indeed, often perpetrated by them. The Kitto name was to become very important to all three of the Hocking writers, and is dealt with later in this chapter.

Eliza fell in love with Jimmy, who had quickly progressed, via a stint as a miner in St Agnes, to later becoming a 'Cap'n'[34] in the Terras and Trelion mining district. As was the case for many miners in the nineteenth century, and as Deacon has shown, income was broadly based on mining activity, but also some farm small-holding and vegetable production, or in his case, an orchard. This 'proto-industrialization' was central in sustaining the Cornish economy, and became increasingly crucial as industrialization faltered from the 1860s.[35] The parish of St Stephen-in-Brannel was in all likelihood, no different to elsewhere in Cornwall.

Upon their marriage, James and Eliza seem to have moved from temporary lodgings in St Agnes and built a stone-walled cottage in Terras. James laid out an orchard there, part of the 'three-life' system of leasehold, which had probably initially been taken out by Thomas Hocking's father (James' grandfather) at the end of the eighteenth century, organised by the local landowners.[36] Most surrounding property was unenclosed (effectively unhedged moorland), so the landowners had considerable monopolistic power over those who needed to lease homes or land. As was the case then, on the expiration of the last life, the house he had built and the orchard he had planted, had to be given up without any compensation, and the property put into complete repair. Clearly it behoved the initial leaseholder to choose 'lives' that would be likely to survive the longest. It was a precarious system, and in the case of James Hocking, it was actually to prove disastrous. The historian John Rowe has argued how outdated the system was:

> *Lives on one lease might expire long before those on another, thereby forcing the tenant to seek a new lease to retain all the lands which he had been working on as a single agrarian unit, or otherwise, adjust his economy to a smaller holding... Such inconveniences probably played no small part in the decline of the life-leasehold system during the eighteenth century in Cornwall.*[37]

The system, however, continued well into the nineteenth century. When Eliza and James were older, the first three-life system was terminated at Terras and after a temporary move to Little Treneague nearby in 1871,[38] they decided to move to another 'new-take' property in the region of Trelion, slightly further south than Terras. James built a new cottage on Broad Moor, near Trenowth, close to where the tin-bronze collar was found, which he had originally leased as unreclaimed, turning it into farmland while still living at Terras and working it for much of his life. The ground-rent receipts describe it as 'Part of Trelyon Common'.[39] The year was 1878,[40] and when finished, the cottage was a good deal larger than the one at Terras, and allowed them to live more comfortably. James had to fence and hedge the Common, and make its roads. He had to drain it and clear away gorse and rocks. He manured the soil and built stables, piggeries and a barn.[41] He had to pay for this a ground-rent equal to that for a good local farm with buildings. The farm labour itself must have near exhausted him.

However, although he had worked very hard to make Broad Moor work, when forty-seven years' lease fell in, which was the maximum that he could obtain, not only had his estate never been able to credit itself with interest on his own capital sunk into the farm, but the whole of that capital and work, and in addition, several hundred pounds later lent by three of his sons, was hopelessly lost. The tragedy of this, and the knowledge of land-owners and the law, remained with Silas, Joseph and Salome for the rest of their lives. It was one reason why villainous landowners and squires were often the targets of their fiction, and why arguments over land law and property became such central themes of their work. All three seem never to have forgiven the parish for this: the system had destroyed their father. For Salome, it was the deciding factor in her later interest in Tolstoyan land schemes.

Who then, were the land owners during this time? The actual landlord at the time of James and Eliza's eviction from Trelion has been difficult to trace. However, as Olver describes, and Smale indicates,[42] much of the whole sett around Trelion was then owned by initially the Pitts, then the Fortescue family of the Boconnoc Estate, near Lostwithiel.[43] The Fortescues owned a considerable amount of land in the Parish, including part of Foxhole, on which is now a housing estate named 'The Fortescues'. This family would seem the likely target for much of Silas, Joseph and Salome's later anger, and the shift in their fiction in the late 1870s onwards to consider more land rights issues. Religious antipathy was perhaps felt as well, since the Fortescues were Anglican.[44] Their name has conveniently been left out of many accounts because the Fortescues covered the living of the parish and sustained the Anglican church of the village. The additional fact that the family at Boconnoc had produced two Prime Ministers may have prevented Silas, Joseph and Salome from being publically open about events.[45] Put simply, from the parish to Westminster, the Fortescues had powerful connections.

The Fortescues, it should be noted, however, were only following the letter of the law in terms of the three-life system, and it would clearly be wrong to suggest here that they were wicked landlords. At the end of the day, it was the system which had destroyed James and his family's work – not the landlords.

This is the overview of James and Eliza's life, but it was never one of complete disaster. Indeed, by all accounts from the time they were married until around 1880, they seemed to have enjoyed a happy marriage together, and like most families then, had several offspring. All the Hocking children were given scriptural names. In order, first came a son Jabez, born in St Agnes in 1846, the second son Simeon, born at Terras in 1848, a third son Silas Kitto, born in 1850, the eldest daughter, Mahala Mary, born in 1852, a second daughter Thirza, born in 1855, the third daughter Salome, 1857 and the youngest son Joseph, born in 1860.

It seems initially that the Hocking family worshipped at a 'Bryanite' Bible Christian chapel at Trelion, which was closer and more convenient for them to attend than the one in St Stephen-in-Brannel churchtown. It had been built by the circuit ministers William Kinsman and Henry Welsh. Kinsman, formerly by trade a mason, procured a spot of ground, and set to work on building the walls. Friends supplied him with food while in his labour and with a horse so he could make his evening appointments. He would get up the next day at four o'clock in the morning to continue his work. Meanwhile, Welsh was begging money towards the cost.[46] After their year in the circuit the ministers moved on. The chapel was not completed but their successors, with the help of friends in Trelion, got it completed with little debt. The *Bible Christian Magazine* of 1903 mentions that Captain James Hocking, his wife and family attended the services in Trelion Chapel for many years.[47] Nothing remains of the chapel today. Its location is marked simply by a public bench. It is close to 'The Stack House' property (originally part of a Terras Mine), where one road heads westwards and the other heads south to the valley bottom – the location of another mine known as South Terras – and then up to Broadmoor, eventually leading to Grampound Road and Tregony. However, it seems later, that as this tiny chapel fell into disrepair, younger members of the family, such as Salome and Joseph, attended the by now, larger Methodist Church in St Stephen's Churchtown. Inevitably, this saw the further decline of the Bible Christians in St Stephen-in-Brannel, and led, as Shaw has shown, to their eventual amalgamation with the United methodist Free Churches in 1907.[48]

As discussed in the Introduction to this book, comprehensive histories of the development of Methodism in Cornwall are offered by many scholars, but for our purposes here, some specific background to the development of Methodism in St Stephen-in-Brannel is useful. John Wesley visited the parish on 25th September 1757. This was the golden age of evangelical Methodism, an era in which many of the Hocking novels would eventually be set. In his *Journal*, Wesley wrote:

At two I preached in St. Stephen's, near a lone house, on the side of a barren mountain: but neither the house, nor the court could contain the people: so we went into a meadow, where all might kneel, (which they generally do in Cornwall), as well as stand and hear. And they did hear, and sing, and pray, as for life. I saw none careless or inattentive among them.[49]

His sermon must have been effective for the first Wesleyan Chapel was soon under construction, and opened twenty-three years after Wesley's first visit, in 1780. The mythology of Wesley's visit must have been known to Salome and Joseph as they listened to the experienced class leaders and preachers at the later Methodist Church in churchtown. Further background is offered again by the *Bible Christian Magazine* of 1903. The magazine interviewed James Hocking about the impressions made on him about Methodist preaching when he was a boy. James humorously comments that 'the ablest preacher was the man who shouted the loudest, and emphasised his words by resounding blows on the bible'.[50] He also remembers with some amusement how his father Thomas would announce the hymn to be sung, then as he thought was proper and fitting, just like the preacher, read two lines, and when the congregation had sung them, he read two more which would be repeated, and so on, until they slowly reached the end of the hymn. The article continues with a recollection of the style of service at the Trelion Bible Christian chapel:

The precentor himself sang treble, an old farmer chimed in with bass, and female voices made out a rather feeble harmony. Hymn books were not so cheap then as now, and the tallow candles would not give so good light as the lamps we have today. Thomas Cooper, the converted infidel, stated that when he was a boy and attended services in a Chapel, one of the most interesting parts of the performance was the man with a pair of snuffers to snuff the candles; on some occasions he snuffed the candles so severely that he extinguished the light [before people had left].[51]

Similar scenes must have been witnessed at Trelion. Perhaps even the candles were not shining strongly enough then for James to see the tin ore, which he was later to discover in the walls of the old chapel. Apparently, James Hocking was a 'class leader' from the age of twenty-five to his death. The magazine also comments that 'he and his good wife took a deep interest in the cause and did their best to improve it'.[52] It was an interest that both Jimmy and Eliza gave to their children.

Trelion Chapel also received a visit from that most famous of Cornish preachers – the celebrated Billy Bray (1794-1868).[53] The so-called 'King's son' came to Trelion on several occasions, but at one evening service, when he came to the chapel door, the building was so packed with people who had come to hear him preach, that he was unable to enter. Small of stature, the wiry and witty preacher made his way in through one of the windows instead, no doubt to deliver another one of his lively sermons. Bray is subject to much mythologising himself. By this stage in his career, he was somewhat 'off-centre', and though a draw, he was actually a poor preacher. Despite this, we can see that the Hocking children grew up in a completely Cornish and fully Methodist environment. Stories of Wesley, the early chapels and Billy Bray must have become part of the Hockings' family folklore.

Alongside the Methodist tradition, mining was also to prove a central theme with the written world of the Hockings, and during their childhood it surrounded them. In the 1851 census, James Hocking describes himself as a miner. The 1861 census lists James, his eldest sons Jabez, now aged fifteen, and Simeon, aged thirteen, all as miners.[54] In 1864, as indicated above, it was James who was the first to discover an area of tin-bearing ground close to the surface about one mile southwards from his first cottage at Terras, at a hillside site which eventually became known as Terras Mine.

The tin is reputed to have been discovered by complete accident.[55] In trying to exact some repairs on the thatched Bible Christian chapel, a piece of stanniferous rock was broken out of the decaying wall and found to contain a considerable quantity of high grade tin ore. Some hundred of pounds worth was quickly procured from both the wall and the nearby quarry. The site become well-known overnight. The 1865 edition of *Mining Journal* describes the site as an extraordinary deposit of tin in an elvan dyke. The elvan is listed as 'more than 25 feet wide, and it is intended to work it as an open quarry'.[56] The report continues by saying that 'we sincerely wish the company success, as it will be the means of restoring the St Austell district to its former celebrity'.[57]

Events moved quickly. In March 1866, an attempt was made to float the Terras Open Workings Tin Company Limited with a capital investment of £30,000 to develop the area. A masterplan was drawn up to make Terras one of the most modern and efficient tin workings of the era, involving considerable expansion and development, including '150 heads of stamps, in addition to those already at work'.[58] Despite the optimism however, this attempt to raise capital was unsuccessful, but twelve stamps already in place, and driven by a water wheel using water from the River Fal, continued for some years.

James Hocking was not around to see these plans. He had made good money from the discovery, and felt, perhaps contrary to the Company, that there was little more tin to be mined easily and cheaply. By the end of 1865, he and his eldest son Jabez, like so many other Cornish of the time, had left Cornwall to work in California. Recent work has documented much of this period of Cornish history,[59] and the rewards that the Cornish might achieve in the mines of Grass Valley and elsewhere in the west of the American continent.[60]

Emigration was, and perhaps still is, a constant feature of Cornish life, expanding and constricting according to economic disadvantage and advantage at home. For the Hockings, perhaps drawing on their own father's experiences, letters and stories, 'abroad' was a place of adventure which could both make and destroy men and women. It offered opportunity, but it had to be seized wisely. Sometimes, it was a mythic learning experience second-to-none, where the frustrations of the Cornish economy and society tempted the individual away to make their fortune, but brought with it sentimental attachment to the homeland and eventual hope of return, having made their riches. Virtually all of the novels about Cornwall, by both Joseph and Silas, feature emigration. It was an experience also captured by many of the poets of the period. A contemporary and friend of Silas, Joseph and Salome was Mark Guy Pearse (1842-1930), whose poetry captures much of the emotional torment men and women endured when they were separated. Here, he writes of the Cornish Miner in California:

> *'Aw my dear life! well, iss, of course,*
> *'Tis very fine, you're right, –*
> *A hundred miles and more of plains,*
> *And then the mountains' height,*
> *The valley and the waterfall,*
> *Besides the towering tree.*
> *But bless 'ee, 'tisn't nothun', sir,*
> *To which I can see.*
>
> *A stretch of furze bush all ablaze,*
> *Another stretch of fern;*
> *A patch of purple heather bloom,*
> *And then you take a turn;*
> *You pass great piles of rubbish heaps,*
> *You pass a bal that's knacked;*
> *And then a whitewashed cottage peeps*
> *From where the corn is stacked.*[61]

Such thoughts may well have run through the minds of James and Jabez as they travelled west. It seems, however, that James kept considerable links with the Mine back at home. In a letter to the Adventurers at Terras, he writes:

> *At the time referred to (the Company having had the advantage of the opening up of the course through my exertion) the elvan was worked upon on the top of this only, as the grant did not extend to the valley, and the consequences was that after I left this country for California, the*

work was brought to a close, as all the stone had been shammelled to the surface.[62]

Five years later, a new company called the *Terras Tin Mining Company* was registered, and in 1870 a new prospectus was printed in the *Mining Journal*. This included interestingly enough, a letter from James Hocking recommending the new Company. Prospectuses for new mines at this time tended to present the mine in the most favourable light possible. It is likely that James Hocking was encouraged to write in 'hopeful' terms:

> *I beg to say that I discerned the elvan course which you have in your sett in 1864... There is not the shadow of a doubt that the average produce from the elvan would not be less than the quantity already stated, and that the whole of the work – including removing of the surface burden, blasting, breaking into siye, stamping and dressing so as to prepare for the market – would be taken readily on tribute, so as to leave a handsome profit for the adventurers. Indeed, I do not believe there would be any tin mine now at work in Cornwall, which in proportion to the outlay would prove as profitable as this mine... I regard this as an investment and not as a speculation.*[63]

It is unclear what part James Hocking played in this new company. Perhaps he saw potential in the old mine, after work in California grew scarce and he became keener to return home. In the 1871 census, he describes himself as a Mine Agent, although he is not listed as the Mine Agent for the *Terras Tin Mining Company*.[64] Nevertheless, "Jimmy Hocky" or not, his recommendation worked. The flotation of the company was successful and the shares were soon selling at a premium. By the end of

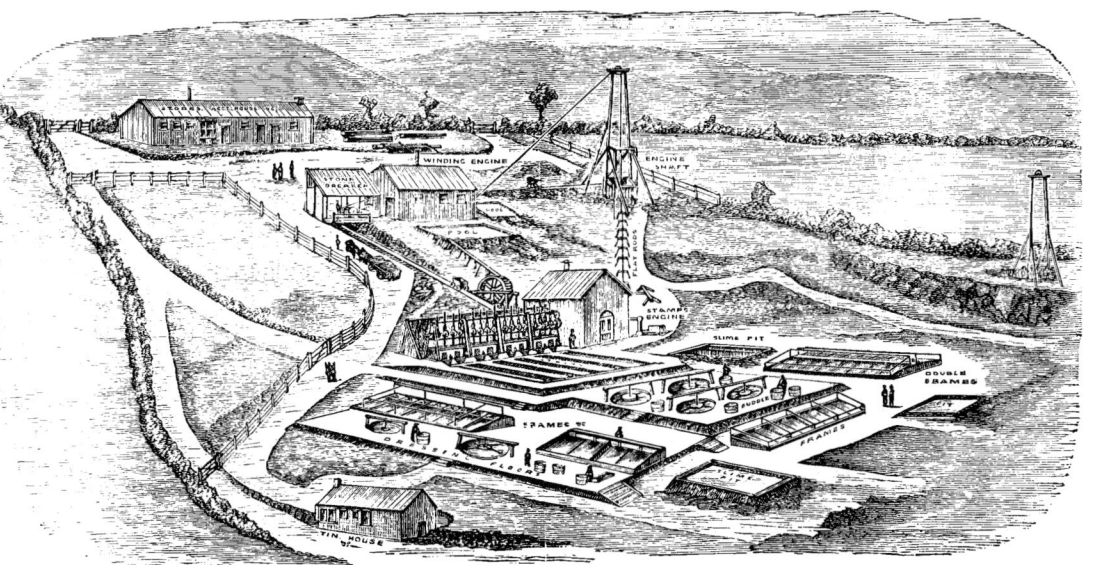

Illustration from *Geology of Cornwall* by Brenton Symons 1884 showing how the New Terras Mining Co. hoped to lay out their mine. This never happened.

1871 steam engines and some tin dressing plant had been swiftly erected on the site. An elaborate drawing had been made of the prospective site, showing how it would look when completed.[65] However, like most mining enterprises of this time, doubts were still being expressed about its viability. Specific criticism though seemed to centre on the financial management of the company, and it was suggested that the share price was being manipulated by dealers. A small quantity of tin ore was raised, but by as quickly as April 1873, mining operations had virtually ceased.

If James Hocking had returned to work the project, then this might have been his reason for switching fully to farming at Broadmoor in the latter days of his life. He knew that mining in Trelion was no longer viable. Despite this generally perceived wisdom, in 1882, a year after James' death, the mine was refloated once again as the *New Terras Mining Company Limited*.[66] According to reports, work did not actually commence until 1884, but the new company was also affected by financial scandal and ceased before the year was out. James had been right. Appropriately enough, these exploits were to provide all three writers with much material for the future, but events at Terras are perhaps best dealt with in Joseph's 1924 novel, *What Shall it Profit a Man?* which draws on his father's experiences.[67]

Tin was not the only mining activity in the region, however, and of the two mines operating in the Fal Valley, it is another, South Terras, which is the more famous, since it mined some of the radium ore used by the pioneering scientist of radioactive physics, Marie Sklodowska Curie, eventually winning with her husband Professor Pierre Curie, and Antoine Henri Becquerel, the 1903 Nobel Prize for Physics. The mine can be observed from the Broadmoor cottage; it is located around Tolgarrick Mill, in the valley of the River Fal, just below the tin mine at Trelion.

According to Courtney V. Smale, who has completed a detailed study of South Terras, its 'active life... spanned six decades, roughly divided equally between iron, uranium, and radium production from 1870 to 1930'[68] – roughly the same period in which the Hockings were writing. A full discussion of the mine's development is offered by Smale,[69] but one or two facts are pertinent to us here. The discovery of uranium at the mine was made public in 1889 in the *Mining Journal* after what Smale describes as the discovery of torbernite – 'an unusual apple-green mineral'.[70] By the following year, a laboratory for the manufacture of the oxide of uranium had been set up by a Mr Benedict Kitto, according to Smale 'a well-known figure in Cornish mining circles',[71] and shortly afterwards uranium ore and oxide began to be sold in significant quantities. The mine closed for a while, but shortly afterwards radium was discovered. Reporters and correspondents descended on South Terras. The 15th January 1904 edition of the *Cornish Guardian* stated extravagantly:

The three great salient features of radium are its enormous energy, heat and light. So prodigious is the velocity of the electrons which radium emits, that if the total energy of one gramme were converted into weight-raising power, it would be able to raise the whole of the British Navy to the top of Ben Nevis.[72]

Without a doubt the impact of the discovery of uranium and radium at South Terras was an immense event. The tiny hamlet of Trelion and the village of St Stephen-in-Brannel found themselves suddenly catapulted forwards into the advanced physics of the twentieth century – with the development of X-rays – and perhaps indirectly to an event with even greater consequence at the end of the Second World War, when on 6th August 1945, the first atomic bomb was dropped on the Japanese city of Hiroshima. How, we wonder, might Silas, Joseph and Salome have responded to such an event, which had some link with their parish?

One final related topic should be mentioned here. In the light of the discoveries made at South Terras, to the south-west of the parish, the October 1921 edition of *Mining World* caused a stir, by suggesting that mid-Cornwall might well have its own bathing facilities, offering the rather tongue-in-cheek headline: 'Cornwall as a Spa Grampound Road as a Health Resort'. Not only does the article assert the convenience of the village being on the main Great Western Railway line, but also refers to the powers of the waters drunk by the young Silas and Joseph in stimulating their imagination:

Grampound Road, a station on the Great Western Railway, between Plymouth and Penzance, viewed from the railway carriage window, sheds a gentle melancholy on the soul. It is one of the most dreary spots from this point of view that can be imagined, and the traveller thinks so as he passes it on his way to Truro some six or seven miles distant... It is true that Grampound Road is undeveloped; that neither the enterprising builder nor his confrère, the jerry-builder, had yet invaded its precincts; that it has no orchestra to emit the "concord of sweet sounds"; that it has no pump room, and, as Sam Weller would say, "no nuffin" – but perhaps to seekers after health it may be more important to know that Grampound Road has an almost unlimited supply of radio-water, and in this respect may at no distant date become a rival even to Bath. True also, Grampound Road has no Beau Brummel, or a promenade upon which he may do a modification of the Piccadilly crawl, and no Beau Nash to exhibit the latest conceits in tailoring; but, at least, it must be credited with having given birth to the famous novelists, Silas and Joseph Hocking, whose imaginative proclivities were no doubt fired, and whose delicate fancies were stimulated by the radio-waters, of which in infancy they may, with more or less discretion, have imbibed copius draughts.[73]

So far, I have considered the influences upon the Hocking trio of writers from the resolutely Hocking side of the family. I now wish to turn to the influences from Elizabeth Kitto, which perhaps had as important a shaping effect on the Hockings' written world as their father and the parish that surrounded them. Indeed, it may well have been a more powerful influence than those 'imbibed draughts' on their developing imaginations.

Elizabeth Kitto was a complex woman whose beliefs and ideology are not easy to surmise. She was originally a Bible Christian, but carried with her some folk medicine and white witch skills.[74] This may seem hard for us to contemplate now, as in present-day Cornwall, for the most part, these seem very much at opposite ends of the spiritual scale.[75] However, like most transitions of faith through the centuries, local pagan beliefs were quickly absorbed into Christianity and reinvented.[76] Put another way, they were given new spin according to the new faith, so Eliza's skills would not necessarily have been classed as evil or ungodly.

As well as this, Eliza Kitto's name merits considerable investigation; also a degree of conjecture and speculation. Her life is not as well recorded as James Hockings'. Even so, it is interesting that the Hocking family – Silas in particular – seemed keen to continue the use of her name.[77] If so, this also brings us to the further folklore of the family, that their ancestors had been both Spanish and Gypsies, and that there was a connection to the Pole-Carews. Cynically, one might argue, that as was fashionable during the late nineteenth and early twentieth century, many people claimed a more noble heritage than actually belonged to them; Thomas Hardy is one striking example of an author who in his life and works sought more glorious ancestry.[78]

Additionally, there has been for many centuries – perhaps since the Spanish landings at Mousehole, Newlyn and Penzance in 1595 – a belief that some Cornish people had descended from the Spanish, folklorically accounting for names such as Kitto, Jago and Jose. This myth is similar to that of the Cornish being one of the lost tribes of Israel – hence many mythic Jewish connections.[79] Such a mythology also accounts for the ethnic darkness readily associated with the Cornish during this period.[80] That said, a Spanish and Gypsy connection was certainly romantic and one which the Hockings may collectively have wished to attach themselves to. Conveniently, it also allowed the Hockings to write about such groups – often negatively. No criticism could be offered, because Silas and Joseph had attached themselves to the legacy. If they criticised 'Spaniards' or gypsies, then it was tongue-in-cheek, because they were writing about their own heritage. Anne Hocking, Joseph Hocking's daughter, was later to reflect on these family connections in 1953:

> *My father [Joseph] always thought that our family had both Spanish and gypsy blood in it. This was during his vague remembrance of stories told about my forefathers, my friend Sir John Squire – who everybody knows is a Devonian – believes it to be perfectly true. The Hockings are related by marriage to the Pole-Carews, and they are directly descended*

from a Cornishman who went to Spain, married a Spanish gypsy queen, and brought her home.[81]

If a Kitto connection is to be argued, then of course, it may have derived from the time that James Hocking was working in St Agnes. The Kitto family, though having connections with St Mawes, had by this time moved to the parish of Gwennap. Gwennap, of course, is only a short distance from St Agnes, and may provide an alternative explanation for Eliza's meeting with James. Further suggestions for family dynasties have been offered by parishioners but none, in this author's view, are fully conclusive.[82]

Her name however, would provide a link to another important historical figure, the celebrated early nineteenth-century Plymouthian author John Kitto (1804-1854), best known now as the author of the first *Pictorial Bible,* but also the respected writer of the *Pictorial History of Palestine and the Holy Land.*[83] His story is worth diverting to, because it does provide some possible connections. As his biographer W.H.K. Wright notes, John Kitto Jr. was the son of John Kitto Sr., a skilled Cornish stonemason, who was born in Gwennap in the later part of the eighteenth century, but who travelled to work in the expanding naval base at Plymouth, as well as helping with the construction of Dartmoor Prison at Princetown.[84]

John Kitto Jr was a sickly child, and while helping to carry slates up a high ladder, he fell, and was thenceforth stone deaf. Now unfit for work, he was sent to the workhouse and then apprenticed as a shoemaker, but in 1824, a kindly Exeter dentist took him as a pupil, giving him board and paying him a small salary, allowing him eventually to be trained in Islington by the Church Missionary Society as a printer.[85] He travelled widely to Malta, Persia and Armenia, and wrote a series of narratives based on the life of the those with visual, spoken and hearing deficiencies, later published under the title of *The Lost Senses.*[86] It was though, his vision of a Pictorial Bible which was to change his life, for the book became an instant best-seller and offered, like the Hockings, a new way of receiving the message of the Bible. Indeed, it is this heritage which Silas may well have wanted to allude to. It would certainly not have done his publishing career any harm to be associated with such an illustrious and influential work.

On 21st September 1833, John Kitto Jr. had married a Miss Fenwick and they had seven children.[87] Kitto himself continued writing although he never reached the level of popularity of his initial work. A projected *Encyclopedia of the Bible* failed to emerge, as did a *Journal of Sacred Literature.* According to Wright, his last work was a series of volumes based on *Daily Bible Illustrations.*[88] These were successful, but by 1851, his health was in serious decline. His only means of support was a small Civil List Pension, which helped pay for medical treatment in Germany. He died on 25th November 1854 and was buried at Canstatt. There ended a remarkable career, immortalised in connection with Biblical study and literature.

The picture is sketchy about what happened to Kitto's family. It is known that they lived in London for some time, though the little evidence that is available, suggests they eventually returned back to Cornwall – maybe to Gwennap or St Mawes. The only other information known is that John Kitto's eldest son emigrated to North America and ran a funeral parlour there. Could it be that Eliza was related in some way to this family? Silas Kitto Hocking, according to numerous observers, always claimed a connection.

Whatever the link, and despite considerable investigation, it has been impossible to precisely pin it down. However, a note of the connection between the Hocking and Kitto families is found in the *Dictionary of National Biography*. Very often a joint reference to both names can be found, and although Cornwall has been slow to respond to the legacy of the Hockings, Plymouth has been rather more keen to link its identity to John Kitto's heritage. In 1884 a Kitto Institute started its life over an onion store in Woolster Street near the Barbican, and was a boys club opened to show them what could be done against all odds – like John Kitto himself. The Institute was eventually taken over and administered by the Young Man's Christian Association in 1909, and in 1974 a YMCA centre was opened at Burrington, Honicknowle, tying in with the later renaming of the Burrington School as the John Kitto School in 1989; now a large, 11-19 community college serving the north-west of Plymouth.[89]

Having considered Eliza's Kitto connection, now let us return to the character of the Hockings' mother. Her magical powers and healing skills are well-recorded, perhaps originally being derived from Spanish and gypsy connections. Several stories are worth exploration here, mainly through a version of her mother's experiences in the part-autobiographical, part-anthropological work, *Some Old Cornish Folk* (1903) by Salome. For example, it was said that on the warm, dry, south-facing slopes of Terras and Trelion, many snakes liked to bathe in the sun. Dogs, having been bitten by such snakes, could be charmed, as could the snakes themselves.[90] At Resugga Lane End, Elizabeth apparently charmed a snake to let a funeral cortège go past.[91] In the same volume there is the story of how 'Richard Bluett and Sam Jones had had the cows charmed for adder stings, and never troubled to send for a farrier; while two of the women knew cases where "kennons" [cataracts] in the eyes and many ringworms had been cured by charms'.[92] In another chapter, headed 'Ferrel's Van', Salome writes of a neighbour, who could charm; clearly an event based on her mother's activities:

> Then there was the well-known case of the boy who had shot off his thumb, and was in danger of bleeding to death before the doctor, who lived five miles away, could be fetched; but a neighbour who knew a

charm for stopping blood had been called in, and the bleeding had ceased.[93]

Charmers such as Eliza could not treat or help her own family, but they could charm out the Brownies; in British folklore, Brownies being pixies who look after the bees, obviously crucial in the process of pollination.[94] They were charmed out by making a loud noise, usually by banging two metal objects together and shouting their name loudly in the place where they were requested to come. Charming tends to follow other patterns of experience across these islands. Where there are small creatures, and a long tradition of folklore and tale, then charming and magic can be found.[95] It appears to go with the territory. Likewise, alongside charming, storytelling skills are often accentuated, as in this sequence from the 1903 volume, in the chapter titled 'Sebudah and Aaron', where two people listen to a story told by an Eliza-like character:

The next scene I have any distinct recollection of is seeing Sebudah and my Aunt Eleanor seated in our kitchen listening to a thrilling ghost story, which my mother was relating, a'propos of some strange event seen in the neighbourhood. I think it is from my mother that we have inherited what little story-telling talent we have. She had a keen eye for dramatic effect, and knew how to work up her audience to the proper pitch of excitement, and leave them gasping and shivering at the climax...[96]

These are neatly fitting Celtic qualities. Since the Cornish Celtic-revival, and in particular, the Cornish Gorseth of 1928,[97] it suddenly became more fashionable for observers to comment on this aspect of a writer's life and work. In 1953 H. M. Cresswell Payne considers the Celticity of the Hockings' skills as writers, relating these to their mother Eliza, as well as a further stereotype of the Celts being good storytellers:

In talking to St Stephens people I always found that [Silas'] father – James Hocking, who was a kind of local "cap'n" of a small tinwork – was held to be man of sterling character and worth. The mother was more gifted and a great strength in the local chapel: her Celtic imagination had endowed her with a rich gift for storytelling. Around the fire on winter nights the family sat as she delighted them with old tales of the country-side: it was from her that the boys – Silas and Joseph – and Salome their sister, inherited the gift for telling a tale.[98]

The Hockings' Celticity is also referred to by Anne Hocking in a 1953 newspaper interview, following a discussion of other Cornish-themed writings. She notes, 'It's the Celt in us. I certainly think it is the case in our own family'.[99] While we are considering the Celticity of the Hocking family, it is opportune here to consider the lives of the rest of the less famous Hocking siblings. We know that both Jabez and Simeon worked as miners abroad. It seems Jabez stayed in California, while Simeon worked in Canada, later dying there. Mahala Mary, the eldest daughter died in 1939, living to the age of 86 – still in the parish of her birth, though little else is known of her life. Sadly Thirza, the second daughter, and a Sunday school teacher, died much earlier aged sixteen in 1872. Elizabeth Kitto, their mother died on 12th May, 1891, aged 69.

As can be seen, the written world of the Hockings was created early on in their lives. They already came from a distinctively literary parish. In many ways, theirs was the classic Cornish industrial childhood; one solidly based on the nonconformist tradition, upon mining and agriculture, the Chapel as community, and of an inherent Celticity. It was also a childhood mixed with emigration, of long separation from their father and brother. At its most devastating, it showed how society and the three life system of leasehold could defeat a man, who had worked hard all his life, who had unconditionally put all his faith in God, and still lost.

Most of all, it taught all the children how to deal with adversity, and that it could hit anyone, even anyone as close to them as their father. It was a swirling mix of emotion, yet it was also a commitment to Christianity that was seemingly unassailable; that emotion and commitment were about to find their way into print in the first of the writing siblings – Silas Kitto.

Notes

1. Silas Kitto Hocking, *Cornish Guardian*, 18th June (1926) p.7. A similarity to the Hockings may be observed in the work of the Welsh novelist Daniel Owen (1836-95), who reacted to similar nonconfomist prejudice to fiction. See Dafydd Johnston (1994) *The Literature of Wales*, Cardiff: University of Wales Press, pp.77-80.
2. Olver, T.J., (n.d.) *An Account of the History of St Stephen-in-Brannel*, St Stephen-in-Brannel: St Stephen-in-Brannel Parish Church Publication, p.10.
3. See Brian Murdoch (1993) *Cornish Literature*, Cambridge: D.S. Brewer.
4. See Lauran Toorians (ed.) (1991) *The Middle Cornish Charter Endorsement: The Making of a Marriage in Medieval Cornwall*, Innsbruck: Institut für Sprachwissenschaft der Universität Innsbruck.
5. Alan M. Kent and Tim Saunders (eds. and trs.) (2000) *Looking at the Mermaid: A Reader in Cornish Literature 900-1900*, London: Francis Boutle, pp.30-31. The piece is considered by some to be a 'fragment' of a longer work.
6. A Jack Clemo Memorial Room was officially opened in 2001 at Trethosa Methodist Chapel. Recent research includes John Hurst, 'Voice From a White Silence: The Manuscripts of Jack Clemo' in Philip Payton (ed.) (1995) *Cornish Studies: Three*, Exeter: University of Exeter Press, pp.125-143; Andrew C. Symons, 'Jack Clemo's Italian Holiday' in *Journal of the Royal Institution of Cornwall* (2000), p.186-96; Alan M. Kent (2000) *The Literature of Cornwall: Continuity, Identity, Difference 1000-2000*, Bristol: Redcliffe, pp.209-14.
7. See, for example, Jack Clemo (1988) *Selected Poems*, Newcastle upon Tyne: Bloodaxe Books, (1948) *Wilding Graft*, London: Chatto and Windus, (1986) *The Shadowed Bed*, Tring: Lion, (2000) *The Clay Kiln*, St Austell: Cornish Hillside Publications.
8. To consider the development of literary criticism, and moves to and from the importance of the author, see John Dixon (1991) *A Schooling in 'English': Critical Episodes to Shape Literary and Cultural Studies*, Buckingham: Open University Press.
9. For a useful introduction to the field, see Scott Wilson (1995) *Cultural Materialism: Theory and Practice*, Oxford: Blackwell.
10. See Caroline and Frank Thorn (eds.) (1979) *Domesday Book: Cornwall*, Chicester: Phillimore, p.121
11. Olver (n.d.) op.cit., p.1.
12. The idea here is that many Britons were pushed across the Channel into Brittany and Northern Gaul following Saxon invasion into the west of the island of Britain. This group became the 'Normans' (although a third of William's army was of Breton stock), who were actually in the Conquest, reclaiming their original land. This is part of the thesis of Geoffrey of Monmouth. See Lewis Thorpe (ed. and tr.) (1966) *Geoffrey of Monmouth: The History of the Kings of Britain*, Harmondsworth: Penguin.
13. Olver (n.d.) op.cit., p.2.
14. Ibid., p.1. See also P. Behenna and Kathleen Caddy, 'Our Village – St Stephen-in-Brannel' in Peter Bishop, Susan Morcom, Babs Bennett, Liz Toms, Liz (eds.) (1994) *A Century of Change: One Hundred Years of St Stephen-in-Brannel Parish Council 1894-1994*. St Stephen-in-Brannel: St Stephen-in-Brannel Parish Council, p.69.
15. Craig Weatherhill (1995) *Cornish Place Names and Language*. Wilmslow: Sigma, p.112.
16. Olver (n.d.), op.cit., pp.4-5.
17. Ibid., p.9. The second Lord Camelford was known as the 'Half-Mad' Lord. For more detail on him, and background to Boconnoc, see Nikolai Tolstoy (1978) *The Half-Mad Lord, Thomas Pitt, 2nd Baron Camelford*, London: Cape, pp.1-16.
18. See C.A. Evans, 'A Tudor Mansion in the Clay Country: The Story of Meledor at St. Stephen' in *Cornish Guardian* (n.d.). Article in possession of the author. For detail and archaeological sketches of the Mansion, see the *Charles Henderson Collection*, Royal Institution of Cornwall, pp.385-404. Henderson felt the features would be destroyed by the expansion of the China Clay workings, but this has not happened. However, Clemo (1948) op.cit. details much of the village of Meledor, which was destroyed by the expansion of Melbur China Clay Pit.
19. For detail on this rebellion, see Kent (2000) op.cit., p.48 and Kent and Saunders (2000) op.cit., p. 267 and p.352.

Chapter 1 – Notes

20. See Evans, op.cit.
21. O.J. Padel (1988) *A Popular Dictionary of Cornish Place-Names,* Penzance: Alison Hodge, p.158.
22. Ibid.
23. Behenna and Caddy in Bishop *et al* (eds.) op.cit., p.69.
24. Padel (1988) op.cit.
25. Olver (n.d.) op.cit., p.3.
26. St Stephen Methodist Church (1970) *St. Stephen Methodist Church Centenary 1870-1970,* St Stephen-in-Brannel: St Stephen-in-Brannel Methodist Church, p.2.
27. Craig Weatherhill (1985) *Cornovia: Ancient Sites of Cornwall and Scilly.* Penzance: Alison Hodge, p.120.
28. William C. Borlase (1871) *Ancient Cornwall, a collection of drawings etc, Original and copied, illustrative of the Antiquities of that County,* MS., I, p.17.
29. Cited in Roger Penhallurick (1986) *Tin in Antiquity,* London: The Institute of Metals, p.190. For an illustration of the collar, see p.192.
30. Ibid., p.190.
31. See A. Douglas Selleck (1978) *Cookworthy: A Man of No Common Clay,* Plymouth: Baron Jay Ltd. Useful background on the operation of the Stannaries in mid-Cornwall can be found in George Harrison (1835) *A Report on the Laws and Jurisdiction of the Stannaries in Cornwall.* London: Longman, Rees, Orme, Brown, Green, and Longman. Certainly much of the early tin works at Terras and Trelion would have been subject to their Jurisdiction.
32. See Charles Thurlow (2001) *China Clay from Cornwall and Devon: The Modern China Clay Industry,* St Austell: Cornish Hillside Publications. A useful archaeological survey of the region is found in Peter Herring and John R. Smith (1991) *The Archaeology of the St Austell China Clay Area,* Truro: Cornwall Archaeological Unit.
33. See Donald R. Rawe (1986) *A Prospect of Cornwall,* London: Robert Hale, p.50. Silt in the River Fal has hampered river traffic to these former quays.
34. Cornu-English terminology for the overseer of a mine.
35. Bernard Deacon, "Proto-Industrialization and Potatoes: A Revised Narrative for Nineteenth-Century Cornwall' in Philip Payton (ed.) (1997) *Cornish Studies: Five,* Exeter: University of Exeter Press, pp.60-84.
36. There are varying views on this. It seems likely that James was the third life, although there is another interpretation. He may have actually had the first life, but having no male children living there to carry on the life, he lost everything.
37. John Rowe (1993 [1953]) *Cornwall in the Age of the Industrial Revolution.* St Austell: Cornish Hillside Publications, p.215. Thomas Hardy also used this theme in his writing. He said of his hero Giles Winterthorne that 'as a story [it is] the best of all'. See Patricia Ingham (ed.) (1998 [1887]) *Thomas Hardy: The Woodlanders,* Harmondsworth: Penguin, rear cover.
38. Little Treneague lies between St Stephen-in-Brannel and Meledor.
39. Fifield, Arthur C. (1927) *Salome Hocking Fifield: In Memoriam.* Coulsdon: Arthur C. Fifield, p.11. Despite considerable research the precise workings of the lease remain a mystery. It seems therefore that James and Eliza were the victims of two evictions – first at Terras, and then at Broadmoor.
40. This date is cared into one of the roof beams of the cottage. According to the *Parish Index* Ref 846, 147-153, Cornwall Record Office, Trelyon [or Trelion] was originally part of the same lease of properties at Goonvean, Stepaside, Penhale and Nazeath from 1758-1859. The *Ground Rent Receipts* collection at the Courtney, Library, Royal Institution of Cornwall, refers to John and Eliza Sharrock of Creed selling Trelion to one Francis Hoblyn in 1603. The Hoblyns were connected to the Pitt family. See above, and below.
41. Although a different area of Cornwall, much of the atmosphere of agriculture at this time is captured in John Rowe (1996) *Changing Times and Fortunes: A Cornish Farmer's Life 1828-1904,* St Austell: Cornish Hillside Publications. See also James Whetter (2001) *The Cornish Farmer,* Gorran: Lyfrow Trelyspen.
42. Olver (n.d.) op.cit., p.9; Courtney V. Smale 'Cornwall's Premier Uranium and Radium Mine' in *Journal of the Royal Institution of Cornwall* (1993), p.311.
43. See Boconnoc, *A History of Boconnoc,* Boconnoc: Boconnoc Church, n.d.
44. Ibid.

Chapter 1 – Notes

45. These were William Pitt, being Prime Minister from 1783-1801 and William Pitt from 1804-06. The Fortescues also had considerable interests in the china clay mining industry. This may be one reason why the Hockings were reluctant to write about that industry during the course of their careers; the early industry being dependant on powerful landowning classes.
46. *Bible Christian Magazine* (1832). pp.143-4. The Chapel opened on 20th November 1831. For interesting insight into the linkages between Bible Christians and politics during this phase, see David Hempton (1984) *Methodism and Politics in British Society 1750-1850,* London: Hutchinson, pp.12-19.
47. *Bible Christian Magazine* (1903). p.176. Part of the success of Methodism was the sheer physical fact that worshippers in large, rural parishes no longer needed to walk several miles on Sunday to the Anglican church, when smaller chapels allowed convenience and proximity.
48. Thomas Shaw (1965) *The Bible Christians.* London: Epworth Press.
49. St Stephen Methodist Church (1970) op.cit., p.2.
50. *Bible Christian Magazine* (1903) op.cit.
51. Ibid.
52. Ibid.
53. Peter Isaac, (2000) *A History of Evangelical Christianity in Cornwall,* Cornwall: Peter Isaac, pp.123-7.
54. *Census* (1861) Folio 104, Cornwall Records Office, Truro.
55. Trelyon Concols (n.d.) *Terras, Hallivick and Trelyon Mines* Grampound Road: James and Company. Pamphlet in collection of the author. Piecemeal mining and tin-streaming had been taking place in this area for a number of years. Receipts for tin bounds renewal from 1806-08 and 1840-1 have survived. See the *Treffry Deeds,* Cornwall Records Office, Truro.
56. *Mining Journal,* 26th August (1865). p.553. Here, Terras is spelt 'Torras', much closer to the Cornu-English pronunciation. An elvan is a porphyry or fine grained granite.
57. Ibid.
58. *Mining Journal,* 24th March (1866), p.181.
59. See Philip Payton (1999) *The Cornish Overseas,* Fowey: Alexander Associates for a comprehensive picture of emigration.
60. See A.L. Rowse (1991 [1961]) *The Cornish in America,* Redruth: Dyllansow Truran, pp.241-86; John Rowe (1974) *The Hard Rock Men: Cornish Immigrants and the North American Mining Frontier,* Liverpool: Liverpool University Press.
61. Cited in Alan M. Kent (ed.) (1999) *Voices from West Barbary: An Anthology of Anglo-Cornish Poetry 1549-1928,* London: Francis Boutle, p.156.
62. Letter from James Hocking in *Mining Journal,* 26th April (1869).
63. *Mining Journal,* 12th March (1870), p.202. A sett refers to the lease stating the boundaries and terms of the ground to mine.
64. *Census* (1871) Folio 33, Cornwall Records Office, Truro. This year the Hockings had temporarily moved to Little Treneague, just up the Fal Valley. Both Censi, list Elizabeth Kitto's parish of origin at St Anthony.
65. This appears in Brenton Symons (1882) *Geology of Cornwall,* London: The Mining Journal, p.137. This is part of a wider survey of the St Austell mining district.
66. *Mining Journal,* 17th June (1882), p.719.
67. Joseph Hocking (1924) *What Shall it Profit a Man?* London: Hodder and Stoughton.
68. Smale (1993) op.cit., p.304. I am indebted to Mr Smale for this survey of South Terras.
69. Ibid., pp.304-21.
70. Ibid., p.306.
71. Ibid., p.307. Probably of no immediate link to the Kittos alluded to below.
72. Cited in ibid., p.311.
73. *Mining World,* 22nd October (1921), p.374. Incidentally, a property in Grampound Road bears the name 'Fentonwyn' [Cornish: 'white well or spring']
74. For a history of witchcraft and healing in Cornwall, see Tony Deane and Tony Shaw (1975), *The Folklore of Cornwall,* Totowa, New Jersey: Rowman and Littlefield and Margaret Courtney (1989 [1890]) *Folklore and Legends of Cornwall [Cornish Feasts and Folklore],* Exeter: Cornwall Books.

75. See regular debate in *Meyn Mamvro.* However, this may not always be the case. The well-known self-proclaimed King, and Archdruid of Cornwall, Ed Prynne, describes his beliefs as 'both druidic and Methodist' – conversation with the author, June 1999.
76. A point well-made in Charles Thomas and Joanna Mattingly (2000), *The History of Christianity in Cornwall AD 500 – 2000,* Truro: Royal Institution of Cornwall.
77. Confirmed by a conversation and correspondence with Molly Richards, 1993. However, to clarify, Silas was christened 'Silas Kitto'.
78. See Kenneth Phelps (1975) *The Wormwood Cup – Thomas Hardy in Cornwall: A Study in Temperament, Topography and Timing,* Padstow: Lodenek Press. This interest is seen most obviously in Tess of the D'Urbervilles. See A. Alvarez and David Skilton (eds.) (1978 [1871]) *Thomas Hardy: Tess of the D'Urbervilles,* Harmondsworth: Penguin, pp.43-4.
79. Deconstructed by various scholars in Keith Pearce and Helen Fry (eds.) (2000) *The Lost Jews of Cornwall,* Bristol: Redcliffe.
80. Best seen in John Beddoes's *Index of Nigresence in The Races of Britain* (1885), cited in James Vernon 'Cornwall and the Engish Imagi(nation)' in Geoffrey Cubitt (ed.) (1998) *Imagining Nations,* Manchester: Manchester University Press, p.158. Cornwall is amongst the darkest regions of the index. See also W.H. Hudson (1981 [1908]) *The Land's End: A Naturalist's Impressions in West Cornwall,* London: Wildwood House, pp.95-6.
81. George A. Greenwood, 'Daughter of famous Cornish novelist writes her 40th book: Anne Hocking's West Reminiscences' in The *Western Morning News,* 2nd December (1953).
82. My research into the family history of the Hockings, is by necessity, introductory. These few remarks may assist other scholars who wish to further trace the Hocking/Kitto lines. Molly Richards believes that Elizabeth Kitto's full name was Elizabeth Kitto Richards, the daughter of one William Richards (1833-1870) who married a Mary Jane Yelland (1832-1904). Dick Smythe adds to this theory by commenting that William Richards had three children: Humphry, Tom and Elizabeth. Humphry married Elizabeth Hooker, but their son and daughter's names are unknown. They may have taken forward the Kitto name. Tom married Belle Ellis and had two daughters – named Gladys Kitto and Virginia Kitto. Tom and his family resided at Spring Farm in Coombe. Dick Smythe also knew of a Joe Kitto who lived at Gloweth, Truro, where coincidentally, there is a Bible Christian Chapel. There was a Barrington Kitto who lived at St Stephen-in-Brannel. He had a son, Murray, who went to South Africa as cinema organist. Although all of this does show a pattern of names across the parish, it does not really move us closer to the more famous Kitto line.
83. John Kitto (1835-8) *The Pictorial Bible, 3 vols,* London: Charles Knight and Co, (1840) *The Pictorial History of Palestine and the Holy Land, including a Complete History of the Jews, 2 vols,* London: Charles Knight and Co..
84. W.H.K. Wright (n.d.) *John Kitto, D.D., F.S.A.* Publisher unknown, pp.1-2.
85. Ibid., pp.3-6.
86. John Kitto (1845) *The Lost Senses,* London: Charles Knight and Co.
87. Wright, op.cit., p.10.
88. Ibid., p.12.
89. See 'Benefactor who beat all odds' in *Plymouth Evening Herald,* 19th October 1990.
90. Salome Hocking Fifield (1903) *Some Old Cornish Folk.* London: Charles H. Kelly, p.126.
91. Ibid.
92. Ibid., p.127. Presumably the farrier would deal with minor veterinary procedures.
93. Ibid., p.126.
94. According to Robert Hunt, 'this spirit was purely of the household, kindly and good, he devoted his every care to benefit the family with whom he had taken up his abode'. See Robert Hunt (ed.) (1865) *The Drolls, Traditions, and Superstitions of Old Cornwall: Popular Romances of the West of England (First Series).* London: John Camden Hotton, p.82.
95. See Hamish Miller and Paul Broadhurst (1989) *The Sun and the Serpent: An Investigation into Earth Energies,* Launceston: Pendragon Press and Nigel Pennick (1996) *Celtic Sacred Landscape,* London: Thames and Hudson. The former book interestingly is very critical of the 'earth energy' found in mid-Cornwall due to the environmental destruction caused by the china clay extractive industry; a view vigorously opposed by this author. The spirituality of the landscape is seen in the work of Jack Clemo.
96. Hocking Fifield (1903) op.cit, p.45.

97. Details of this are outlined in Kent (2000) op.cit., pp.149-153.
98. H.M. Cresswell Payne, 'Pages from the Book of Memory: A Cornish Novelist' in *Cornish Methodism,* 24th December (1953), p.4.
99. Greenwood (1953) op.cit.

Silas Kitto Hocking, a photograph when middle aged.

Chapter Two

Who wants to be a Million-Selling novelist?: The Life of Silas Kitto Hocking, 1850-1935

> *"The novels of Silas K. Hocking*
> *Don't mention the village of Stocking.*
> *When he learnt that there were*
> *Not one but a pair,"*
> *He said, "This nomenclature's shocking."*
> *Yvette Tuke laughed, though she had missed much of the point,*
> *none of Mr. Hocking's hundred novels having come her way.*
>
> Douglas G. Broome, *Too Many Cousins*, 1948[1]

Silas Kitto Hocking was the first novelist in the world to sell a million copies of one title – his 1879 novel *Her Benny*.[2] We tend to think of the other better-known British novelists of the nineteenth century – Charles Dickens, George Eliot, the Brontës and Thomas Hardy – as selling many more copies, and probably, over the course of time, they have, but by the end of the nineteenth century, nothing, not even these literary heavyweights could touch the sales of Silas Kitto Hocking. A million copies may not seem that many, in today's best-seller world of *Harry Potter* and cinema tie-ins, but the sheer physical quantity of books sold, indicate massive interest in the author's work during his lifetime. Silas Kitto had probably wanted to be a novelist since childhood. The story of how he achieved both this incredible statistic, as well as many other notable publications, not to mention a ministerial, political and pacifist career will be the subject of this chapter.

The elder of the two writing brothers, Silas Kitto Hocking, was born on the 24th March 1850 in the middle of a tempestuous and ever-modernising century. As both Jones, and McCord note, Britain had to take notice of the wider world stage: France, Austria and Hungary had all undergone new revolutions; France was setting up the Second Republic, the Austrian Emperor Ferdinand had abdicated in favour of his more democratic nephew Josef, and Hungary sought a new constitution for itself outside the reins of Austrian control.[3] Close by, events leading to the Crimean War – and perhaps even to World War One – started to brew in Russia and Turkey. Despite these internal changes, Europe as a whole, had become the overlord of the rest of the world. Britain itself, was fully confident of its own imperial power.[4] A year after Silas's birth, the Great Exhibition was held in London, celebrating Britain's prowess and technological achievement. Cornwall meanwhile, was still in the boom years of metal mining; the economic decline beginning in the second half of the nineteenth century[5] – a culture that was to have a major impact on the young Silas Kitto Hocking's work. In many ways, it was both these wider world events and those in Cornwall which would contribute to his success as a writer, yet in the parish of St Stephen-in-Brannel, Silas's childhood was seemingly at a distance to these huge world events.

Unlike Joseph and Salome, Silas Kitto was to write an autobiography, *My Book of Memory*,[6] published in 1923, but unfortunately it tells us little about his youth, and, in general, its tone is distant from Cornwall. A second collection of reminiscences, *Looking Back*,[7] was published 1936, and though again, offering a useful general picture, its use to the biographer remains limited. Much more can be gleaned about his early years from interviews given to newspapers and magazines later in his life. Silas actually resisted the importunities of his friends to write an autobiography, since he felt uncertain about it as a genre, feeling it was too egotistical for him. The resultant two texts are not autobiographies in the conventional sense, since they spend more time on other figures and events happening around Silas, rather than placing himself centre-stage. However, this is not to distract from both of the books' worth, for in them, we see a Cornishman's ability to overcome numerous obstacles, his literary skill and development, and above all, his resilient faith. Silas was actually a very private man, who acknowledged the fame that accompanied his literary success, although very often, he felt constrained and even manipulated by it.

My Book of Memory is characterised initially by an enthusiastic young man, eager to succeed, but later, particularly after three events – his resignation from the ministry, his crisis over the Boer War and then the death of his son – feels less confident and certain of the world. At its most devastating, it sometimes feels as if the public, and perhaps even all he had been preaching in his fiction, had somehow failed him. Publicly, as Jack Clemo argues, it looks as though Silas loses the thread,[8] but privately, as we shall see, the picture, is much more complicated.

In our story, we shall move from his beginnings at Terras and Trelion, through a highly successful writing career, to what Silas considered to be the 'World's Hope' – the League of Nations. It was as massive a leap as any Cornishman might have made in the end of the nineteenth – and the opening decades of the twentieth centuries. To begin our story of the first writing sibling, we return to the parish of St Stephen-in-Brannel in the middle of Cornwall. Silas, like all the Hocking siblings spent his time roaming the tin streams, fields, moorland and woodland of Trelion and

Terras, following his father's tin and farming exploits and listening to his mother's stories, undoubtedly intrigued at his Kitto family connections. He was later to recollect this innocent time:

The days of my youth were spent in a remote Cornish village, five miles away from the nearest lamp-post, two miles and half from the nearest railway station, and about mid-way between the Atlantic seaboard and the English channel.[9]

Perhaps for effect, his description of his childhood, is a little laced with romance. In Britain, Cornwall by now, was expected to produce as such, but nevertheless he makes connections to what is known about his mother and early narrative influences:

In such an environment, life was not exactly exciting. Nevertheless, it has its interest, and occasionally, its touch of adventure. There were smugglers all around the coast. Travellers crossing the fields and moors at night were led astray by mischievous pixies; witches still dwelt in lonely huts in secluded glens... and gypsies pitched their tents outside the village and told the fortunes of the lads and maidens who were rich enough or foolish enough to cross their palms with silver. I never had any communication with smugglers though I frequently saw them. They looked more like gamekeepers than anything else. They usually wore a loose coat with large inside pockets, the better to conceal articles of contraband, especially the skins of brandy they carried.[10]

Unlike many children of the parish – from the age of seven he received a private education at a parochial Dame School in the village. The cost was 'tuppence a week, and for this fee Silas was drilled in reading, writing and arithmetic, as well as Scripture. His education lasted there until 1863, by which time he was thirteen. Then he passed into the private and influential tutorship of Mr. T.N. Andrews, a local man, of whom we know little, yet presumably it was during this period, that Silas expanded both his Christian convictions as well as his interest in literature. (Some sources allude to Silas attending Grammar school, but I can find no such evidence[11]). Visitors, seemingly staying in his grandfather's smithy captured the young boy's imagination, as did the canon of literature:

In those days story-books for young people were few and far between, though story-telling was common everywhere. Occasionally, a down-and-out sailor would straggle through the village, and sometimes find a night's lodging in the smithy. In such occasions, we boys would gather round for a yarn, which we generally got apocryphal, no doubt, for the most part, but not the less interesting on that account. When there was no-one to weave yarns for us, we wove them for ourselves, evolving them out of our inner consciousness. On rainy or stormy evenings we would gather in a barn and tell stories by the yard. I was generally regarded as pretty good at this particular form of entertainment. We would start off not knowing whither we were going. Often the stories were not finished

> at a sitting, but were announced 'to be continued in our next', like a regular serial... When I had pocket-money of my own, I invested the greater part of it in cheap paper-covered books. One of my first purchases was Shakespeare's plays. I bought nearly all Scott's novels, some of Dickens's books and Fenimore Cooper's tales. I read also Goldsmith's 'Vicar of Wakefield', 'Uncle Tom's Cabin' and of course, 'Queechy' and 'The Wide Wide World'. I made a dash at the poets and read Byron, Cowper, Milton, Young's 'Night Thoughts' and the 'Proverbial Philosophy of Martin Tupper'.[12]

This is a fascinating insight into the shaping of Silas as a writer. Even in childhood, he had an incredible awareness not only of storytelling, but also the mechanisms of keeping an audience on the edge of its seat, and the process of literary production in the form of serial magazines. The influence of Sir Walter Scott, was massive in terms of the shaping of his later adventure stories, and in his wider education. Silas remained with Mr Andrews until 1866 when he began work as a mining surveyor.[13] This may have been influenced by his father's career as Mining Cap'n and Agent, as well as the industrial activity around Terras, Trelion, and elsewhere in Cornwall.

However, while still a teenager, he had undoubtedly been treated to the preaching of figures such as Billy Bray at Trelion Chapel, as well as a leading young Methodist traveller by the name of Amos B. Matthews,[14] who preached regularly at St Austell. As a young man, Silas heard Matthews on numerous occasions, and Matthews took an interest in him, knowing he was attending a private academy back in St Stephen-in-Brannel. Matthews had grown up in similar circumstances in Plymouth, so a bond of understanding developed between them. Their friendship was to last throughout their lives. Matthews was crucial in influencing Silas to enter the Ministry.

In *My Book of Memory,* Silas makes some allusions to this time in his life. In the chapter titled 'Beginnings' he explains his desire to become a public speaker and that he would tramp miles across the mid-Cornwall landscape to listen to what he terms the 'temperance orator, returned missionary, political aspirant or budding social reformer'.[15] He admits his own early attempts at speaking were dogged with failure, and though he sometimes planned certain speeches to last for an hour, he found he finished them within only twenty minutes, with nothing else to say, but accept questions. Fortunately, he tells us, that one day at Grampound, he began to develop the skills of oration properly.[16] We may wonder if the high moral stance of some of these early speakers actually helped or hindered him.

Alongside his quest to become a preacher, we learn much of his earliest literary attempts. The Band of Hope Union offered one hundred pounds for the best story illustrating the evils of strong drink, and Silas was determined to have a shot at it.[17] Having read Scott, and Fenimore Cooper, alongside Harrison Ainsworth, Wilkie Collins and Bulwer Lytton,[18] no doubt he felt it would be as easy as falling off a stool. He spent several days devising a suitably tragic and blood-curdling plot, but as he later reflected, the novel's conversations lagged and his characters had little to talk about. Suffice to say, he did not win the prize money.

Aged eighteen, Silas was accepted as a local preacher in the expanding St Austell circuit. Sundays were spent preaching, travelling as far afield as St Columb Major,[19] while during the week he prepared sermons and read commentaries of the Holy scriptures. In addition to this he attended Temperance Meetings and Mother's Groups. After six months, he became an auxiliary preacher, giving him added duties, and more travel to and fro across Cornwall. Already some conflict of interest was developing; Silas on occasion preferring the open platform to that of the pulpit, a platform which was eventually to become his writing:

> *The platform seemed to offer more freedom of expression and a better opportunity of seizing points and illustrations that might occur at the moment. In the pulpit one had to move along clearly defined lines, to stick more or less closely to the text, to observe all the conventions. On the platform one was less concerned about form. It was like a galloping across the open country instead of running between fences.*[20]

Another story of this time relates to the many occasions when Silas rode on horseback to the location where he would be preaching. One windy Sunday October morning, he was riding across a broad plateau – perhaps Hensbarrow Downs – sparsely covered with gorse and heather. Suddenly, a gust of wind caught his bowler hat and carried it over a shallow ditch, beyond a fence, and left it stranded in gorse bushes some fifteen or twenty yards away. Retrieving the hat would be tricky. His horse, Bess, was not the most amiable of creatures, and to leave her standing in the road, while he went to search for his hat would be to court disaster. There was no tree nor gate to which Silas could fasten her. In the end, he jumped the ditch and fence and managed to retrieve his hat. Upon completing this, he tried to ride on again, but Bess was uncooperative. She reared, and only when Bess decided they should go, did she jump back over the fence. Silas describes the ride back as being like 'an indiarubber ball'.[21]

Clearly Silas worked hard during his training, reading a number of books, studying for examinations and preaching several trial sermons while being observed. Within two years, in 1870, aged just twenty, he was ordained in the United Methodist Free Churches' Ministry. There is not the space here to enter into a full discussion of the origins and aims of the United Methodist Free Churches. Beckerlegge's 1957 account provides much of this.[22] It is, however, worth reasserting at this stage, their commitment to democracy and to greater local independence. In relation to this, two issues should be borne in mind. Firstly, although it had been James Hocking's wish for Silas to start a career in mine surveying, no doubt he would have been delighted to see his third son enter the Methodist Ministry. Secondly, given the circumstances and opportunities in mid-Cornwall during this time, one of the few ways for the aspiring intellectual to broaden his horizon, was to enter the Ministry. This was important, since in general, the Anglican church in Cornwall and elsewhere, tended to select those who would progress educationally. The Ministry was a way of subverting this tendency. His first appointment came quickly, actually before he was properly ordained, in 1869, when he was aged only nineteen. He left Cornwall for another Celtic territory – Wales.

There, he was stationed at Pontypool, in the Newport Circuit,[23] where the mining-Methodist and nonconformist culture existed in a similar way to that of Cornwall. Here, however, it was not tin, copper or clay that was mined, but coal. It was during this time that the Reverend Silas Kitto Hocking was to first grow his characteristic long beard, which over time gave him his patriarchal appearance. It is very likely that he first grew the beard to look older, so he could gain more respect as a Minister. His stipend at Pontypool was fifty-five pounds a year, out of which he paid six shillings a week for his room. How the Welsh community would have responded to this young Cornishman is difficult to assess, although we may conjecture that it would have been a trial by fire. Life would not have been easy for Silas. Despite the similarities to Cornwall in the valleys, no doubt he felt very isolated. There is one suggestion that Silas made friends with some students of the local Baptist College and that he most likely attended lectures organised by worker's educational groups.[24] To make ends meet, he began to write – at first, only for parish magazines and newspapers – yet his initial foray into the world of pulp publishing had been made. None of these articles have survived, but they were probably of the short, sermonising kind. However, as was customary in Methodism, his stay was a short one, and he was to leave Wales after only a couple of years.

While at Pontypool however, we learn a good deal in *My Book of Memory* about Silas's early influences, his developing theology and philosophy. Silas never felt God had called him in the way that some Preachers had, though later did admit that 'my gift clearly indicated the work for which I was intended and that I should do wrong to resist the call of the Church'.[25]

While alone in his room, he made good acquaintance with the novels of George MacDonald (1824-1905), explaining that they were 'a light shining in a dark place'.[26] MacDonald, the son of a Scottish miller, was briefly a Congregationalist minister, but had been rejected by his congregation, and had to support his family of eleven children by writing alone.[27] He was a founder of the so-called Kailyard ('cabbage patch') school of fiction who wrote stories exploiting a sentimental vision of small town life in Scotland, but is now perhaps best known for his children's stories.[28] It was MacDonald's compassion for humanity and nature that Silas enjoyed. Here, in these earliest reflections upon religious experience, there is much similarity to Jack Clemo.[29] They have the same questions needing answering. Silas read Tennyson's *In Memoriam*, but did not enjoy it. Dante's *Inferno* and Milton's *Paradise Lost*, he enjoyed more – prompting, like Clemo, much debate. Within him, there was an inward revolt, at this time vague and wholly inarticulate, but Silas records lying awake for hours trying to reconcile 'infinite mercy' with 'eternal torture', finding that at the end of this mental conflict he was 'up against a blank wall'.[30]

It was George MacDonald, with his sceptical views of extreme Calvinism, who cut through Silas's mental tangle. He was aware that at this time, MacDonald's teaching was heterodoxy, but that did not bother Silas. Besides, in the early twentieth century, the whole Protestant world actually came round to MacDonald's way of thinking: that to God, all people, not just Calvinists, reach perfection, even if through suffering, to attain final salvation. Fifty years earlier however, he fought hard for a foothold, and always ran the risk of excommunication. Looking at Silas's later career, this battle with religious authority must, even then, have seemed attractive. MacDonald was a major influence on the young Silas. Crucially, as Reis, his biographer was to later note, MacDonald 'felt he had to find another medium through which to disseminate his essentially religious message, and he chose literature as that medium'.[31]

Silas admits that he left Pontypool, 'as he entered it, without observation',[32] but was presented with an illuminated address and a complete set of Bell's Aldine Poets, which were to accompany Silas throughout his life and travels. After leaving Pontypool, Silas had a three week break before he was due to take up his new appointment. He spent the interim at home in Cornwall, and though he found it delightful to be back in his home Parish, he observes that although nothing had changed, things were not as they had once been. He tried in vain to recover whatever was lacking, but confesses that the two years away had wrought a massive change:

I had seen a little of the great world outside, had mixed with people in other spheres of life and work, had found new interests and had looked at life and the world from a fresh standpoint. It was a joy to see the old faces, to sleep in the old bedroom, to look at the old orchards and field and hills, to talk to my father and mother about my work, and all that it meant: but all the while I was conscious that nothing was quite the same, and that I would never be content to live at home again.[33]

His move in 1871 took him to a completely different environment from

Illustrations from *Her Benny*, 1879, based on Silas's experience in Liverpool.

Cornwall or Wales. Following the Stationing Committee's wishes, Silas moved to the wide, undulating landscape of the Lincolnshire Fens, of which the Spalding circuit formed a part.[34] He was Second-in-Charge in the Circuit, living in Holbeach. It was here, more than anywhere else in his life, that with some twenty-one Chapels in very small country villages, that the young Minister discovered that walking was by far and away the best form of transport. It is no wonder then, that many of Silas's future novels were to feature characters walking immense distances. As was usual then for peripatetic ministers in large circuits, he was hosted by various families on his travels. His experiences in the Fens were to be influential – a few novels were set there – and he used the two years experience wisely, building his reputation as a sound preacher and orator. Working at his outer career, Silas's writing continued behind the scenes.

The greatest challenge of his career however, was to come his way when he received a call to minister in Liverpool. It was a quickly urbanising Liverpool, with its sea-port, docks and cosmopolitan population, which was eventually to hold him in high esteem longer than any other place, including Cornwall. On reflection, the whole experience of his time at Liverpool was to change the course of his life, and paved the way for his literary career. As Silas himself later commented:

> *In Liverpool, I found my wife, the greatest good fortune that has ever come to me... [and] the writing of Her Benny proved the beginning of such success as has come to me.*[35]

Perhaps the strangest thing about the position in Liverpool was that Silas had previously received an offer to go to another country circuit around the River Humber, which he actually accepted, but providentially this letter of acceptance was not posted by his landlady in Lincolnshire, and in the meantime, the invitation to go to Liverpool had been received.

This came from one Richard Lloyd, the Circuit Steward of the Grove Street Methodist Church,[36] part of an area which embraced some five ministries in the city, stretching across the Mersey into Birkenhead. Lloyd had seen the Cornishman in Nottingham, when Silas had been sitting his annual examination, and knew of his abilities. Lloyd was so keen to see Silas appointed he even paid for a new suit for him. Silas had particular care of Russell Street church, as well as the Wellington Road chapel. In sight were the southern docks and the Pier Head.

Russell Street was what we might now call an 'inner city' church, embracing both the docklands and some of the poorer districts of the city. Quickly, Silas had to get to grips with tenement housing, slums, dirty streets, orphans and prostitution. Urban poverty abounded, in ways he had not experienced in Cornwall, Wales and Lincolnshire. Alan Brack has detailed the state of Liverpool during Silas's ministry, and those people who to the Victorians were known as 'the submerged tenth':

It was a period which saw Liverpool's population rise to more that six hundred thousand and the merchant princes begin to move away from the over-crowded city centre into the cleaner air of the leafy areas to the south and 'over the water' into Wirral. It was also a period when Liverpool for all its wealth had the biggest workhouse in Britain, the highest infant mortality rate and more than three thousand prostitutes, while a large part of its population lived at near-starvation level in squalid, foul-smelling cellars or in crumbling houses in the notorious 'courts'. Many were even without a roof over their heads and men, women and children alike spent their nights huddled in shop doorways, in narrow alleyways, under arches, on basement steps and in any corner which afforded some protection from the elements.[37]

While working in Liverpool Silas became particularly appalled at the way children were treated. Children from the slums were taught how to beg and steal. They had to earn a living, perhaps by selling matches, standing by the Landing Stage of the ferry, or outside the train station. Selling matches was not the only way of earning a living. As Brack notes, 'rag-collecting, shoe-shining, carrying travellers' baggage, street-singing, turning cartwheels, picking pockets, snatching from market stalls and barrows, robbing drunks who had fallen unconscious in the street, and stealing from the docks were all prevalent'.[38] Reform was on-going, but moving far too slowly for Silas's liking. Interestingly, when Victoria ascended the throne in 1837, there was no such offence in English law as 'ill-treatment' of children. She was aged 70 before the Better Treatment of Children Act became law in 1889.

When Silas Kitto arrived there one morning in 1873 he would not have known that the social and economic conditions that he was to encounter would form the basis of many of his future novels. Liverpool was full of activity. He embraced the culture of the city by visiting its art galleries and listening to the city's philharmonic orchestra and choir. He witnessed the arrival of the American evangelists Moody and Sankey, though remained sceptical about their success and impact,[39] as well as religious factional fighting between Catholics, Jews and Protestants. This fighting would also provide him with much material for later books. The busy atmosphere of the port is captured in Silas's autobiography as he takes the ferry across the River Mersey one dark and foggy evening:

> *The Liverpool lights had disappeared, the Woodside lights had not yet come into view. The river was full of craft. From every side came the hooting of sirens and the screaming of whistles. Big ships were at anchor, smaller craft were trying to feel their way up or down the river, while our lumbering ferry was aiming to nose her way straight across.*[40]

Silas worked hard at the Ministry,[41] and was introduced to Esther Mary Lloyd, the youngest daughter of Richard. They soon fell in love and became inseparable. She was aged eighteen when they met. Their marriage took place in 1876 (Silas was aged twenty-six) at the Grove Street Church. Other changes were on the way. Silas was on the move again: this time to the town of Burnley, where he was to be in charge of Brunswick Chapel, his congregation being composed of the newly-emergent social classes of manufacturers, mill operatives and shopkeepers.[42] As we shall see in Chapter Three, Burnley itself is from this time onwards, intimately connected with the story of the Hockings, since Joseph, was later to take over Ministerial duties there, following the family tradition.[43] After a year in post Silas and Esther's first child, Bertha, was born on 27th July 1877, their marriage producing three other children: Ernest, Eunice and Arthur Vivian.

Having now passed further examinations, Silas Kitto was accepted in what is known in Methodist circles as full connexion with all its added privileges and status. Silas now had much experience as a Minister, and his time at Burnley proved to be the starting point for his writing. Initially, he had completed a few short stories for the *Methodist Magazine*, but had been working on a larger project, his first novel. For its setting, he chose Cornwall, a landscape and a people he knew intimately, but his pulp Methodist career began in earnest, when in 1878, the story – *Alec Green: A Tale of Sea Life* – found its way into Burnley's local newspaper, *The Advertiser*, as a weekly serial.[44] Burnley was not as challenging as Liverpool had been, and Silas freely admits he had more time for himself and his young family. So the story goes, *Alec Green: A Tale of Sea Life*, was written one night, when after opening the door to go out on a round of visits, he was greeted by a deluge of rain and a raging wind. For a while, apparently, he sat staring into the fire, listening to the wind rumbling in the chimney and the rain against the window. Silas comments:

> *Perhaps it was the sound of the wind and rain that sent my thoughts trailing back and back to the days of my boyhood. Suddenly I had a*

Frontispiece from *Alec Green: A Tale of Sea Life*, 1878

picture of a little fishing village on the north coast of Cornwall, with the waves breaking on the rocks outside. Then I saw the beginning of a story.[45]

Whatever its compositional history, *Alec Green: A Tale of Sea Life* was an immediate success, and Silas Kitto began to understand there were methods of preaching other than at the pulpit. The Burnley congregation began to take note of their celebrity Minister, a man who preached and dared to write fiction as well. No doubt, not all were in favour of this tendency.

Back home in Cornwall, Silas' father was unimpressed.[46] He thought his foray into fiction was putting his career into jeopardy. Traditionally, many nonconformist households had a dim view of fiction, considering it as immoral as the theatre. In some ways, James Hocking's view was to be justified – the fiction was a radical departure. However, the strategy could work. One time when Silas was preaching in a town close by to Burnley a lady said, 'I would like to meet some of the kindly people in his books'.[47] Silas was not put off by his father or other detractors. *Alec Green: A Tale of Sea Life* quickly found acceptance with Frederick Warne and

Company who paid fifteen pounds for the copyright.[48] This was the first remuneration that Silas received for his writing; the novel appearing later that year in Warne's Star Series, selling for one shilling and sixpence. The link with Frederick Warne was to prove enormously lucrative for both author and publisher. For more than half a century this firm were to produce edition after edition of his novels.

Destined to become his million-selling book, the writing of *Her Benny* (1879)[49] came about, not while he was in Liverpool, but actually during a period of great unrest in Burnley. There had it seems, been a spate of agitation amongst the mill operatives, culminating in street riots and a very serious strike, events which were repeated in other major northern English towns and cities.[50] Strikers stood outside factory gates while night-watchmen lit braziers. Silas referred to it a miniature war and military forces were even called in at one point.[51] Given his own background, it would be fair to say that he had substantial sympathy with those campaigning for better conditions and rights. Back home in Cornwall, James Hocking was struggling with the three-life system.

Such was the background when Silas began *Her Benny*; the chief characters being two street waifs, who are used as a mechanism against hardship and poverty in the docklands of Liverpool. Despite the success of *Alec Green: A Tale of Sea Life*, Silas experienced great difficulty in convincing his then Connexional Editor, Reverend J.S. Withington to publish it as a serial in their *United Methodist Free Church Magazine*. Apparently, newspapers were one thing; the magazine another. No such thing as a novel had been published in a religious magazine before. When Silas first talked to Withington, and was told that no fiction had ever been admitted into its pages, Silas, with a gleam in his eye, responded with, 'What about the obituary notices?'[52] Withington took a lot of convincing, but eventually relented. *Her Benny* followed the success of *Alec Green: A Tale of Sea Life* in its serial form, and Silas was soon paid twenty pounds by Frederick Warne for the novelisation proper.[53]

In its hardback form, *Her Benny* sold incredibly well, instantly reverberating with readerships in Liverpool, the north-west in general, but also at home in Cornwall. Other novels came quickly, which followed the blue-print established by *Alec Green: A Tale of Sea Life* and *Her Benny*. These were *His Father or A Mother's Legacy* (1880), *Reedyford or Creed and Character* (1880), *Chips: A Story of Manchester Life* (1881), *Ivy: A Tale of Cottage Life* (1881), *Poor Mike: The Story of a Waif* (1882) and *Sea Waif: A Tale of the Cornish Cliffs* (1882).[54] All the novels set simple, poor, waif-like characters within moral dilemmas, their settings in the north-west of England or in Cornwall. By 1882, Silas had become a major novelist in these islands, his popular pulp Methodism capturing public mood and interest. His finger was on the pulse of a nation-state rapidly industrialising, yet witnessing all kinds of social inequality and injustice. Despite this, the sentimental and sermonising narratives were perfect for a confident, Protestant Britain.

In Burnley, one of Silas's more interesting friends was J. Marshall Mather. Mather was another United Methodist Free Churches minister, and something of an intellectual, having a keen interest in literature, and in particular, non-standard Englishes.[55] He found great empathy with Silas's Cornu-English and the pair struck up a long friendship. Mather knew Lancashire like the back of his hand, and understood the idiosyncrasies and peculiarities of the Lancashire people. Mather's friendship was to be helpful when Silas tried to imitate that speech in his novels, yet Silas also encouraged Mather to put his knowledge of Lancashire into a book, lest it should be forgotten (a process then occurring in Cornwall, with writers such as Hunt and Bottrell, and Forfar and Tregellas[56]). Mather was always doubtful of his own abilities (perhaps made worse after the runaway success of Silas's *Her Benny*), but some years later, Silas was delighted to receive a manuscript called *Owd Enoch's Flute,* eventually published under the title *Lancashire Idylls.*[57] Mather's work is well-known in Lancashire, but still, like Silas, under-rated.

Another interesting acquaintance of Silas at this time was Mark Guy Pearse, who would come to know both him and Joseph very well. Pearse was already a popular preacher, writer and lecturer.[58] A Cornishman, born in Camborne in 1842, he knew how to entertain Cornish audiences 'abroad', whether in England or as he did more regularly, in North America. Silas recollects how once, during a visit to the far west of Canada, Pearse visited a mining camp to which a number of Cornish miners had emigrated, and there, gave his usual lecture on 'The folks at home'. At the close of the lecture, a Cornishman came up to Pearse and with misty eyes, shook him heartily by the hand, saying:

"Lor, Maaster Pearce. It's like being down to home again to hear 'ee spaik, and I've been wondering all the while how you do do it. You bain't livin' in Cornwall be 'ee when you be to home?

"Oh, no, I live in London."

"Well, now, there 'tes. An' yet you do remember everything. 'Zactly like they used to was. All they curious words; and all they funny little turns. Lor, how I ded laugh. I caan't think how tes you ain't forgotten them 'em oall. Why, Maaster Pearse, I hadn't been out of this country six months before I'd forgot every bit of my Cornish."[59]

Such hilarity is a trademark of Silas's memories. He was far removed from the stern patriarch he is often visually seen as, and though outwardly it may appear that he had neglected his Cornish roots, inwardly, they went deep, and he himself loved to hear such stories. Elements of them are found in many of his Cornish novels. All the Hockings had a particularly good ear for catching Cornu-English dialect in prose, bettering most other nineteenth-century novelists who wrote about Cornwall (who with the notable exceptions of Edward Bosanketh and Arthur Quiller Couch) were mainly English or Scottish.[60]

Despite meeting such famous names as Mather and Pearse, Silas also worked hard in the north-west. Burnley had many connections with Manchester, and being the large manufacturing centre that it was, had its fair share of social problems and deprivation. In 1880, Silas and his

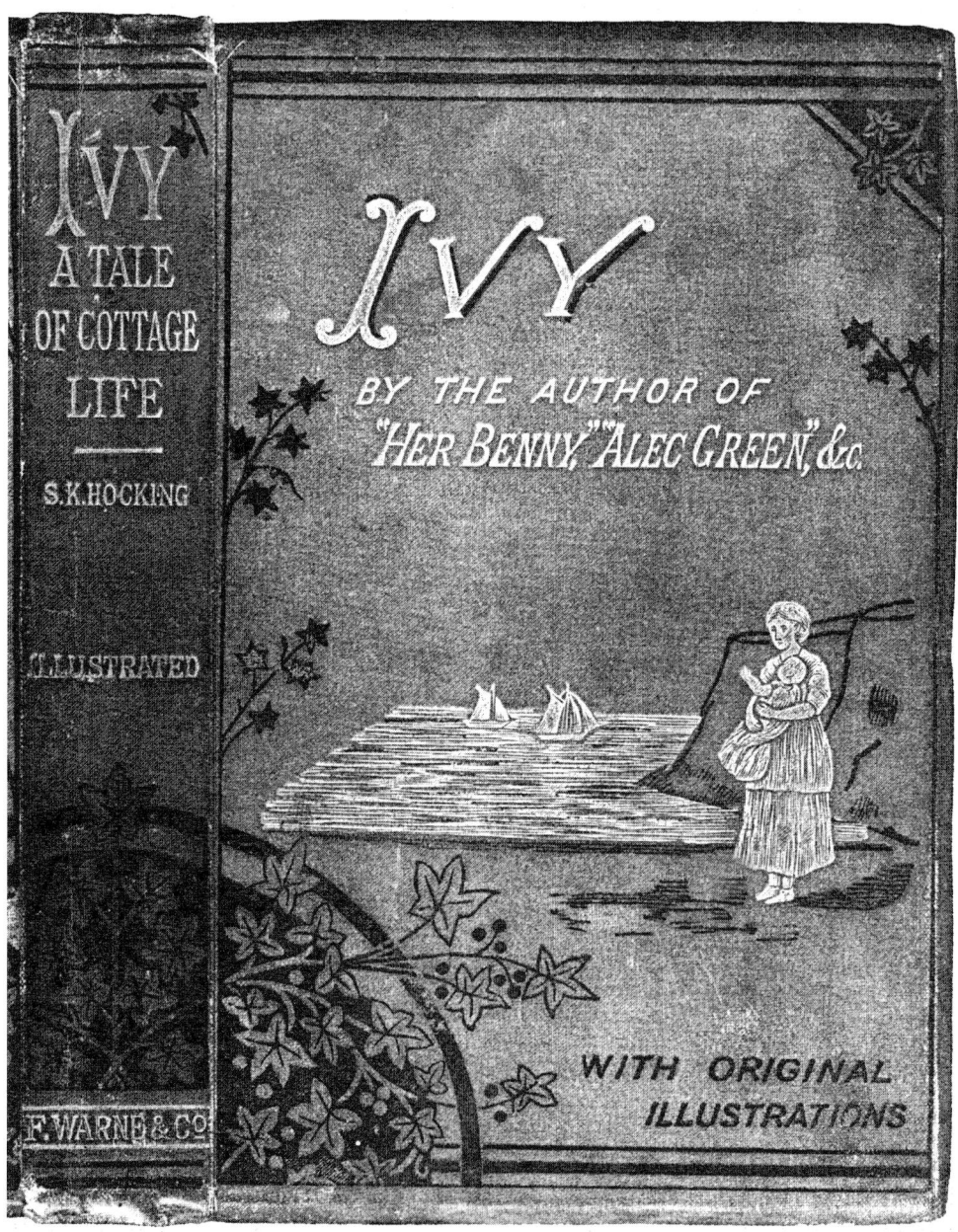

Cover of *Ivy: A Tale of Cottage Life*, 1881.

growing family went to live in Manchester. The stipend and his earnings from his early novels had allowed life to be comfortable in Burnley, but here, he was appointed to a Circuit position, meeting those of high standing in society. While there, he was also to become re-acquainted with his brother Joseph, who by 1891 was attending the United Methodist Free Churches College. When Silas had first left home, Joseph was only nine years old, and they met frequently – Silas was convinced that whatever else the College might make of his brother, they would never shape him into a mould. Like his elder brother, he was too much of an individual. Neither of them were sufficiently malleable to be licked into any kind of orthodox shape.[61] During this phase, the injustice and fate of their father back home must have formed much of their conversation, as did discussion of their sister Salome, whose own literary career had taken off in the past decade.

By now, Silas had a good deal of experience of how best to deal with social deprivation and offered his services to the City Mission there. Silas worked on the streets with others, between ten o'clock and midnight, his pocket full of cards of invitation to a supper of cocoa and coffee, buns and sandwiches at the Friend's Meeting House in Mount Street. Eventually Silas and his companion encountered the prostitutes of the city. He recollects that initially he would 'never have recognised these women as being what they were' and that they were 'all too thinly clad for such a bitter night'.[62] Walkowitz, and Fisher have drawn attention to the widespread prevalence of Victorian prostitution, yet also that society's ambivalence in solving the problem.[63] Here, we perhaps see a combination of caring Methodism and protective Cornishry, such that most of the girls accepted the Mission's offer. At the supper, the hymns provided all the preaching that was necessary. No doubt was left in Silas's mind as to the sad upbringing and fate of these women:

> *At the close of the meeting some forty or fifty girls remained behind. Three or four hailed from Burnley. One of them told me she had been a scholar in the Brunswick Sunday School. Others came from such towns as Rochdale, Bacup, Bury and Accrington. Love of finery, the hatred of mill work, the lure of a big city and the treachery of male acquaintances had been the chief factors in their fall. Next day about twenty of them were restored to their homes, and others taken care of in the Mission's Refuge. If only one girl was rescued it was worth all the labour and expense.*[64]

For Silas, his fiction was concerned with the prevention of such problems, and we may posit that his experiences on the streets of Liverpool and Manchester form a crucial ideological backdrop to much of his work. In this sense, though on the surface, Silas might seem as far removed from contemporary feminism as is possible, he was an early supporter of Women's Rights, and throughout his fiction, continued to identify and criticise the evil and corruptive dominance of men in society. A full investigation of Prostitution in Silas's fiction was not possible however. In *Her Benny,* Nelly's fate if she became a prostitute could only be hinted at.[65]

Liverpool, then Burnley and Manchester, had given rise to his success, though Silas was soon to leave the latter for another circuit. On reflecting on his time in the city, he was later to comment that 'Manchester did not suit my health', perhaps because of its factories and industrial pollution, although it seems he still had a hankering for Liverpool.[66] The year was 1883 (Silas was 33 years old) and he and Esther eventually made a move to the seaside resort town of Southport, just north of Liverpool facing the Irish Sea.[67] Although his longest lasting ministry, it was also to be his last. Moneyed Southport was undergoing its own transition into a retirement town. Its promenade, gardens and scenery made it attractive to the Hocking family, so they moved to 21 Scarisbrick New Road. Here, he was in charge of Duke Street United Methodist Free Church, yet all was not as it seemed. The Church was in debt, due to a problem in the lease, and Silas was having a problem with his throat – a serious issue for any preacher.[68] A doctor diagnosed rest and a holiday, and he and his family travelled to the United States and Canada, attending a British Association meeting in Montreal, and then through the Rockies on the Canadian Pacific Railway. It was just what he needed. After the summer, Silas was soon back in action. As ever, Silas proved a draw and soon bankruptcy was avoided and the debt repaid. This was completed by remodelling the Church allowing extra people to be seated and by judicious business acumen. He continued his often controversial sermons, still packing the place. By the end of the decade there was a spate of reprinting of his earlier novels.[69]

While at Southport, Silas was to solidify his reputation as a novelist, broadly writing two novels a year for the next thirteen years, as well as completing his Ministerial duties. In 1895, just as Joseph Hocking was taking up his post at Burnley and was about to make his first steps into a literary career, Silas had made his mind up to leave the Ministry. However, the Church officials persuaded him to stay on for another year, brought about by the fact that ministers in the United Methodist Free Churches were usually booked anything up to two years in advance for their next ministry.

At this time, Silas was receiving dozens of appointments to lecture and preach, and became an extremely busy man. The demands made upon him, coupled with his views on the United Methodist Free Churches, forced him to resign in 1896. This was Silas's first crisis. It is clear that there was no love lost on either side. For their part, the United Methodist Free Churches had, over the past decade, reacted badly to Silas's celebrity status. On Silas's part, he had started to find the Connexional rules hampered his work, and that he was not conscious of any 'call' to ministerial work away from his writing. Justifiably, Silas felt his call was to use fiction as the teaching device, but this was a progressive and radical position. A passage in *My Book of Memory* clarifies Silas's views:

> Many of our Ministers seem to live in a little world of their own, an intellectual world it may be, but essentially narrow. They spend their days with critics and commentators and theologians. Biblical criticism and theological niceties have become an obsession with them. They seem unable to get out into that greater world of men and women, and the things that matter.[70]

For Silas, the United Methodist Free Churches had seemingly become too institutionalised. He believed it was moving towards Anglicism, alienating the very population it needed to target. For him, there was also the Anglo-Catholic threat. Silas's writing was not afraid to step into that 'greater world'. As Bennett argues, popular fiction 'matters'.[71] Silas knew it mattered. He must however, have had mixed feelings. It was a moment of deep spiritual and ethical crisis for him, but he felt he had made the right decision. It also concerned him, for he knew that it was a crisis which his brother might have to face as well. His resignation gave him freedom though. He no longer had to attend dull leaders or trustee meetings, nor those of the Quarterly or District meetings. It is clear also that Silas was becoming increasingly frustrated with the way the United Methodist Free Churches operated. He disliked the 'itinerant system intensely'[72] and remained committed to his principles: 'The difference between state-churchism and free-churchism is fundamental. What is sacrosanct to the one is almost anathema to the other'.[73] Silas, of course, never wore clerical dress throughout his career, so as to be indistinguishable from the layman. Whereas before, he had been 'restricted', now he could be open in what he said and did.

For the past decade, while at Southport, Silas could afford to travel abroad, helped by earnings from his writing without the financial embarrassment which dogged his earlier efforts to visit the continent, while still a relatively lowly paid minister. He had visited North America, and a number of other European destinations, including Norway, Germany, France and Italy, as well as a trip to Algiers and Malta (interestingly following in the steps of his namesake John Kitto[74]). The outcome of one such holiday (while he still was Minister in Southport) is told in an early piece of armchair travel writing, written in 1886, from notes he had taken during a summer vacation in Germany and Switzerland, and bearing the title *Up the Rhine and over the Alps*.[75] On this occasion his was accompanied by his wife Esther, and his brother Joseph, with his fiancé Annie Brown, who were to be married the following year. It was on this trip that Silas met Arthur Conan Doyle (1859-1930), best known for his Sherlock Holmes detective novels. While standing at the Findelan Glacier, Conan

Doyle confessed freely to Silas that he was tired of his own creation:

> "The fact is," he said, "he has got to be an 'old man of the sea' about my neck and I intend to make an end of him. If I don't he'll make an end of me."
>
> "How are you going to do it?" I asked.
>
> "I haven't decided yet," he laughed. "But I'm determined to put an end to him somehow."
>
> "Rather rough on an old friend who brought you fame and fortune?"
>
> We reached a wide crevasse and stood for some time on the brink looking down into its bluey-green depths.
>
> "If you are determined on making an end of Holmes, why not bring him out to Switzerland and drop him down a crevasse? It would save funeral expenses."
>
> "Not a bad idea," Doyle laughed....[76]

Whether or not Silas's suggestion had anything to do with the eventual fate of Holmes is still conjecture, but Conan Doyle did bring Holmes to Switzerland a few months later and caused him to disappear over the Reichenbach Falls. Of course, the 'old friend' was to reappear shortly afterwards in *The Hound of the Baskervilles* (1902) part of which was set on Dartmoor.[77] Conan Doyle and Silas actually had much in common. With early literary success, Conan Doyle was later to turn his work onto public themes, in much the same way as Silas, including an influential pamphlet on 'The War in South Africa' (1902), which Silas is bound to have read, as well as eventually, a long history of the French and Flanders campaign in the First World War.[78]

Following his long stay in Southport, Silas and Esther travelled south, making their home at 'Heatherlow', 10 Avenue Road, Highgate, north London, where he was to be based for the rest of his life. In many ways, it was a completely new start, since he had served in the Methodist Ministry for a period of twenty-six years. As he was later to reflect:

> I was giving up a certainty for an uncertainty, sacrificing a regular income for the hazard of public favour... For twenty years I had lived in a circuit house, trodden on circuit carpets and slept in a circuit bed. Now I was to have a house of my own and my own furniture.[79]

Now at the age of forty-six, the pen would provide all his living. In 1896, Silas also founded, with Frederick Anthony, the highly influential and hard-line Protestant periodical, *The Temple Magazine*.[80] Silas was at the height of his powers. As well as the demands on him as a speaker, he still found time to write short essays and articles. The 1896 editions of *The Temple Magazine* contain his novel *In Spite of Fate*, in its initial serial form, while the following year it was published as a book.[81] The sheer mechanics alone of managing so much writing put incredible demands on Silas. *The Temple Magazine* also included two popular series entitled 'Under the Greenwood Tree' and 'Round the Study Fire' which were a set of essays

Frontispiece from *The Heart of Man*, 1895, pehaps reflecting the conversation with Conan Doyle.

on topical issues, many containing helpful advice to young authors. The sub-heading for the magazine was *Silas K. Hocking's Illustrated Monthly*, his name clearly hoping to pick up readers. For a short while, Silas continued to edit *The Family Circle* magazine by Christian World, but this folded by 1903.[82] Meanwhile, the novels, quite literally were 'cranked out', sales of *Her Benny* now exceeding one million copies.

Honours came thick and fast. He became a member of the Royal Literary Society, mingling with Charles Kingsley, Mark Twain, W.W. Jacobs and George Bernard Shaw, the latter who by now was also a friend of Silas's sister Salome. A Dr. Parker asked him to preach at the City Temple.[83] He was offered an honorary Doctor of Divinity degree from Columbia University, but declined.[84] Silas was very sceptical of such a practice, which he was later to describe in 1907's *A Modern Pharisee*.[85]

Further invitations came for him to lecture in America and Canada, travelling aboard Atlantic liners. He managed to convince the United Methodist Free Churches that he should be a minister without charge, though still remained very active. He helped Walter Besant to form the Atlantic Union and assisted his brother-in-law, Salome's husband, Arthur C. Fifield, in Fifield's publishing enterprises.[86] As a 'layman', he preached virtually every Sunday until aged seventy, and 1900 saw him elected as a lay member of the executive of the National Council of the Evangelical Free churches, and he remained a member for some twenty-five years.

For a while, Silas kept in regular contact with the congregation at Southport. At one point in *My Book of Memory* he details a train journey he made between London and Southport. At Crewe, an Anglican clergyman and two ladies got into the compartment in which Silas was seated. One of the ladies took a book from her bag and began to read. Silas was intrigued to see that it was one of his own publications. The clergyman then began talking to the lady and suggested that such books were very harmful. The lady told him she felt they were very moral. The clergyman however, felt that that was their chief danger – people were taken in, deceived as it were, by the poison lurking underneath. At this point, Silas joined in with the conversation, still not revealing his identity. Still the clergyman continued, saying how laymen could not be expected to understand theology, and thus Silas K. Hocking was a dissenter and a schismatic. The clergyman was to leave the train at Rugby. Silas and he continued their conversation to the carriage door. Just as the train was about to pull away, Silas handed the clergyman his card, leaving him on the platform with an exceedingly puzzled expression on his face.[87] This may be a piece of nonconformist propaganda within his autobiography but it is certainly an amusing tale, showing us more of Silas's playful nature.

Soon after settling in London, he was ready to embark on the second phase of his career: politics. In many ways, it was to be as controversial as the first few decades of his life. When not writing, for the next two years, Silas was using all his spare energies to build up Liberal interest in him as a parliamentary candidate back home in Cornwall, in Helston and Camborne.[88] While in London, he made contact with David Lloyd George, who saw him as a serious political contender and encouraged him to stand as a Member of Parliament. On many occasions, Silas and Lloyd George were on the same platform together. Silas remembers how Lloyd George's oratory relied very much on the inspiration of the moment. At one event, the Welshman began by saying he had just seen a picture of Silas with the caption underneath it, reading 'The Silent Man'. Lloyd George went on to say that he had known Silas in various parts, known him as a pacifist, a social reformer, a stubborn fighter and a politician. But as a silent man, No! He was the very opposite.[89] This was greeted with much laughter by the audience, yet these words would come to haunt Silas for the rest of his days. His political career was not to go smoothly. Far distant activities on another continent were to have massive repercussions for Silas in Cornwall.

In 1899 the Boer War broke out in South Africa. As part of the nineteenth-century 'scramble for Africa', as far back as 1877, Britain had annexed the Boer (Dutch) South African Republic (the Transvaal) with Boer agreement, but in 1880, Paulus Kruger and other Boer leaders proclaimed independence again. The British were defeated by Boer forces at the battles of Laing's Nek and Majuba Hill, and in 1881, Britain signed the Treaty of Pretoria, restoring Transvaal's independence, with Britain interestingly, supervising foreign affairs.

But as Richard Dawe details, when gold was discovered in the Transvaal in 1886, thousands of *Uitlanders* (foreigners), including many Cornish people, went there to work in the mines.[90] Denied civil rights by

Plate from *A Bonnie Saxon*, 1903, a moral fiction?

the Boers, the *Uitlanders* set about revolting. Cecil Rhodes, the British Cape Colony's prime minister, promised them a military force led by Leander Starr Jameson. At the very last moment, the *Uitlanders* decided not to rise, but Jameson, went ahead with his raid – disobeying orders. After only four days, he had to surrender and was jailed, while Cecil Rhodes resigned.

Britain continued to persuade the Boers to give rights to the *Uitlanders*, but the Boers declared war in October 1899, invading Cape Colony and Natal, besieging the towns of Mafeking, Ladysmith and Kimberley, winning several battles. As a consequence of this, in 1900 Britain sent over many more troops; the Boers reverting to guerilla warfare prolonging the conflict until they surrendered in 1902. Britain annexed the two Boer republics – Transvaal and Orange Free State – but later amalgamated them with Cape Colony and Natal to eventually form South Africa. Caught in this conflict were thousands of Cornish people. It is not surprising that the Cornish miners, who had travelled to South Africa to work in deep hard rock mining, showed no enthusiasm for 'liberation' at the hands of Rhodes and Jameson. When the War proper, broke out, most of them returned home. At the General Election of 1900, sentiments in Cornwall were sharply divided, although most sympathy went with the miners who had been denied opportunities.

At Liskeard, a meeting against the Boer War was organised by the Conservative Member of Parliament Leonard Courtney and the Humanitarian, Civil and Women's Rights activist, Emily Hobhouse (1860-1903),[91] with Arthur Quiller Couch as the chairman. David Lloyd George was the speaker for a 'Stop the War' agenda, with Silas Kitto Hocking standing as Liberal Party candidate in the Helston and Camborne constituency. Lloyd George's position was not popular in Cornwall and the meeting broke up. Hobhouse, who herself, was born in St Ive, near Callington, and who then was the Honorary Secretary of the Women's branch of the South African Conciliation Committee gives some flavour of events in east Cornwall:

In July... I went down to Liskeard with Mr Lloyd George to speak at a meeting. The meeting, under the auspices of the Women's Branch of the S.A.C.C. was organised mainly by the Quakers in the vicinity. Mr. Quiller Couch (now Sir Arthur), the distinguished Cornish author, was the Chairman. We needed one with tact and patience and he had both, but even he could not cope with the planned and prepared rowdyism which disgraced Liskeard that day. Not one of us was allowed really to deliver a speech. Some never uttered a word. The hall was crowded and round about the platform were thronging friends from my childhood, people who had walked in from St. Ive to hear me once more. Their tears fell as the mob of roughs howled us down. These finally stormed the platform, hurling forms and chairs at our heads. Mr Lloyd George spoke no syllable, he who could so have charmed! I can see him now, facing the storm, erect, courageous but stern and absolutely mute...[92]

Such feelings were affecting Silas's election campaign. As a Christian pacifist, he made clear his views on war and his abhorrence of it. In the mining towns of Helston and Camborne, this guaranteed his ostracization, and despite courting the Constituency for two years, he found it necessary to take drastic action. He resigned as the Liberal candidate, commenting that while he…

…won back the Constituency to its old allegiance I have not the least doubt, but I was not permitted to reap what I had sown.[93]

Silas was threatened with violence, and on several occasions, after lecturing, had to leave buildings by the back entrance, to escape and attack. He later reflected, 'I became a target for every Jingo in the land to shoot at'.[94] A crowd of youths actually hoped to wreck his house in London, on Mafeking night, but confused the location, and stoned the property across the road.[95] A number of windows were smashed. For some time afterwards, Silas was given police protection. He was a man of high principles however, and despite the interests of the Cornish in the Boer conflict, he had to do what his Christian conscience told him was right.

To add salt into the wound, as it were, Silas had controversially chosen to set one of his projected novels in South Africa, during the war against the Boers. *Meadowsweet and Rue,*[96] as it became, shows clearly the author's revulsion at cruelty and his abhorrence of all violence. That said, the novel vividly portrays the dilemmas and subterfuges that followed in the wake of the rival factions of the Boer conflict. The novel was clearly written around 1899-1900, but he was unable to find a publisher for it until 1904; the text being too contentious. Once published the book was shortly withdrawn from sale. Only one edition was ever produced, so copies of this text are rarely found today. The fact that the wider public seemed to assume erroneously that he was Pro-Boer only made things worse. The novel is an interesting work, but Silas returned in his next few novels to less controversial subjects and reverted from Unwin, to Frederick Warne his usual publishers. The nightmare was not over though. Letters reached him in a steady stream from all over the country once his stance in Cornwall became better known. Some churches and venues cancelled forthcoming engagements fearing trouble. Some booksellers even refused to stock his work, or removed their copies from shop windows.[97] It looked as if the British public meant to starve Silas into repentance for what he had said. The repercussions continued long afterwards.

A decade later and Britain was at peace again; the Boer war somewhat forgotten. Silas though, had developed a work titled *Sword and Cross,*[98] which had as its central theme, war and conflict, the author endeavouring to portray these themes from a Christian standpoint. He felt that the public were looking for guidance which would bring about mutual trust, based on the ethics of love for one's fellow man, until war became outlawed. But the idealistic subject matter was too close to the earlier controversy and events in contemporary Europe. Again, he had difficulty placing the book with a publisher, until Stanley Paul intervened. In the event, it was published in the Spring of 1914, just before the outbreak of the First World War. To Silas, the timing was perfect. The public did not agree. For a second time, he had failed to capture Britain's mood. The book never made it to a second edition. The novel itself is a rather black and white account of a young minister who preaches pacifism to a fashionable congregation which happens to be doing very well out of the Boer War. As the congregation dwindles, he is forced to relinquish the pastorate. It is certainly one of his most autobiographical novels, but, in his lifetime, made him no new friends, either in the politics of Britain, or at home in Cornwall.

In the wake of his earlier resignation and the fate of *Meadowsweet and Rue*, this was not, as might be supposed, the end of his political career. Silas could be both obstinate and determined. When peace had been restored in South Africa, he twice fought unsuccessful campaigns as a Liberal, in 1906 for mid-Buckinghamshire (Aylesbury), being beaten by Walter Rothschild, and again in 1910 for Coventry. In the 1910 election, he almost gained election as a Member of Parliament, losing by only 216 votes.[99] Silas felt he had redeemed himself, though following this defeat, he did not put up for election again. Like Joseph, Silas continued to support the Liberal cause whenever he was able to do so.

His decision to resign back in 1900, allowing Sir Wilfred Lawson to win, alongside his second defeat in Buckinghamshire, made Silas the target of much political commentary in 1906. In that year one edition of *Vanity Fair* features Silas Kitto as part of its 'Men of the Day' satirical series. Leslie Ward, drawing under the pseudonym of Spy, completed a comic chromolithographic illustration of him, making Silas look rather gnome-like. The associated lampooning text upset him, and he commented wryly, 'I never felt any inclination to frame a copy for myself'.[100] Nevertheless, the fact that he was featured in the series and the anonymous author of the text knew so much about him, proves Silas's status at the time:

> He first joined one of the oldest of Cornish families at St Stephens six-and-fifty years ago, and his mother being related to that Dr. Kitto who commented so much, and the men of Cornwall having a taste for Biblical names, he was naturally also called Silas. After a course of grammar school he desired a surveyorship of mines, which, had he achieved it, might have kept him out of Vanity Fair. But nature will out, and he was turned aside into the ministry, and at nineteen became a candidate for the Methodist itineracy. There followed charges in Pontypool, Spalding,

Who wants to be a Million-Selling novelist?: The Life of Silas Kitto Hocking, 1850-1935

Cartoon of Silas Kitto Hocking by Spy in *Vanity Fair*, 1906

Liverpool, Burnley, Manchester, and Southport, in each of which places, no doubt, he did much good among those of his own persuasion who had ears to hear him. But the evil habit of writing came upon him, and at forty-six he was again diverted – to what he calls literature, in which he is still prolific, after having supplied the world with over thirty novels with more or less curious titles and large circulation, as well as with much ephemeral work in the Press. At the game of politics he was a failure. He once stood for the Helston Division, but effected a strategic defeat in favour of Sir Wilfred Lawson; then he was rash enough to fight a Rothschild in Bucks, and getting badly beaten, was guilty of more novels. Nevertheless, he was a member of that deputation which presented its case so strongly to Mr Birrell as to make the Education Bill quite inconsistent with that Education Minister's speeches. For he is a forcible fellow, as well as a Passive Resister, who had sealed his faith with his goods, and a fluent preacher who, notwithstanding the grace of retirement, may still be heard at the City Temple and in other high places of Nonconformity. Yet he is not to be confounded with his brother Joseph of "No Popery" fame; for he is cast in a different mould, being an active yet less perfectly sincere upholder of Nonconformist habits, who was once more or less adequately described as a haggard Anabaptist. He has now written himself into something more than a competence, and accordingly lives in luxury on the Northern Heights.

He talks his writings with much assiduity into a phonograph, and they are said to be much read by people who like their fiction hall-marked with religion. He is nevertheless a bright and cheerful fellow who has travelled and plays golf. Lately he has taken to visiting music halls in order to see life.[101]

All this said, on the whole Silas tended to be very pragmatic about both journalists and critics. They could be very cruel to him, but Silas simply responded with his sales and popularity. However, in post-Boer War Cornwall, at least, Silas' sales must have dropped. Certainly, his reputation had been marred by events in 1900 and may be one contributing reason why he chose not to retire there, and why Cornwall features so briefly in his autobiography. Despite writing about Cornwall for a lifetime, the memories there were no longer positive. One of the few politicians Silas actually admired from back home was Leonard Courtney, who had been there at the Liskeard débâcle. Even though Silas and he did not always agree, Courtney at least understood and sympathised with Silas' position when he was ostracised. Silas never lost his humour though, chaffing Courtney for being a true Conservative:

"How?" Leonard questioned with a smile.

"You never change the colour of your waistcoat."

"And you never shave," Leonard laughed.[102]

Other commentators of the day, were more praising than those back home, and *Vanity Fair.* In *The Secret of Upland Farm* (1903), David Lyall observes that...

> ...on the 24th March, the Rev. Silas Kitto Hocking will complete his fifty-third year. He is usually described as a minister of the Methodist Free Church[es] without a charge. As a matter of fact, Mr Hocking has the whole nation as an audience, and if today he has not as much time to preach or lecture, it is only because his written Gospel is so much in demand. His mother was a Kitto, and hence, perhaps, Mr Hocking's literary bent. A native of Cornwall, he was intended for a surveyor of mines, but preferred the pulpit. Then it was a shower of rain that started Mr Hocking story-writing. He was once weather-bound at Burnley, and jotted down some curious stories he had heard from an old seafaring uncle. A local editor accepted the tales, and from that day to this, Mr Hocking has had an ever-increasing audience among English-speaking people.[103]

After his political career failed, Silas entered upon a new endeavour. It was one that had been the very reason for his political resignation; that of an Ambassador and a worker for Peace. As events in South Africa began to fade from memory, Europe seemed to grow restless. Silas was one of the delegation representing the churches of Great Britain, which visited Germany in 1909 in the interests of peace and goodwill, meeting both Admiral Von Tirpitz and the Kaiser.[104] However that peace was not to last long. In 1914, after war was declared, Silas's patriotism overcame his earlier Liberal scruples and he joined in wholeheartedly with war-work in Britain.[105] Despite being elderly, under the auspices of the Young Man's Christian Association, he also travelled thousands of miles throughout the Continent, visiting hospitals and Segregation Camps.[106]

Thus, at the start of the First World War, Silas experienced a second phase of spiritual turmoil. The idealism of the New Testament bore no relation to the reality of the Western Front. The Kaiser's imperialism tested him. Accordingly, to Silas, the state of the world was so dreadful that the Sermon on the Mount seemed, for the first time, unworkable. Controversially, as usual, Silas questioned the very relevance of preaching mercy and goodwill, pouring instead, scorn upon the enemy.[107] The result was that, though not ever losing his faith, he finally gave up preaching. It was as if the modern world was taking away a great deal of what he had struggled for. After the Armistice, Silas spent six months lecturing to Canadian troops, although it remains unclear what the topics of these lectures were. Presumably, they were peace-related.[108]

One of Silas's great disappointments and a time of immense sadness for the novelist, was the early death of his youngest son, Arthur Vivian, aged only twenty nine. He was to have this in common with his brother, Joseph, who also lost his young son. His passing, it seems, left an immense void in Silas's family, one that obviously influenced his later writing and politics. Like his father, Arthur Vivian had started to carve out a career in writing, publishing short plays and essays, after initially training as a barrister. He had seen service with the Inns of Court Officer Training Corps during the First World War, being invalided out as a result of a heart weakness. Arthur Vivian lived to see the end of the conflict in 1918, but in the succeeding February during a severe epidemic, was struck down by influenza, from which he never recovered.[109] Silas's novel of that year, *Nancy* (1919), with much of its action based on Newquay, was dedicated to his son's memory with the words, 'To live in hearts we leave behind, Is not to die'.[110]

The year was not all bad news however, since Frederick Warne sold the film rights to *Her Benny* for £200 to the Diamond Super Film Company.[111] Having been somewhat mismanaged, Warne publishers had been in financial trouble for a number of years, so this helped them out of difficulty. In January 1920, Silas's story was released as a British-made silent film. Produced by W. H. Baker and directed by A.V. Bramble, the film was widely distributed, with Sydney Wood playing Benny and Babs Reynolds as Nellie. Silas makes no comment about the production in any of his writings or memoirs, perhaps because he was to receive no further monies from Warne. By this time, of course, *Her Benny* had sold well in advance of one million copies, and despite Silas's bad publicity (or perhaps in spite of it – since he was featured in magazines and newspapers so often), continued to sell well. In essence, Baker and Bramble knew that the novel had all the elements of a 'feel-good' film for post-Great War cinema. The five reels of the film have not survived, but 1920's *Bioscope* gives a useful summary, as well as a somewhat favourable review:

> *Benny and Nellie Bates are the victims of their stepmother's idleness and drunkenness and cruel treatment drives them running away to the kindly sheltering care of Joe Wragg, a night-watchman. Nella, an angelic child, meets with a street accident, and dies in hospital, and Benny is desolate. A rich little girl, touched by his story, begs her father to give him a chance, and Benny is made an office boy. Later he is wrongfully accused of robbing his employer of a £5 note and sent to be tried in the Juvenille Offenders Court. He escapes from endurance vile, and gets away into the country, where a kindly farmer finds him in a state of collapse, and afterwards offers him a home and work. He grows up into manhood, and one day rescues a rich girl from death through a run away horse. His bravery cost him a broken arm, but lead up to a meeting with the rescued, and the intelligence that his innocence of theft has long been proved by her father. A year later he married his good Samaritan of youthful days... The outstanding characterisation of the play is presented by C. Hargrave Marshall, whose study of the gentle and philanthropic night watchman is convincing and delightfully human. The girl and boy of Babs Reynolds and Sydney Wood are exceptionally appealing,*

although little Nellie is much too clean for a child who roams the highways of a muddy city in winter time. Robert Villis is convincing as the brutal father, and Anthony Johnson's Artful Dodger an oft met type of precocious criminal. The staging throughout is good, and the photography far above the average. The first few reels are inclined to drag, and a little judicious pruning of the incidents which occur on "their day's outing" would certainly improve the film.[112]

Kinematograph magazine is more praising, commenting on its 'wholesome' qualities, as well as being less critical of the editing. With such a review, it is perhaps interesting to speculate why more of Silas's stories did not make it to the big screen. Clearly, *Her Benny* was expected to do well at the box-office:

The exhibitor who has on ounce of business acumen will not only book and show "Her Benny". He will regard it as a privilege to do so and thus honour alike his commercial shrewdness and his profession. The film represents the best possible type of popular screen entertainment. It taps the most fundamental instincts of the homely, kind-hearted and rather sentimental race to which we belong.[113]

Such praise would have sat well with Silas. The overwhelming factor about him during this final phase of his career is that he genuinely carried with him a hope that men and women of differing nationalities and creeds, might one day, be able to live together in peace. The phrase 'sentimental race' would have appealed to him. It is not surprising then, that Silas placed great faith in the work of the newly formed League of Nations, taking his stand among those men and women of his day, to whom this cause was dear. At the end of the First World War, statesmen from many countries decided to form an international organization designed to keep the peace, and the League of Nations came into existence on 10th January, 1920. Silas's 1920 novel, *Watchers of the Dawn* expresses much of this hope.[114] One of the men most concerned to form the League, President Woodrow Wilson of the United States, could not persuade his own country to join, so this weakened the League from the start. Eventually a number of countries withdrew, including Germany, Italy and Japan. The League of Nations settled some small disputes in its early years but despite its idealism, it lacked the power to enforce its decisions and by the late 1930s, Silas saw few countries paying it any attention. Little did he know, that when earlier referring to the League of Nations as the 'World's one hope',[115] that within the space of sixteen short years, the world would again be convulsed with another catastrophic upheaval in the Second World War. However, retrospectively, it is possible to see the transition the League of Nations made upon the world, being replaced in 1946 by the United Nations Organisation to which Silas would have given approval.

By 1930, Silas was approaching the end of his career. As a result of his preaching, writing, political life and pacifist stance, Silas became one of the most respected figures of early twentieth-century British society. He sat in fine philanthropic company, knowing the Rowntrees, George Cadbury and Storrs Fry, as well as many prominent Quakers.[116] Largely as a result of his political associations with influential members of the cabinet, his name was put forward for the Honours list of 1908, while the Liberal Sir Henry Campbell-Bannerman was Prime Minister. This was to be in recognition of his literary skill in providing healthy fiction for the young people of Britain. However, the honour was never actually bestowed upon him because Campbell-Bannerman died and was then replaced by Herbert Asquith. It is probable that Asquith had his own friends who he felt were more deserving of the honour. In his autobiography, Silas comments that he lost little sleep over it, but the snub must have hurt.[117] Reading between the lines, Asquith seems to have felt that Hocking spoilt his political career costing the Liberals votes at the turn of the century.

Although elderly, Silas's writing did not slow down. As well as continuing his legacy of fiction, he was finding time in 1930 to continue the *Temple Magazine*-style advice in newspapers such as the *Sunday Guardian*. An article by Betty Riddell titled 'Is the Modern Girl looking for Trouble?', is supplemented by a commentary by Silas. Although in the wake of the roaring 1920s, writing about 'flirting', there seems a mellowing in the nonconformist manner of old from Silas, counteracting the earlier observations of Douglas G. Broome at the beginning of this chapter, that Silas, being a Preacher and a writer of moral novels, could never deal with 'stockings' let alone 'young ladies':

> *The modern girl is certainly a much-talked about young lady. "She is brazen," says one. "She is a flirt," says another. Well, why not? Here flirting at its worst is harmless and naïve and she takes no pains to conceal. Her Victorian sister flirted and simpered behind her fan, or from behind tea cups and thin bread and butter, and made countless secret assignations. She affected horror if a young man chanced to catch a glimpse of her pretty ankles beneath a flowing skirt... Mademoiselle of 1930, I take my hat off to you!*[118]

Unexpected as this passage is, it is arguably, Silas attempting to keep abreast of the latest fashions, and perhaps he had even been asked to comment, since he then represented the establishment. Such articles also kept him in the public eye throughout his remaining years, as the sales of his books started to steadily decline. The *Daily Mail* published an article on Silas's career in 1934, when he was in his eighty-fifth year.[119] It is a treatise on the 'Art of Growing Old Happily'. This was a theme further expanded in a 1935 article for the *Cornish Guardian*,[120] in which he asks elderly people not to work too long in their own lives; contradictory advice given his own workaholic tendency. He was actually to comment a short while before his death, 'that I have been temperate in all things – except work'.[121] Two years earlier he had written, 'Never insure old age by 'safety first' slogans; they are damning as they are decaying. Living is an art. To achieve the art of living is to achieve a great victory'.[122] In another newspaper article of the time, evidently written around Christmas time, Silas, now described as the 'veteran novelist' warns his readers of the danger of losing the warmth of the family circle, perhaps recalling his Cornish childhood:

> *Has youth forgotten how to revere the peace and solemnity of our ancient customs: is there nothing left of the past which they hold sacred? One last word: I think the spirit of Christmas is more deeply felt and more truly exemplified among the lowly and poor, particularly in remote villages and small country towns, than among the leisured and well-to-do of our big and crowded cities.*[123]

Writing featured heavily in Silas's life, though he did find time, as *Vanity Fair* had noted, for recreation and relaxation. Presumably, *Vanity Fair*, had found it amusing that the hard-line nonconformist, could find time to visit the theatre, although, from his childhood, neither he, nor his family had actually been opposed to such recreation. His political career had gained much ground from being a member of the exclusive Whitefriars Club, where he mixed with other luminaries of the day. The 1905 magazine *Leisure Hour*, however, reveals interesting background about both Silas, and his younger brother, Joseph, who are pictured enjoying a round of golf under the heading 'Some Popular Authors at Play'. The caption under Silas's photograph reads 'Rev. Silas K. Hocking plays golf with skill and enthusiasm alike', while that of Joseph reads 'Rev. Joseph Hocking taking a rest after a game of golf.' A further photograph shows a rather windswept Silas, high on a crag, with the caption 'Rev. Silas K. Hocking is fond of mountaineering'.[124] Equally, in his later years, he had taken up bowls, which he said was 'the most sociable game' he knew.[125]

Despite his socialising, Silas continued to write prolifically. One of the tools of his trade is worth mentioning. Several sources claim that no less than forty of his novels were written, not only with the same pen, but also with the same nib.[126] He was very proud of this fact, his Will distributing his pen collection to various friends and family.[127] In his lifetime he had earned over £60,000 from his writing career.[128] It is with this that we come to the final year of Silas's life, when his health rapidly deteriorated. He died peacefully in his sleep on Sunday 15th September 1935, at his Highgate home, in the presence of his daughter.[129] He was aged eighty-five. Even in his ministerial days, and like a number of United Methodist Free Churches Ministers, he had never been in favour of clerical dress, since he felt it alienated his congregation, so his last request was that no-one should wear mourning for him. The same request had been made at his son's funeral, just over ten years earlier.[130] The funeral was held at St Pancras Cemetary, London. It seems Joseph did not attend, since he too, was unwell.

Silas's achievement had been outstanding. He had crammed into his eighty-five years, more activities than any other figure of his era. He had felt the highs and lows of a career that had witnessed massive transformation of British and world society. Assessing his life is not easy, since there are so many phases of it and so much that could be said. However, one interesting article in the *Methodist Monthly* magazine of 1894 covers much about Silas's skill as a preacher (perhaps bringing to mind the words of his father, James Hocking):

> To anyone who cares to know Mr Hocking, the secrets of his success are not hard to discover. Like his great predecessor, Marmaduke Miller, the eye is a most effective adjunct in his public utterance – it is, indeed, the eagle eye; and from first to last his audience cannot, even if they would, withdraw themselves from its spell. As a speaker, he is master of the secrets of emphasis. He knows the word that tells, and he knows how to make it tell. He can linger on it, or play passionately upon it, or bring it off sharp and suddenly, and so gain splendid effects thereby. Running through all his sermons is a pictorial element, always severe enough to be artistic, and yet always simple enough to arrest the heart of the multitude. He can paint a picture, describe a character, and build up a peroration without effort; indeed we do not notice he is doing these until we awake from the entrancement which has so subtly wrought upon us. But more than all, Mr Hocking introduces into every sermon a great human principle. His preaching is practical, and philosophically practical. He is not the man who strings the commonplaces of life together as a number of varicoloured beads, but rather the man who seizes some common error, some national sin, some heart-subtlety, and so exposes, condemns, rebukes, and warns, until the sermon arouses all the moral instincts in his hearers, and furnishes their intellectual faculties to boot. We generally hear Mr Hocking preach twice a year, and on each succeeding year we not only noticed these elements, but we have noticed them strengthening and developing as his ministry grows in age. At present there are no signs that Mr Hocking has reached his zenith.[131]

The author of the article recognised Silas's oratorical skills; perhaps picked up a long time ago, home in Trelion Chapel, shaped by Amos B. Matthews, and refined by his experiences in Pontypool, Spalding, Liverpool, Burnley, Manchester and Southport. As a writer, the article continues by showing Silas at the pinnacle of his career, justifying the reasons for his popularity, while alluding in passing to his inherent Celticity:

> The charm of Mr Hocking as a writer is his touching simplicity. He tells his story, he does not make it up. He give us life in its infinite pity

and pathos. Those who smile at his success as a novelist, and content themselves by saying, "There is nothing in his books," always remind us of the young preacher who expressed his astonishment that the Parable of the Prodigal Son should be called "the pearl of parables", because, as he said, "It was nothing but the story of a naughty boy." Just so. The criticism condemns the critic. And so with those who condemn Her Benny. It is only the story of a waif, but we venture to prophesy that the English-speaking youth will read it until the day dawns when youth, owing to an advancing education, ceased to be youth, and babies are born with Gladstone Heads and Edison intelligences. In Her Benny the secrets of Mr Hocking's powers are discoverable; and, if a young man were to ask us "What book must I read to learn to tell a story?" we should refer him to this, the most popular, and yet, perhaps, the most crude, of the many works of this famous novelist.

Mr Hocking is an endless worker, but first and foremost come his Sunday sermons. These are not only carefully thought out, but for the most part committed to Ms. This is a safeguard against all slipshod work. Indeed, Mr Hocking's best work is in his sermons. The preparation for the Sunday over, he devotes himself to his four hours' desk-work. This is followed – ill or well as systematically as sunrise and sunset. Mr. Hocking glues and screws himself to the chair until the number of folios are ready for the printer...

Mr Hocking's most delightful characteristics are seen in the home-life. By his children he is beloved; all the domestic tenderness of his writings springs for the sacredness of his own fireside. He may not have a very wide circle of friends, but those whom he had, he grapples to him with hooks of steel. The apparently cold exterior of the man, no doubt, repulses many, and his native self-assertiveness has begotten him enemies. He is a Celt, and has all the idiosyncrasies of his countrymen; and these are always showing themselves. But under all beats a manly, tender heart, and where duty, or affection, or right calls, no sacrifice would be deemed too great on the part of Mr Hocking. Unknown to the world, it none the less is true that Mr Hocking is a poorer man, both in purse and reputation, because he has preferred to follow conscience rather than fame. Of course, morally speaking, this counts for very little; only when there are those who suppose that all successful men are selfish men it is as well to bear these things in mind.[132]

This is an interesting assessment, where we learn much about Silas's working methods, and which again permits the alignment of Protestantism with Celtic, as well as indicating that Silas's idiosyncrasies and conscience prevented him from earning more money. This article was written before the events of 1899-1900, but even so, assigns these characteristics to him. In actual fact, the Christianity that informs Silas's writing is the turn of the century manifestation of a continuum going back to the

Medieval period, but like most nonconformist Methodists, Silas deployed it to combat the newer evils attendant upon mass industrialisation and urbanisation; empathy with people's inhumanity to others; in his own words 'ethical fiction'.[133]

Silas's high principles brought him much trouble and heartache in his life, yet his fiction, as we shall see later in this volume, was to be a staple diet of the reading public for some fifty years. He had not intended to be a million-selling novelist. Society had made him so, yet he was not the only Hocking to become essential reading for generations. His younger brother Joseph, also managed to make the courageous shift from pulpit to the pen. It is his story that I turn to next.

Notes

1. Douglas G. Browne (1948) *Too Many Cousins,* London: MacDonald, p.150. I am indebted to K.C. Phillipps for drawing my attention to this source.
2. A statistic well-attested in H. M. Creswell Payne, 'Pages from the Book of Memory: A Cornish Novelist', in *Cornish Methodism,* 24th December (1953), and in Silas K. Hocking (1900) *When Life is Young.* London: Frederick Warne and Company, p.275. It is also confirmed in Arthur Mee (1967 [1930]) *The King's England: Cornwall,* London: Hodder and Stoughton, p.251. Silas was also at one time 'said to be the best-selling English [sic] novelist'. See *The Dictionary of National Biography.*
3. Ben R. Jones, *A Political, Social and Economic History of Britain 1760-1914: The Challenge of Greatness,* London: Hodder and Stoughton; Norman McCord, Norman (1991) *British History 1815-1906.* Oxford: Oxford University Press.
4. See L.C.B Seaman (1973) *Victorian England: Aspects of English and Imperial History 1837-1901,* London and New York: Routledge.
5. Philip Payton (1992) *The Making of Modern Cornwall: Historical Experience and the Persistence of 'Difference',* Redruth: Dyllansow Truran, pp.99-118.
6. Silas K. Hocking (1923) *My Book of Memory: A String of Reminiscences and Reflections,* London: Cassell and Company.
7. Silas K. Hocking (1936) *Looking Back. London:* Cassell and Company. This Silas K. Hocking text is now very rare.
8. Jack Clemo (1969) 'The Hocking Brothers', in *Cornish Review*, Spring, pp.36-41. It is clear that Clemo felt Silas forgot about Cornwall. The reality was that after events of 1899-1900, Cornwall wanted to forget about Silas.
9. See 'In the Days of his Youth' in *Cornish Guardian,* 25th June (1926), p.14. Much of this article is taken from Silas's 1923 autobiography.
10. Ibid.
11. See 'Men of the Day' No. 1040, in *Vanity Fair* (1906). The nearest 'grammar' school was possibly at St Austell, and unless Silas was a boarder and James and Eliza could afford the fees, it seems unlikely. Most education ended at eleven.
12. *Cornish Guardian* (1926) op.cit. 'Queechy' and 'The Wide Wide World' were religious periodical magazines. Edward Young (1683-1765) was a dramatist and poet. His poem *Night Thoughts* is composed of 10,000 lines of didactic blank verse, meditating on death and mortality. Martin Farquhar Tupper (1810-89) wrote maxims on life in poetic forms, becoming a best-seller in Britain and in America. The aliases frequently used in Silas and Joseph's novels owe much to Walter Scott.
13. Ibid. Silas clearly was ready for his career. He notes here, 'My time being in Cornwall, I acquired some knowledge of geology and mineralogy'. The newspaper does not make reference to Grammar School.
14. See John Matthews (1992) *Amos: Amos B. Matthews, Victorian Methodist Traveller,* London: Bryant, pp.34-5. Matthews' importance in Cornwall is neglected.
15. Hocking (1923) op.cit., p.2.
16. Ibid., pp.3-4.
17. Ibid., p.6. Silas was aged between seventeen and eighteen years old.
18. Harrison Ainsworth (1805-182) was most famous for his highwayman and swashbuckling novels. Interestingly, he also wrote about the Lancashire witches – a story set on Pendle Hill, close to Burnley. Wilkie Collins (1824-89) is best known for writing mystery and detective fiction, though in 1851 he completed a book on Cornwall. See Wilkie Collins (1948 [1851]) *Rambles Beyond Railways,* London: Westaway Books. Bulwer Lytton (1831-91) wrote long verse-romances.
19. See Hocking (1923) op.cit., p.7.
20. Ibid., p.8.
21. Ibid., pp.11-12.
22. Oliver A. Beckerlegge (1957) *The United Methodist Free Churches: A Study in Freedom,* London: Epworth Press.

23. Hocking (1923) op.cit., p.19.
24. Ibid., p.20
25. Ibid., p.17.
26. Ibid., p.28.
27. For a useful account of MacDonald's life, see Richard H. Reis (1972) *George MacDonald,* New York: Twayne Publications.
28. See, for example, George MacDonald (1865) *Alec Forbes of Howglen,* London: Hurst and Blackett, (1883) *The Princess and Curdie,* London: Chatto and Windus, (1886) *At the Back of the North Wind,* London: Blackie and Son. The first book is a notable influence on Hocking's *Alec Green* novel.
29. See Jack Clemo (1949) *Confession of a Rebel,* London: Chatto and Windus, (1986 [1958]) *The Invading Gospel: A Return to Faith,* Basingstoke: Marshall Pickering. In these volumes, Clemo reflects on much of his spiritual debate. John C.C. Probert argues that it is hard to truly appreciate the Hockings' writing without knowledge of Dante and Milton. However, most people knew these texts very well during this phase.
30. Hocking (1923) op.cit., p.28. The point here is that one does not have to accept 'hell-fire' gospel.
31. Reis (1972), op.cit, p.2. MacDonald's views on salvation are very modern.
32. Hocking (1923) op.cit., p.29. This means that no one from the United Free Methodist Churches came to observe or examine him.
33. Ibid., p.30.
34. Ibid., pp.32-3.
35. Ibid., p.42.
36. Ibid., pp.44-5.
37. See Alan Brack (1983) *All they need is love: The Story of the Liverpool Society for the Prevention of Cruelty to Children.* Liverpool: The Liverpool Society for the Prevention of Cruelty to Children, cited in Liverpool Empire Theatre (1994) *Her Benny: Programme.* Liverpool: Liverpool Empire Theatre Publications, p.6.
38. Ibid., pp.6-7.
39. Hocking (1923) op.cit., p.50. After they had returned to the USA, he notes how 'emotion had exhausted itself'.
40. Ibid., p.53.
41. See numerous references to Silas's work in *Liverpool Mercury,* 17th July (1876).
42. See Brunswick Chapel (1959) *Brunswick Chapel 1869-1959 and the original Mount "Pleasant",* Burnley: Brunswick Chapel.
43. Ibid., p.10.
44. Hocking (1923) op.cit., p.69-71.
45. Ibid., p.68.
46. *Cornish Guardian,* 18th June (1926), p.7.
47. Brunswick Chapel (1959) op.cit., p.9.
48. Silas K. Hocking (1878) *Alec Green: A Tale of Sea Life,* London: Frederick Warne and Company. This was the only payment Silas received for all the sales of this novel.
49. Silas K. Hocking (1879) *Her Benny: A Story of Street Life,* London: Frederick Warne and Company.
50. Hocking (1923) op.cit., pp.73-4.
51. Ibid., p.77.
52. Ibid., p.81.
53. Ibid., p.83. Despite the success of *Her Benny,* Silas received no more money after this sale of copyright for ten pounds. He later realised how naïve he had been. The novel was translated into many languages.
54. Silas K. Hocking (1880) *His Father or A Mother's Legacy,* London: Frederick Warne and Company, (1880) *Reedyford or Creed and Character,* London: Frederick Warne and Company, (1881) *Chips: A Story of Manchester Life,* London: Frederick Warne and Company, (1881) *Ivy: A Tale of Cottage Life.* London: Frederick Warne and Company, (1882) *Poor Mike: The Story of a*

Waif. London: Frederick Warne and Company, (1882) *Sea Waif: A Tale of the Cornish Cliffs.* London: Frederick Warne and Company.

55. Hocking (1923) op.cit., pp.87-9. Between 1892-1907 Mather was the Connexional Editor.
56. See Alan M. Kent (2000) *The Literature of Cornwall: Continuity, Identity, Difference 1000-2000,* Bristol: Redcliffe, pp. 119-30.
57. Hocking (1923) op.cit., p.88.
58. I am much indebted to Derek R. Williams for his detailed knowledge of the life of Mark Guy Pearse. For an example of Mark Guy Pearse's written work, see Mark Guy Pearse (1902) *West Country Songs,* London: Horace Marshall and Co.
59. Hocking (1923) op.cit., pp.118-9. Clearly, Hocking and Pearse got on very well together.
60. See Kent (2000) op.cit., pp.130-141 and pp.165-9. Though from London, Charles Lee's work shows some of the finest fictional representation of Cornu-English.
61. See Silas' observations in Hocking (1923) op.cit., p.100.
62. Ibid., pp.97.
63. Judith R. Walkowitz (1983) *Prostitution and Victorian Society*, Cambridge: Cambridge University Press; Trevor Fisher (2001) *Prostitution and the Victorian,* Stroud: Sutton.
64. Hocking (1923) op.cit., p.99.
65. Hocking (1879) op.cit., p.16. Joe comments 'I wonder what will become o' her when she grows up?'
66. Hocking (1923) op.cit., p.103.
67. Ibid., pp.102-7.
68. Ibid.
69. This can be gleaned by correlating dates of editions with original publication dates. The earlier novels were sometimes in their tenth or eleventh impression by now.
70. Hocking (1923) op.cit., p.64. Beckerlegge records that Silas 'withdrew to devote himself to literature'. See Oliver Beckerlegge (1968) *United Methodist Ministers and their Circuits 1797-1932,* London: Epworth Press, p.113. Silas also related how he was unable to 'burn the candle at both ends'. See *Cornishman*, 19th September (1935), p.9.
71. Tony Bennett (ed.) (1990) *Popular Fiction: Technology, Ideology, Production, Reading,* London and New York, Routledge, p.ix.. For useful background here to Silas's agenda, see P. McCann (1977) *Popular Education and Serialization in the Nineteenth Century,* London: Methuen.
72. Hocking (1923) op.cit., p.103.
73. Ibid., p.196.
74. It is very probable that Silas Kitto visited John Kitto's grave in Canstatt.
75. See Silas K. Hocking (1886) *Up the Rhine and Over the Alps.* London: Andrew Crombie and the Denominational Press of UMFC. The word Alps is of Celtic origin and is closely related to the Cornish language word for cliff: *als*. Silas regularly climbed high into the mountains with other British adventurers.
76. Hocking (1923) op.cit., p.153. A similar death is featured in Silas K. Hocking (1895) *The Heart of Man,* London: Frederick Warne and Company.
77. Arthur Conan Doyle (2000 [1902]) *The Hound of the Baskervilles,* Harmondsworth: Penguin.
78. See Arthur Conan Doyle (1902) 'The War in South Africa', Pamphlet, (1917) *The British Campaign in France and Flanders 1915,* London: Hodder and Stoughton.
79. Hocking (1923) op.cit., p.164 and p.168.
80. See *Temple Magazine: Silas K. Hocking's Illustrated Monthly.* Between October 1899 and March 1902, it ran under the title *Temple Magazine for Home and Sunday Reading*, then reverted to its original title.
81. Silas K. Hocking (1897) *In Spite of Fate,* London: Frederick Warne and Company.
82. See *Family Circle* magazine. This need not be confused with the later Women's magazine.
83. Payne (1953), op.cit.
84. See Hocking (1923) op.cit., pp.115-6.
85. Silas K. Hocking (1907) *A Modern Pharisee,* London: Frederick Warne and Company. This novel was also intensely critical of the legal profession.
86. Hocking (1923) op.cit., pp.220-2.

87. Ibid., pp.165-8.
88. Ibid., p.178. Silas terms this phase 'a fresh start'.
89. Ibid., p.174-5.
90. Richard D. Dawe (1998) *Cornish Pioneers in South Africa: Gold and Diamonds, Copper and Blood,* St Austell: Cornish Hillside Publications, pp.135-91. Dawe's book is an excellent examination of the Cornish in South Africa.
91. For specific comment on Hobhouse's role, see ibid. pp.176-181. Hobhouse's bravery was especially noted by Ghandi. She was thirty nine years old when the Boer War began, and through her mother, was reputedly a direct descendent of Sir Jonathan Trelawny. Her uncle was Leonard Courtney.
92. See Rybie Van Reemen (ed.) (1984) *Emily Hobhouse: Boer War Letters,* Capetown and Pretoria: Human and Rousseau, p.81. This is a fascinating collection of correspondence, making her, and Salome Hocking two of the most radical women activists during this phase of Cornish history.
93. Hocking (1923) op.cit., p.178. For an interesting perspective on this incident, see John C. C. Probert 'Recruiting for the 1914-18 War and the 1851 Religious Census Etc' in *Journal of the Cornish Methodist Historical Association,* No.4 (2000), p.134. Here Probert observes that *'The Cornish and Devon Post* 12/10/1901 quoted a complaint in *The Birmingham Gazette* saying that the Cornish miners who had fled the Rand precipitately for the comfort of England, when the Boer War broke out, had now returned and described them as members of a great empire run on commercial lines alone'.
94. Ibid., p.179.
95. See *Cornubian,* 8th June (1900), p.7.
96. Silas K. Hocking (1904) *Meadowsweet and Rue,* London: T. Fisher Unwin.
97. Hocking (1923) op.cit., p.183. Earlier that year, Silas also spoke at a meeting in Exeter Hall, London. His views were unpopular. The same newspaper details lots of flags out in support of the Pro-Boers on Ladysmith Day at St. Just Wesleyan Chapel. See *Cornubian,* 8th March (1900), p.5 and p.7.
98. Silas K. Hocking (1914) *Sword and Cross,* London: Stanley Paul.
99. For statistics, see Harman MS. The source for these is unclear. See also 'Sixty Years a Bestseller: Silas Hocking's 100 Books' in *Daily Mail,* 16th September (1935), p.2.
100. Hocking (1923) op.cit., p.230.
101. *Vanity Fair* (1906) op.cit. The angle was very similar to the present-day *Guardian's* 'Pass Notes'. It is interesting that the magazine should mention his famous relative John Kitto. Clearly the connection was still significant.
102. Hocking (1923) op.cit., p.216.
103. David Lyall (1903) *The Secret of Upland Farm,* London: United Methodist Free Church, p.65. This unusual volume was a bound book of compiled monthly parts; a popular format at the time.
104. Hocking (1923) op.cit., pp.231-241. Silas seems to have had more respect for the Admiral than the Kaiser. In 1910, Silas returned to Germany with friends to see the Oberammergau Passion Play. See p.241.
105. Ibid. p.276.
106. Ibid. p.277. Segregation Camps were effectively Prisoner-of-War Camps. The Boer War had greatly influenced Silas' position and he had much sympathy with the German prisoners.
107. Ibid., pp.273-5. The historian of Cornish Methodism, Cedric J. Appleby has completed a detailed analysis of the relationship between the Hockings and the First World War. For Silas's role, see Cedric J. Appleby (2001) *The Hockings and the First World War.* Unpublished paper, pp.18-21. Broadly, Silas questioned his faith and became more committed to peace, whereas Joseph became more 'gung-ho'.
108. Hocking (1923) op.cit., pp.287-92.
109. Ibid., pp.280-1. For other information on Silas's children during the war, see p.282. Both Esther and his family contributed much to the war effort. Arthur Quiller Couch's son, Bevil, also died of influenza at the end of the war in January 1919.
110. Silas K. Hocking (1919) *Nancy.* London: Sampson Low, Marston and Company, p.i. Later editions did not carry the dedication.
111. For full details, see Audio Visual sources in Bibliography.

112. See *Bioscope,* 22nd January (1920), pp.53-4.
113. See *Kinematograph,* 22nd January (1920), p.117.
114. Silas K. Hocking (1920) *Watchers in the Dawn,* London: Sampson Low, Marston and Company.
115. Hocking (1923) op.cit., p.298.
116. Ibid., p.196, and p.180.
117. Ibid., pp.210-1.
118. See 'Silas K. Hocking Raises His Hat to Miss 1930' in *Sunday Guardian,* 30th November (1930), p.12.
119. *Daily Mail* (1935) op.cit., p.2.
120. *Cornish Guardian,* 30th May (1935), p.9.
121. *Cornish Guardian,* 19th September (1935), p.9.
122. *Daily Mail* (1935) op.cit.
123. *Cornish Guardian* (1934), op.cit., p.10.
124. *Leisure Hour* (1905). The only material relating to this publication forms part of the Harman MS. – some poorly photocopied pictures of the article. Both Silas and Joseph were golfing enthusiasts, although their playing of the game on Sundays, caused much consternation. See *Cornishman* (1935) op.cit., p.9.
125. *Cornish Guardian* (1935) op.cit., p.9
126. Ibid.
127. See *Last Will and Testament of Silas Kitto Hocking,* Probate Registry, Bodmin. Silas bequeathed the sum of four hundred pounds to his wife. Each of his children received one hundred pounds. To Arthur C. Fifield, he bequeathed his scarf ring and any books from his library.
128. *Cornishman* (1935) op.cit. Interestingly, Silas's funeral ceremony was taken by the Secretary of the Congregational Union, Dr S. Berry. Of course, the Secretary might have been a friend, but the fact that a Methodist was not asked to take the ceremony is significant.
129. *West Briton,* 19th September (1935), p.6. Silas's wife, Esther died in 1940. See *Dictionary of National Biography.*
130 Ibid.
131. See Methodist Monthly (1894), pp.40-1.
132. Ibid., p.41.
133. See Daily Mail (1935) op.cit.

Joseph Hocking, a photograph in middle age.

Chapter Three

Cornish and Christian Venturer: Joseph Hocking, 1860-1937

> 'Sometimes when reading a novel aloud my father would skip about a dozen pages – much to my mother's disgust: 'Father, you can't skip all that – it spoils the story.' 'Oh,' he would reply, ''Tis only an old Joseph Hocking. You can tell what's coming a mile off.'
> K.C. Phillipps, *The Western Morning News*, 1976[1]

Despite the views of Ken Phillipps' father, Joseph Hocking was an extraordinary Anglo-Cornish writer whose achievement was to steer the Cornish 'pulp Methodist' novel away from religious tract, to full-blown historical romance.[2] He effectively is the most important and most successful Cornish novelist of the late nineteenth – and early twentieth-century and as consumers of these texts, we are still feeling the effects of his life and work. More secular, and to an extent, more modern and contemporary than his brother, it is Joseph's work which had a great effect on how the Cornish perceived themselves in fiction, and how others perceived the Cornish. You *could tell* what was coming a mile off: for Joseph, that was the point. As in most popular culture, in all Joseph Hocking novels, prediction and confirmation are more important to the genre than novelty or originality. To have shaped such a fascinating collection of work was a major accomplishment, and in this chapter I will explore his life.

Mapping Joseph's life has been more challenging since there is no equivalent autobiographical volume to Silas's *My Book of Memory*. The youngest son of James Hocking was born at Terras, St Stephen-in-Brannel on 7th November 1860. Joseph, like his other brothers and sisters helped their father on his farm, but also showed early signs of creative talent at school. From all the evidence, Joseph must have been a very sociable and gregarious boy. He had a number of well-documented friends – Richard Curnow, Harry Clemo, David Truscott, Samuel Truscott and 'Nor' Truscott. Speaking in 1937, just after the author's death, the latter, the village cobbler, recalled his schooldays with Joseph Hocking:

> In that school across the way, Joe Hocking and I went to school. The school has been much enlarged since then: the old part where we went to school, is that small middle section, where four windows look on to the road beyond the playground.[3]

This presumably refers to the beginnings of the old Primary School – a Victorian Board School, which following, the building of a new Primary School to the north of the village (near the Creakavose housing estate), still stands, but was converted into small industrial units in the 1990s.[4] As well as his regular secular education, Sunday School was also an important early influence on Joseph's life. Like most children of the village, and indeed, children all over Cornwall, he joined his local Methodist Church. Extracts from the Church Sunday School minute books reveal both his involvement, as well as latent literary talent. On the 1st January 1877, aged seventeen, he was appointed to 'Write the books quarterly' and on 29th December the same year, he was made 'Secretary to the Band of Hope'.[5] These were serious responsibilities in village and parish life, but by this time, Joseph was probably already thinking of following a career in the Ministry. In the 1867-8 St Austell Circuit of Methodist Churches, Silas is mentioned under the heading 'On Trial' meaning he was active as a trainee preacher. Later records have not survived, but we may say with certainty that at some point, as a young man, Joseph would also have been on trial in the same circuit.[6]

Like his writing siblings – Silas and Salome – the parish of St Stephen-in-Brannel proved to be an enormous influence on the young Joseph. In an article in David Lyall's *The Secrets of Upland Farm* (1903), the journalist John Dunnerdale considers the lifestyle and work of Joseph Hocking. Dunnerdale argues that because of his background, Joseph was able 'to weave a fine romance out of the tangled skein of human life'. The journalist, obviously writing from the perspective of England, rather romanticises the parish (in actual fact, some seven miles away from the ocean), using vocabulary that could be from any one of Joseph Hocking's novels:

> The home in which Joseph Hocking first saw the light still stands overshadowed by an ancient sycamore tree, and surrounded by fields, from which, when the stars are out and all things are still, one may hear the wild threnody of the sea and waves tossing in fury upon the shore.[7]

The romance of the place did, however, affect Joseph, as Andrew Symons has argued, that the St Austell and mid-Cornwall area has affected many Cornish writers over successive centuries.[8] Joseph was later to recall how his earliest memories were of 'sitting in the old chimney corner with a log on the fire and my mother telling me ancient Cornish stories of wizards, wreckers, ghosts and haunted houses'.[9] Michael Dorey has suggested that these crucial story sessions, often completely ignored by Silas until he was sentimental and elderly, may well explain why Joseph's books contained more Cornish content than his brothers, and perhaps even his earlier interest in literature.[10] In our story of the Hockings, this further demonstrates the importance of Eliza's influence on her children, as both storyteller and healer.

Joseph, like most boys of his age who could read, had devoured almost all of Walter Scott's works, before he was twelve, and would walk twelve miles locally – to and from St Austell market – to obtain cheap reprints of classic novels, an event confirmed by Norman Truscott: 'Oh yes, we thought nothing of walking into St Austell in those days. Why my uncle used to walk to Plymouth – he used to walk it in a day'.[11] Joseph's favourite books at this time were not surprisingly Scott's *Kenilworth* (1821) and Harriet Beecher Stowe's *Uncle Tom's Cabin* (1852) (a book which he would continue to refer to in later life as life-changing).[12] At this age, Joseph set about writing his first novel, which he later said was 'not a success'.[13] As Dunnerdale outlines, this was probably the projected three-volume work entitled *The Fisherman's Children*.[14] However, his elder brother Silas read the ambitious manuscript and promptly had it destroyed. Dorey outlines what he terms 'the minefield of conjecture' this act invokes:

> *Could it be that, as [Silas] suggested, it was unpublishable or was there some other reason, at which we can only guess. Whatever it was, it apparently had the effect of temporarily curtailing [Joseph's] literary ambitions.*[15]

This entirely fits our knowledge of Silas' character, since he seemed to feel he was the only family member who was going to have a literary career. The two brothers in fact, fought like cat and dog throughout their career, putting on a very public face of unity, but the tension behind the scenes is clear to see. He did not, it seems, at this stage want a younger brother pushing through behind him. The destruction of the manuscript was possibly quite devastating for Joseph, and relatively little is heard about Joseph's later teenage years. Norman Truscott recollects however, that Joseph always took his stories and essays to show his friends at Sunday School: 'He was always ambitious, even as a lad. He always said he wanted to write. And he did what he wanted to do and made a great success of it.'[16] Truscott probably heard and saw drafts of *The Fisherman's Children*.

Aged sixteen however, there was little Joseph could do to realise his ambition as a writer. He opted instead for a brief career in land surveying. This period of Joseph's life is not well-documented, but a few observations can still be made. Surveying of course, was a traditionally Cornish career. The young Joseph had observed numerous surveyors working around the Terras mining district, yet perhaps his decision in 1878 to enter this occupation may have been influenced more by the fact that, in 1880, the first major Ordnance Survey of the country around St Stephen-in-Brannel was due to be published.[17] This would have been an exciting event, with outside figures entering the community, to document the landscape. Knowing the area intimately, Joseph would have been a useful asset to the team – understanding peculiarities of the area, as well as place-names and boundaries. Like everything he turned to in his life, Joseph worked hard, but just like his elder brother, he soon felt that the call to the Ministry outweighed anything else.

In order to enter the Ministry he needed private tuition (in his time with the Survey he really had not risen above workman), and though there are no records of this time period, and education, he appeared to have studied well, for in 1881 he was accepted at the United Methodist Free Churches College, Victoria Park, in Manchester.[18] The move to Manchester meant great change for Joseph. From the still rural Cornish parish where mining and farming seemed in a relatively happy union,[19] he was thrown into the urban sprawl of a northern English city. Joseph, like most Cornish people 'abroad', succeeded well however, winning, as Dorey details, the Cuthberton Prize in his first year there.[20] It remains unclear what the prize was for, but such an award was bound to increase the rivalry between Joseph and his brother. After a year at Victoria Park, he then moved to Owens College, at the university, attending Arts degree classes there until 1884.

By now, of course, both Silas and Salome had embarked upon successful careers as writers. Salome's first novel was published in the same year that Joseph entered the Ministry of the United Methodist Free Churches. It must have been both a busy and frustrating time for him at his first station in Birstall in Leicestershire. On the one hand, he was seeing his siblings succeed; on the other, he was establishing his ministerial career. Little is recorded of the latter in Birstall. Indeed, it was hardly likely to have been, since he was still an entrant into the profession. However, it was whilst at Birstall that he met his future wife. She was Annie Brown, the elder daughter of a Leicestershire Justice of the Peace, Joseph Brown, who he married in 1887. Again, very little is recorded of their courtship, but just before their marriage, as Dorey notes, Joseph travelled extensively in the Middle East,[21] a tour which would provide many of the settings, adventures and characters for his novels, as well as material for his lectures and sermons in the future. The tour was probably of the kind that many male novelists undertook during this time period, providing stock and clichéd locations for 'boys' own'-style adventure novels and stories,[22] not to mention broadly unflattering portraits of many distinguished cultures still under the command of the British Empire.[23]

Around 1886, Joseph made a move south to London, where he spent some nine years, comprised of two in Chelsea, and seven in Thornton Heath. Despite much attempted research, this period is undocumented in Joseph's life. Possibly this was because he was settling into married life, and then was completing much needed work in the city, of the kind Silas had already performed in Liverpool and elsewhere. Peter Ackroyd, in his study of London, shows the degree to which poverty was still rife there in the late nineteenth century.[24] It was, however, during the time he was living at Thornton Heath that he started writing in earnest, grabbing time between his ministerial duties. A religious novel, actually a classic of its genre – *Jabez Easterbrook* – was published in 1890,[25] and is generally thought to have been his first.

Four other novels, however, were actually produced and published prior to this one: *Harry Penhale: The Trial of his Faith* in 1887, *Gideon Strong: Plebeian* in 1888, and in 1889, two works: *Elrad the Hic* and *From London to Damascus*.[26] The latter work was an account of his trip to the Middle East, with spiritual and geographical observations along the way. From this, we can see that 1887 was an important year for Joseph – he had become married and his first novel was published. Several of Joseph's early novels were serialised in journals such as *The British Weekly*, and as noted earlier, this was still an important literary form – collectable, cheap and accessible to a wide proportion of the public. As literacy levels in Britain

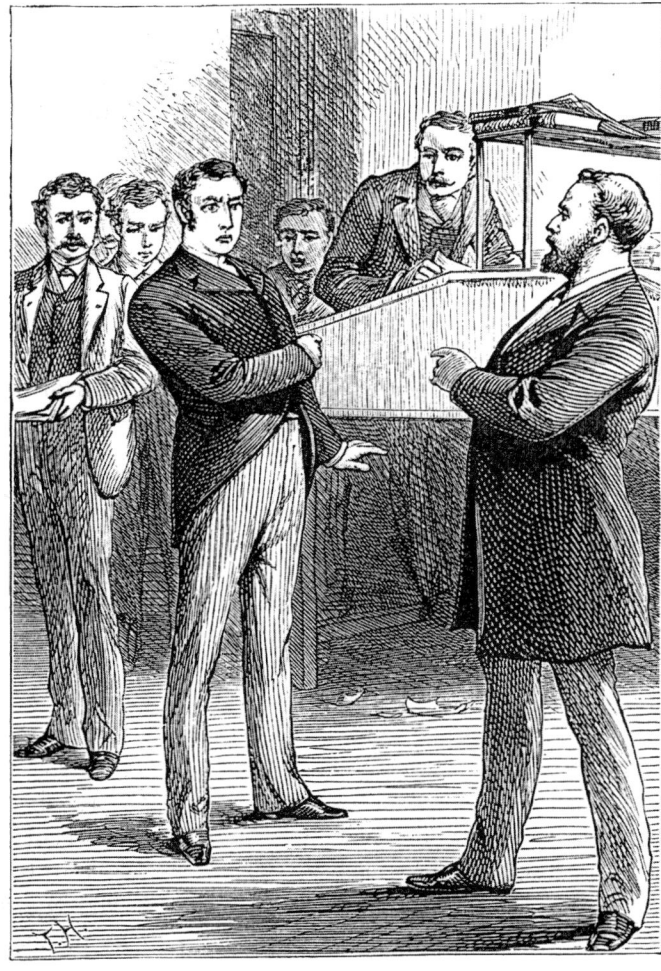

Plate from *Harry Penhale: The Trial of His Faith*, 1887.

began to grow, like his brother, he soon began to regard fiction as a highly effective medium for conveying his Christian message to the public. These early novels were didactic in the extreme, yet still made good use of serialisation and suspense. With the release of *Jabez Easterbrook,* Joseph finally started to emulate the success of his brother. It must have been an enormously satisfying time for him.

Joseph and Annie's time in Thorton Heath witnessed the birth of their first daughter, Anne, who grew up to also become a famous novelist. Joseph's thoughts on her are remarkably silent through the years, though he was keen to send her to a Quaker school in Somerset for her education. According to Anne, reflecting later on her childhood, apparently, Joseph did not care much for sectarian teaching,[27] though possibly it had more to do with the school offering stability in a time when Joseph knew he might be moving. Annie and Joseph had a further three daughters, Elizabeth, Alison and Joan, and a son, Cuthbert, who was killed in action during the last few days of the First World War. The life and work of Anne is given more discussion in Chapter Six.

Change, however, was on its way. The industrial north, as crucial to his brother's work, as Cornwall was to his own, seemed to beckon. Burnley in Lancashire was a growing textile town,[28] experiencing the kind of rapid urbanisation, and often industrial unrest,[29] which had once effected parishes such as Gwennap in Cornwall.[30] As Silas had already encountered, Burnley already had a tradition of textile working – wool being replaced by cotton – but it was its proximity to coal deposits that made it ideal for expansion. In 1851 the population was more than 10,000 and by 1901 was over 50,000. By then it was the largest producer of cotton cloth in the world. In Burnley, Brunswick Chapel seemed the perfect place to take his message.[31] Joseph and Annie found themselves in a community which was already aware of his reputation as a lively and thought-provoking preacher and writer. Right away, Joseph, using his instinct of old from St. Stephen-in-Brannel Sunday School, took over the junior classes on Thursdays nights and made an immediate impression on the young people of the community; many of whom who were already engaged in the looms of the textile industry, receiving poor wages for hard labour.

While in Burnley, Joseph gave a number of sermons on 'Ideals', one succeeding another, appropriately enough like a book, chapter by chapter. He urged the congregation to attend regularly lest they miss the continuity of the work. Much of this period of Joseph's life is encapsulated in a later novel, *The Eternal Challenge* (1928).[32] It is chiefly of interest now, since its semi-autobiographical narrative follows the life of a young minister and his experiences in a northern town during times of political and industrial unrest. All writers draw on real life, but this way of drawing in very personal experiences and either changing the settings or time periods, had become the hallmark of much of Joseph's fiction by now.

One major controversy surrounds Joseph's three years at Burnley; this being with the then Canon Morrisey of St Mary's Church, Burnley.[33] Rivalry between Methodism and the Church of England would seem to be the root of the argument, since we know that Brunswick Chapel was full to overflowing while Joseph preached there. The same could not be said for St Marys. Sadly, Brunswick Chapel was demolished in 1965, and Chaddesley House built on the site – currently headquarters for Social Services in Burnley.[34] Joseph remained there until 1898. It was then that he accepted his only Pastorate (a one chapel circuit); a position which would take him south again.

Joseph Hocking and family c.1900. Left to right; Elizabeth & Anne (daughters), Cuthbert (son) Annie (wife), Joseph.

The Woodford Green Chapel in Essex, known as the London Ninth, was a Union Church, under the auspices of the United Methodist Free Churches, and it had quite a chequered history in itself. In particular, from 1842-75, its minister had been William Burnett. Burnett was a great reformer, and as a result of his activities, had been expelled from the Wesleyan Ministry in 1852.[35] The church remained independent until 1871, when it eventually came to join the United Methodist Free Church. The congregation at the time of Joseph's pastorate consisted mainly of those of Congregational persuasion and Free Methodists, and although they had some differences in belief, apparently they worshipped amicably in the post-Burnett era. Interesting material has come to light documenting Joseph's time at Woodford Green. R.L. Galley has written an extensive history of the Chapel and records the importance of Joseph's time there:

> *No long gap of anxious searching and enquiry for a new minister separated the ministries of George Atchinson and Joseph Hocking. When George Atchinson conducted his farewell service in July 1900, arrangements were well in hand for introducing his successor, and in September Joseph Hocking preached for the first time, although no decision regarding his appointment was made for several months. He was then forty years old and had been a successful novelist for nearly ten years and, like his elder brother Silas, regarded fiction an effective medium for conveying religious ideas in a popular form to a wide audience.*[36]

For the biographer, this is too interesting an observation to let go. One can almost hear the church elders and Deacons pondering over whether 'a novelist' was the correct Pastor to employ. We should remember that the novel as a medium of instruction, was still very much a controversial form. Would literary 'rebellion' be suitable for the London Ninth? That said, some United Methodist Free Churches could be very open-minded and they may have been keen to employ him. Joseph too, had his stipulations. Galley details that he would only accept the pastorate 'if the Deacons agreed to build a new church'.[37] Inevitably they knew that despite being a practitioner of 'pulp Methodism', Joseph was a draw. In 1901 they agreed to plans for a new building, and a site was purchased in September that year for £1,000, the gift of a Mr. J.R. Pascoe, a Cornish-sounding supporter. A public appeal for its construction was then launched the following year. By this time, Joseph had succeeded in filling the old church to overflowing and could say with complete truth that it was inadequate for its purpose. Indeed, it was not uncommon for people to faint during services. A note written by him says:

> *It is badly built as a church and most difficult to ventilate. The excursion traffic along the Woodford Road has now assumed almost alarming proportions. It is necessary during the summer months to keep windows closed to exclude dust and prevent the noise from grievously interfering with the service. The state of the atmosphere on a July morning can be better imagined than described.*[38]

A fete was held in the three acre grounds of Trevanion – Annie and Joseph's residence at Woodford Green.[39] As Galley observes, 'the neatly printed programme on thick, good quality paper exudes an air of comfortable, Edwardian well-bring; the air of a society confident of its own future'[40] and the opportunities, local, national and personal, afforded by the beginning of a new century. Galley records that:

> *The architect of the new church was C. Harrison Townshend, whose best-known work now is the Dulwich Art Gallery. The Gothic revival which had so greatly influenced Victorian church designers was now on*

the wane, and other styles were coming into fashion. A first glance at the church may give the impression that the architect had purposefully chosen a style that was very modern in 1901, but it owes more inspiration to one of the oldest forms of Christian architecture in the world – the Byzantine style – which had developed from the fourth century onwards.[41]

In one aspect however, the first plans were altered. This was in the quality of the wood chosen for the seating. Galley records how 'the estimates had provided for seats and screens made of deal',[42] but Joseph gave his vote in favour of oak. It is due to Joseph's reasoning that the Church today, still enjoys comfortable and spacious seats made of oak. Maybe Joseph had remembered sitting on the seats in St Stephen-in-Brannel a little too long. A plaque on the porch reads:

> To the Glory of God this church was erected during the
> Ministry of the Rev. Joseph Hocking.
> Memorial Stones laid June 11th 1903.
> Opened for Public Worship April 28th 1904.
> Architect: C. Harrison Townshend.
> Builders: Vigor & Sons.[43]

When the new church was completed, Joseph's effective leadership filled it quickly, with people often travelling long distances to hear him. When he arrived at Woodford, the membership totalled one hundred and fifty. By this time, numbers had trebled. The influential publisher Joseph Malaby Dent (1849-1926), founder of the Everyman's Library, was one of the leading members of the congregation. He and Joseph were members of a flourishing Book Society at the Church. Dent and Joseph gave talks there on 'Jane Austen', and 'Novels and Novelists' respectively.[44] Another speaker at this time was the popular novelist and short-story writer, W.W. Jacobs (1863-1943), now most famous for his 'Claybury stories'.

From Woodford Green, Joseph was also making many journeys around Britain to promote his views and give sermons. In 1954, the Cornish writer H.M. Cresswell Payne reflected on an encounter he had with Joseph during this period, when he returned on one of his fairly frequent visits to Cornwall. Payne is a reliable, if sometimes critical narrator, but his observations on Joseph, and to a certain extent, also on Silas, are worthy of our consideration. Payne also provides useful context for Joseph's position on the Jesuits and Roman Catholicism:

> *I first heard Joseph Hocking speak in the Public Rooms, Bodmin, in the early years of this century. Disturbed at what he considered the insidious encroachment of Jesuitry in Britain and the growth of Roman Catholicism, he had written some of his successful and anti-catholic novels. He was then a minister in the U.M.F.C. and still at Woodford Green, where he had a successful ministry and was instrumental in building a new church. I read the first of these novels, The Scarlet*

Chapter 3

Woman, in the Temple Magazine where it was published serially. This strongly Protestant journal was edited by his brother Silas K. Hocking. In The Scarlet Woman, and in other novels, which followed it, Joseph introduced his best-known character – Father Antony Ritzoom – the intellectual and intrepid Jesuit.

At this time when he was thus boldly entered in the lists as a Protestant champion, The Puritan, a new monthly journal, was launched. It was a promising venture, but its appeal was too limited to ensure for it a long life. The journal, however, was responsible for sending Joseph Hocking on a visit to Rome in order that a true and vivid picture of life at the centre of the Catholic Faith might be presented to its readers. So The Puritan published a series of papers which received considerable attention, but their author gained also much material for further novels.

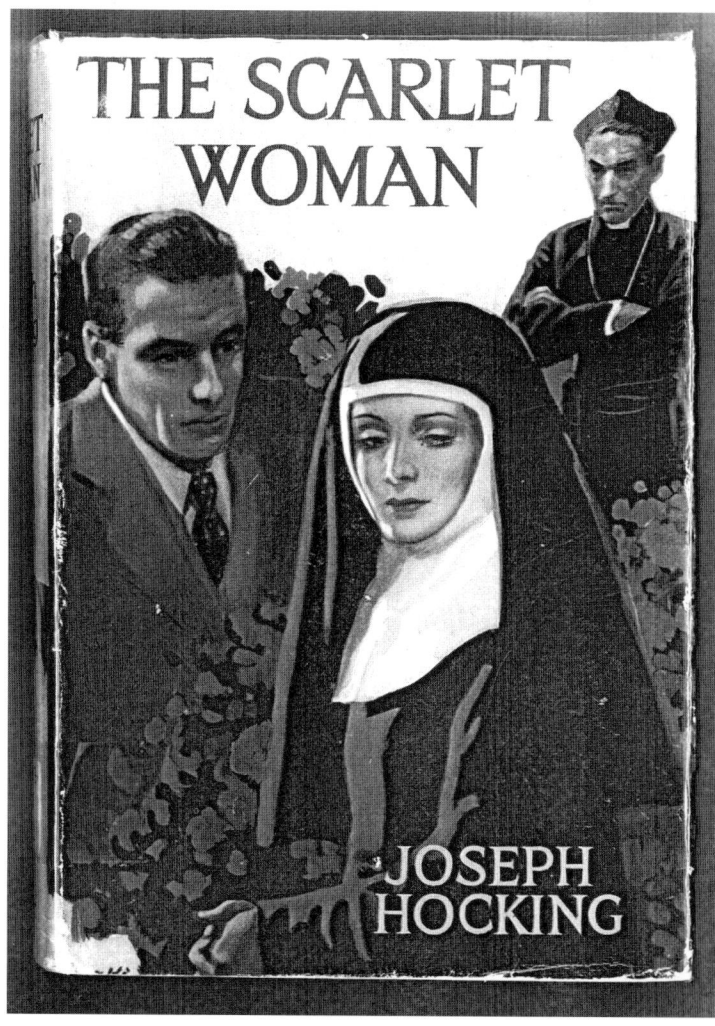

Jacket illustration for
The Scarlet Woman,
1899.

Out of the experience, too, Joseph Hocking prepared a notable lecture which he called 'A Protestant's Pilgrimage to Rome', this lecture he gave in many parts of Britain, and this was his subject when he spoke in Bodmin. It was with powerful utterance backed by Celtic fire and great enthusiasm; the audience were quite evidently impressed, but since it was made up almost wholly of Free Church men, little lasting result, as far as I could judge at the time, was made.

Joseph Hocking's books had been known to me for many years before I had heard him speak. I had forsaken much earlier, the books of his elder brother for his own. He was to me, quite a different author: his work I thought distinctly nearer to real literature, though as the years went on I concluded that he would never stand on the high rungs of the ladder.

There was much truth, however, in what Dr Roberston Nicoll wrote of him when he said: "Joseph Hocking never wrote a dull story, he could tell a good tale." Whereas Silas remained mainly a writer of the purely 'Sunday School type reward for older children' type of book, Joseph soon broke away into the purely romantic novel but he never forsook his high sense of purpose and idealism. Joseph Hocking struck a happy vein when he wrote a series of novels with a historical setting: stories written around some period when religious strike and upheaval characterised our national life.

I recall in early youth going week by week to Old Pentevale ostensibly to visit my grandmother but having in mind all the time that I would read the new instalments of Joseph Hocking's serial running in the Christian Globe – my relative's favourite paper. Here I read Lest We Forget, a really stong tale of the reign of "Bloody Mary": and at another time – not far separated – Follow the Gleam – an exciting and well sustained story of Roundhead and Cavalier in the time of Cromwell. There were other titles – now out of print I'm afraid! – all of which met with considerable sale in book form.

In my teens when Cassell's Magazine (more or less on the lines of the better known Windsor Magazine) was launched, its long serial was Joseph Hocking's 'Trevannion'. The title was changed to Mistress Nancy Molesworth when it appeared in book form: this story aroused considerable hope among many of the author's well-wishers – some of whom had vision of him doing for Cornwall what Hardy had done for Wessex but, although the book became popular and is still in print – it cannot be placed as high as his early admirers had hoped. This book was followed by many romantic tales – most successful being The Birthright, The Spirit of the West and The Sign of the Triangle.

In no field did Joseph Hocking attract so many readers as in those novels dealing with religious themes and problems which were usually first published in well-known weeklies. Outstanding in this category was All Men are Liars – the title alone was challenging. I have very vivid memories of visiting the house of friends on the evening when the British Weekly arrived. Here, at the head of the table the master of the house would read aloud to the assembled large family the latest chapter of the Joseph Hocking serial. So I listened (at times) to such of the stories as The Man Who Rose Again, The Soul of Dominic Wildthorne *and (I think)* The Man Who Found Out. *How popular he was in thousands of homes!*[45]

Such best-selling success and the expansion of the church led to many changes. Joseph was still particularly active in his work with children and teenagers. Galley records how a Young People's Society was formed as part of a Young Christians Class.[46] Joseph was still writing and preaching however. As time went on, he began to feel the strain of actively leading the church as well as writing a novel or two a year. His health suffered,

Frontispiece from *Follow The Gleam: A Tale of the Time of Oliver Cromwell*, 1905

and an Assistant Minister, Archibald Reith, was appointed in 1908, staying until the following year.[47] By this time, Joseph had reluctantly decided to resign from the Methodist ministry, a decision, which despite their initial concerns about employing 'a novelist', was received with great regret, as that year's Methodist Conference minutes confirm:

> The Conference accepts with regret the resignation of the Rev. Joseph Hocking on the ground of impaired health... The Conference prays for him the restoration of his health which will enable him to render occasional services in the churches in preaching, and trusts, also that by the continued exercise of his literary gifts he may be the means at once of interesting his extensive circle of readers and confirming them in their attachment to the Protestant religion.[48]

This does not tell the full picture. It seems Joseph was actually somewhat frustrated at the lack of progress he was making at Woodford Green. The church had grown enormously and was successful, and yet Joseph was to comment:

> Perhaps the people of Woodford are somewhat slow to move, they are not enthusiastic. Woodford is a well-to-do suburb, and the bulk of the Church are comfortably off, and as a consequence, one could not arouse the same enthusiasm as in a provincial town.[49]

Woodford, it seems, was not offering Joseph a challenge anymore. Another perspective on this change is given by his daughter Anne. She writes of how Joseph was 'told he would have to stop'.[50] Who is doing the telling is unclear. Perhaps it was his family, perhaps it was the Church authorities, who may have grown increasingly frustrated with his controversial anti-Catholic activities. Joseph was looking away from London toward the provinces, moving initially to Totteridge in Hertfordshire. Upon his subsequent recovery, he became a much sought-after preacher across Britain. One location where he found himself was at Sheringham in Norfolk, alongside his brother Silas. They conducted services in the United and Primitive Methodist chapels, while spending holidays there. Again, like his brother, Joseph travelled widely, reaching Egypt, Palestine, Syria, Turkey and Greece.

He continued to write, with more and more novels being received with acclaim; the religious press seeing no signs of abating. By now, Joseph had altered the subject matter of his writing. Gone was the overt preaching of earlier texts. The inclusion of the message had, with years of practice, become more sophisticated. His fiction was now incorporating the sociological and industrial upheavals of early twentieth-century Britain, as well as some of the gathering political clouds, which would lead ultimately to World War One. The War itself was to prove enormously inspirational for Joseph, like many other writers and poets, and many of his novels deal with events during the conflict and its aftermath, themes dealt with more fully in Chapter Five. After the war, society began to return to normal again, and Joseph returned to the speaking and lecturing circuit. Humour is perhaps something we may not readily associate with Joseph, though once again, the evidence runs to the contrary. Joseph was a witty man and when he spoke at a Cornish gathering in London on 23rd December 1921, he was in fine form:

Mr Hocking said there was only one county, and the future address of England should be: "A piece of land not far from Cornwall." (Laughter)

"We are wonderful people, we Cornishmen – the most wonderful people in the world. We are philosophers. What philosophy means I do not know, except you do not pledge yourself." (Laughter)

"The Cornishman is also a critic. A great preacher went to Camborne and asked an old man, Harry by name, what he thought of his sermon, and Harry replied, "Well, I don't think there was nothing to think about." (Laughter)

"Some years ago I happened to be the guest of the Cornish Association at Birmingham. I did let myself go. I said that Cornwall really is a king of pivot. We founded the British Navy; it was founded at Fowey (Cheers). I let them have it strong, and I spoke of Cornish pluck, telling how when Bishop Trelawney was in trouble there were 20,000 Cornishmen to support him." (Laughter)

"Mr Jesse Collings' turn came, and he said: "I was very much interested in what Mr Hocking said about Cornish courage. There is no doubt Cornish courage is very great, but I should like to ask Mr Hocking if he has ever heard about Devonshire. I went to Exeter Cathedral last week, and looking over some old registers I found the name of John Snell who in Exeter Cathedral married his own mother-in-law. (Laughter). Think of the brave noble soul marching up the aisle with his mother-in-law on his arm, and I would like to appeal to Mr Hocking where he knows in all the annals of Cornish history one whose heroism equals that of John Snell." (Loud laughter). "Of course, there I gave it up. I had to. You see, Devon men are a bit thick, and we are very keen." (Laughter).

Other witty stories followed, including one which Mr Hocking heard from Sir Arthur Carkeek. respecting the new spirit which has come over Cornwall. An old Methodist was deploring the new life, and said he saw a lot of boys playing football. They were nearly naked, with short trousers that did not come down to the knees. "Indecent," he called it, and when he asked them what it was all for, they replied, "Recreation". "Recreation," said the old man, "why, when I was young it was exercise. I got my exercise every Sunday morning at 6.30 by wrestling with the Lord." (Laughter).

Mr Hocking told another story he said he heard from Mr Boscawen, rector of Longstone. A member of Parliament was returned for one of the divisions of Cornwall, and to one of his supporters, a farmer named Josiah Liddicoat, a good substantial man, he said: "When you come to

London, just look me up." He never thought anything more about it, but one evening, when he was entertaining friends in Eaton Square, Josiah made his appearance. He was shown into the dining-room and given a chair, but not asked to dine.

Invited to tell good things about Cornwall, he said some things were good and some things were bad. He first told of the farming and said: "My old sow had a litter of fifteen." "Come," said the M.P., "that is not so very bad." "But she had thirteen teats," replied Josiah. "Well," said the M.P. "that is rather awkward. What did the other two do?" "Oh, they sat down and watched others eat, as I do." (Loud laughter)[51]

Possibly it was these meetings with Cornish people again, sharing their very particular form of humour and views on life, which tempted Joseph back over the River Tamar. Now in his seventies, he finally decided to return to Cornwall, but it was not to be to the parish of his youth. Instead, he elected to move further west, to a large dwelling named Penmare (now ironically a public house and night-club) at the eastern end of Hayle. While there, he took a great deal of interest in Cornish affairs, being returned as the County Council member of the Hayle Division in 1931, having defeated his opponent, Mr R.A. Kevern by some 180 votes.[52]

He was also present, as a member of the audience at the initial Cornish Gorseth held on September 21st 1928 at Boscawen Ûn stone circle, an observer at the time commenting how he regretted that Joseph, along with Crosbie Garstin and Mark Guy Pearse were not admitted as bards.[53] In fact Mark Guy Pearse was to be made a bard of the Cornish Gorseth the following year, but neither Silas nor Joseph were admitted as bards. This tells us not only of Joseph's probable disinterest in the 'Anglo-Catholic' Gorseth, but also of the schism between the Methodists (deriving from the Englightenment), and the Revivalists (deriving in part, from Romanticism) in Cornwall during this phase. Not that this lack of recognition in Cornwall would have worried him, but misfortune seemed to follow Joseph for a while. After a slight stroke, brought on, perhaps, by the death of his son at the end of the First World War, he was then involved in a motoring accident, which meant that he did not seek re-election to the County Council in 1934. Besides this, he had moved further eastwards, back up the north-Cornish coast to Perranporth, his house there being named Bodvean (Cornish: Little Abode). Like Silas however, he still found time to support the Liberal cause in the Camborne division, and then later, in St Ives.[54]

The motoring accident actually resulted in his being the subject of a faith healing. Perhaps Joseph remembered the abilities of his 'healing' mother and felt that some 'magic' might do him good. He was taken from Cornwall to a community in Tunbridge Wells called 'the Seekers', where after a laying on of hands, he temporarily recovered.[55] However, later that year, the *Cornish Guardian* detailed a report with the headline 'Illness of

Mr Joseph Hocking: All-Night ambulance journey to Cornwall'. A member of the family at the time told the newspaper that…

> …Mr Hocking had been pining to get back to Cornwall and went down from his house at Tunbridge Wells in a motor ambulance on Sunday, travelling all night. The car left at 10.30pm and arrived at Perranporth at 9.30am the following morning. He stood the journey, more than 240 miles, remarkably well and is far happier in spirit.[56]

Once back in Cornwall, Joseph seems to have regained his strength somewhat. As to whether the faith healing had been successful, we can only speculate. More importantly, back in Perranporth, Joseph had a visitor. It was his old schoolfriend, Norman Truscott, who recalled how he…

> …met Joe Hocking not so very long ago over at Perranporth. He attended chapel there with his wife. When I mentioned that I was from St Stephens, he said, "Who is it?" I said I was 'Nor' Truscott and he remembered me then and said, "I am so glad you spoke to me."[57]

Joseph's words here seem to encompass a great deal. Not only do they indicate his meeting up with a long lost friend, but also because Joseph seemed to realise his time was short. He was starting to view Cornwall and his childhood with more sentimental eyes, and the late novels are packed with reminiscence and disgust with change and development in his homeland.[58]

Despite his personal misfortune and wider mistrust of Cornwall's future, one event must have brought enormous joy to Joseph towards the end of his life. This was the Union of the Methodist Churches which formally took place in September 1932 at the Royal Albert Hall in London. It was a landmark in modern Methodism, bringing together all three of the separate churches: the Wesleyan, Primitive and United, all under one movement. This union formed the focus for his novel *Not One in Ten* (1933), which featured a picture of the celebration inside the Hall on the dustjacket.[59] The prior novel to this, *The Eternal Choice* (1932), appears to contain Joseph wrestling with these very issues of unity and division, while *No Other Name* (1934) continues the Methodist 'feel-good factor' of the previous year.[60] This merger would have delighted Joseph, knowing that he was approaching death, yet knowing that the Methodist church was very strong.

In 1936, Joseph and Annie moved permanently to St Ives; this time their house being named 'Bodanna' (Cornish: abode of Annie). This was a dwelling that they had bought some years earlier and had previously used as a holiday cottage.[61] During this phase, the reinvention of St Ives was beginning. It was being promoted as both a bohemian artists' colony, a holiday destination and a town ideally situated for recuperation if one was ill or unwell.[62] Perhaps fittingly, this was where Joseph was to write his last novel, *Davey's Ambition*, which was published in 1936.[63] He died

Jacket illustration for the 1970 edition of *Davey's Ambition* first published in 1936.

on Thursday 4th March 1937, aged seventy seven. A special memorial service was held at Truro's St Mary's Methodist Church on the following Tuesday, during the time of his cremation at Plymouth Crematorium. The Reverend T. Wearne delivered an address in which he said the congregation met, representing the life and interests of the Duchy, to express their sense of loss in the passing of one of the most widely-known Cornishmen of their day.[64] After the cremation, Joseph's ashes were brought back and buried close by the members of his own family in the local cemetery at St. Stephen-in-Brannel. Placed over his grave is a stone largely of rough Cornish granite. After his burial, the following comment was made of his achievement as a novelist:

In all his writings there was evidence of the spirit of clear conviction concerning the great moral and spiritual principles of Christianity. His books were clean and in a time like today, to have any writers whose books could unreservedly be commended, was a high tribute to him.[65]

Praising as this tribute was to Joseph, it perhaps says more about literary appreciation and censorship in the late 1930s, than the full impact of his work. It brings to mind another novelist with Cornish connections – D.H. Lawrence (1885-1930). Lawrence, along with his German wife, was to spend World War One at Higher Tregerthen near Zennor.[66] He later described the experience as a 'nightmare'.[67] Lawrence, however, was perhaps better known in Cornwall then, for the controversy over his 'unclean' novel, *Lady Chatterley's Lover*, which although published in Florence in 1928, with an expurgated version in London in 1932, still signified the kind of controversial fiction which it was felt improper to read. The full text of Lawrence's novel was not published in Britain until 1960.[68] Lawrence must have been aware of the Hockings as novelists; even more so their Cornish connections, neither approving very much of the other. They were writing at opposite ends of the spectrum of taste. Annie, Joseph's widow, did not have much time to reflect on Joseph or his achievement. Though still active in the Liberal movement and in the Women's Institute, within the space of two years, she had also died, leaving their daughter Anne to continue the family occupation of writing.

Now that we have covered Joseph's life story, let us consider the character of the man himself. According to Dorey, during the bulk of his career, Joseph achieved his prodigious output…

…by first dictating a chapter to his secretary. The following day he would revise and correct the transcript, and then dictate a further chapter. This way he managed to maintain an output of roughly two books per year, as well as his sermons and other work.[69]

In both his fiction and sermons, it is clear that Joseph was extremely outspoken, completely convinced that his own views were right. As I have indicated, this caused considerable tension between himself and the established United Methodist Free Churches. In Free Church circles his works were often severely criticised, sometimes for being too strongly Protestant. The dangers of fads like Theosophy (the philosophy professing to attain the knowledge of God by direct intuition or spiritual ecstasy) and Spiritualism (the belief that the spirits of the dead can communicate with the living), as well as materialism, modernism and pessimism were all regular targets. As Dorey observes, 'Joseph purposely never wrote on a high intellectual or artistic level',[70] but wrote instead so that the more poorly educated could understand the underlying ideas in his fiction. All told, it was a masterful ploy and it worked well throughout his career.

Most observers of the Hocking brothers find Joseph the better storyteller of the two.[71] Traditional literary criticism, which attacks the 'sameness' in his plots,[72] perhaps misses the point, for they were writers to reaffirm convictions and attitudes in a popular, pulp format. At the same time, as Dorey notes, 'Joseph was concerned there were not more writers like him, with his sense of high moral purpose, with a vision of the truth, who would not pander to the low tastes of man'[73] – and therefore declined to enter the emerging form of the realistic novel – best seen in the work of writers like Hardy and Lawrence. When we come to consider Joseph's fiction, Dunnerdale is again illuminating, maybe even ironic, yet at the same time, intimately aware of how the narratives worked:

> *The books written by Mr Hocking are full of originality in conception and structure... The beauty of the world is seen through his own eyes, and the passions of love and hatred which sweep like a hurricane or gentle breeze across the field of every life are truly interpreted in his novels. He has all Thomas Hardy's insight into the depths of human character – without his pessimism, and all the skill and ingenuity of Conan Doyle or Hall Caine in working out his plot. The baneful influence of what is called "the realistic novel" is largely counteracted by such writers as Joseph Hocking. I once heard Dr. Lorimer say that the novel of the future would be more idealistic and less realistic. To those who are at all acquainted with the average novel of today, the coming of that time is much desired.*[74]

Dunnerdale and Joseph Hocking may have been disappointed, since the novel has not moved towards idealism. Rather, through modernism and post-modernism, it has become if anything, more realistic – even in so-called 'magical realist' texts.[75] It is intriguing to see Hardy singled out for criticism in respect of his pessimism; a trend thought to be prevalent at the time.[76] Yet Hardy was not entirely a pessimist in the way Joseph thought if we consider his poetry:

> *If way to the Better there be, it exacts full look at the Worst.*[77]

This is not pessimism, but more a realistic acceptance of what life is actually like. Hardy aside, Joseph's optimism and faith are again well-documented by Dunnerdale:

> *He sees life clearly, and sees it whole. No pessimism blinds his vision to the grandeur and dignity of men. You will find that the light of humour is not lacking in his books; but Mr. Hocking is not of those who think that the province of the novel is primarily to amuse. His purpose is only realised when he enables the reader to see that human nature, however base and ignoble will respond to the call of love when nothing else in all the world will move it, and that He whose throne is set amid the flaming stars claims to be the eternal Master of the soul.*[78]

As to the matter of Joseph's personal character, Dunnerdale offers us interesting observations, initially comparing him to the territory of Cornwall. He was interviewing and observing Joseph just as the new church was taking shape at Woodford Green. The toll of creative work and ministerial duty seem not to have had effect yet and we see Joseph at the height of his creative powers:

> *Something of the elemental nature of that rock-bound country seems to have entered into his life. He is a man of fine healthy physique, one who believes to his finger tips in the value of athleticism... [His] study is a veritable literary workshop. A photo of Mr Coulson Kernahan stood upon the mantel-piece. The first few chapters of his fine new story The Coming of the King which is to appear in serial form in The Crusader lay upon the table, and shelf upon shelf was lined with books... Mr Hocking is a most painstaking and tireless worker, yet like most men of dreamy and imaginative mind, much subject to the moods of the day. He will sometimes sit at his desk for hours and few thoughts bearing upon the story cross the pathway of his mind. At another time under the inspiration of the hour the words flow easily from his pen, and he writes with great rapidity.*[79]

A talk given by Joseph at Woodford Green is referred to earlier in this chapter. It was titled 'Novels and Novelists', and was originally commissioned by the *Methodist Monthly* in 1894, just after the release of the second phase of his work, such as *Ishmael Pengelly: An Outcast*, *The Story of Andrew Fairfax* and *The Monk of Mar-Saba*. The talk was given by Joseph on numerous occasions and probably went through further drafts and revisions to suit the time and place. However, the fact remains that it stands as a fascinating insight into the production of fiction during this phase, as well as being one of the first pieces of literary theory written by an Anglo-Cornish novelist other than Arthur Quiller Couch.[80]

I have taken the liberty of reproducing much of it verbatim, while attempting to provide a brief commentary on its contents. However, the writing alone merits considerable interest. The article begins with a philosophical debate on the function of the novel, (despite its relatively recent emergence as an actual literary genre) justifying the value of pulp Methodism:

Novels as a class of literature will never die. The love of the narrative is embedded in our nature. Children demand a story as soon as they can in the most vague way connect cause and effect, and the oldest of us are only children "grown up". I pity the man or woman who is too much grown up to appreciate a story. The writer of the Arabian Nights expressed a profound truth concerning men, when he showed how the Eastern Sultan of romance, who had taken an oath to marry a new wife each day, and to put her to death the following morning, was turned aside from his purpose when one beguiled him with a story, and then broke it off in the middle, telling him she would finish it the following night. Of course, the irate Sultan wanted to know the end of it, so does the reader. We do not wonder that she kept him interested for a thousand and one nights, by which time his anger was gone. It is true to life; and while men and women are what they are the novel can never be destroyed.

And this is true largely because novels deal with life in the concrete. A truth stated in the abstract appeals only to the few; the same truth expressed in the story of some life appeals to the multitude. An argument, however cleverly worked out, however faultless its logic, affects us but little; the same argument expressed in a story stirs our emotions, fires our imaginations, and enkindles our enthusiasm. Far be it for me to say that the logician, the metaphysician, has done his work, and has had his day; but if I understand the signs of the times, the future will be moulded more by the poet and the novelist than by the metaphysician. For, say what we will, the novel is read when other books are allowed to lie dusty; it is the class of book which appeals to the popular taste; it is the form of literature, either for good or for evil, which is influencing the minds of the million. There is a story told, how far it is true I cannot say, that William Black, the novelist, sent a copy of his latest novel to Thomas Carlyle, and, after a few days called to know what the Nestor of History had to say about the work. Carlyle, so the story goes, tried as well as his dyspepsia would allow him, to say some kind things about the story, and then burst out savagely: "But why don't you quit this stuff and write a real book, man?" Very good, but why can't a novel be a real book? Nay, is not the novel among the most real books of the age?

Broadly speaking we need three things. We need to be amused, we need to be taught, we need to have our sympathies and emotions aroused. Is not the novel, rightly understood, among the most potent factors in our life in supplying these needs? Of course, I refer to the unlearned many, to the ordinary individual, rather than to the learned few and the people of extraordinary attainments.

That people need to be amused is a fact which we need not discuss. Not one in a million will subscribe to the teaching of Wesley's hymn, in

> which it is stated that there is 'No room for mirth or trifling here'. There may be no room for trifling, but there is for mirth, there is room for recreation, and while we are what we are, people will seek these things until they find them. This being so, is not the novel among the most pleasant and healthful forms of recreation? I am of course, aware that fiction has been abused, and that day by day a vast amount of poison is issued in this form. I quite concede the fact that hundreds of young people's minds have been unhinged and their morals sullied by the trash of the time. No one will deny the importance and need of the newspaper, and yet a vast amount of evil is wrought by that form of literature. Who shall calculate the evil that is effected by the sporting and society newspapers, which sell by hundreds of thousands? But we do not condemn the newspaper because of this. Nay, rather we say let us try to purify and uplift this class of literature. The same applies to the novel.[81]

Joseph's comments are interesting. As well as saying how all of us need to be 'taught' (in the Protestant faith of course), Joseph continues to neatly justify the process of developing ethical fiction for the purposes of character development and the process of teaching good citizenship. It is intriguingly a very contemporary argument considering the development of English and Citizenship within the context of the National Curriculum for schools in England and Wales. It is a mechanism of instruction foremost, not imparting knowledge to the cultured few, but instead to many.

This is, in actual fact, underpinned by a philosophy that went against much of the intellectual imagining of the masses in Britain by the literary and philosophical intelligentsia, as 'semi-human swarms, drugged by popular culture'.[82] Joseph Hocking had no time for this. The novel had other social uses. Joseph's was also a view against the grain of some of the intellectuals, such as George Bernard Shaw (who paradoxically ran in the same circles as his sister Salome) and many other canonized writers like D.H. Lawrence and Virginia Woolf:

> Moreover, is not the novel one of the greatest reforming forces of the time, and thus is not the novelist among our greatest reformers? Here again, we need only reflect a few minutes before the answer comes to us. History had revealed this fact: before any abuse can be removed, before any wrong can be righted, sympathy must be realised, conscience must be aroused. Think, as an instance, of the cruel fact of slavery in the Southern States of America. Three million human beings were bound by cruel chains, crushed by tyrannous laws and corrupt customs. Before the evil of slavery could be realised, men had to be made to feel the condition of the slaves, had to see with their eyes and to feel with their bodies. Well, Mrs. Harriet Beecher Stowe wrote Uncle Tom's Cabin, and now it is a recognised fact that the novel had more to do with the arousing of public conscience than perhaps any other influence of the time. Indeed, it is

impossible to estimate the power of her book in sweeping away one of the greatest abuses of our generation.

I need not enlarge upon this, and I have already used all the space at my disposal. We have only to think of the influence of Charles Reade's Never Too Late to Mend *on the prison life of the land, of Charles Dickens'* Oliver Twist *on the Poor Laws in England, or of Walter Besant's* All Sorts and Conditions of Men *in the East End of London, to realise that the novelist had in his hands not only the "Sword" which strikes at the hoary head of abuse, but the "Trowel" which helps to build up a new and better state of things.*

Novels, then I claim, are among the most potent influences of our life, and as such we must regard them. Fiction used rightly is destined to become in God's hands one of the great means in the future for teaching and uplifting the life of the people. The work of the storyteller, rightly understood, is more effective to teach than that of the teacher at his desk, and not less sacred than that of the divine in the pulpit.[83]

This last statement fully encapsulates Joseph's ideology and justifies the 'pulp Methodist' methodology of all his fiction. Certainly Joseph ide-

Gravestone for Joseph and Annie Hocking at St Stephen-in-Brannel churchyard. All other records, including the *Census* and the *Dictionary of National Biography* list Joseph as born in 1860.

alised chapel life, and appealed to the belief of his readers in an illusory Golden Age of Methodism, enjoyed by their fathers and just around the corner for them. Despite this, and possibly even because of it (in its reflection of an idealised eighteenth and nineteenth-century Cornish lifestyle, still romanced by many contemporary Cornish writers and academics[84]), Joseph's fiction had remained more popular than his brothers after their deaths.

As Harman records in his notes on the Hockings, a serialised *Jabez Easterbook* found its way into the *Sunday Companion* during 1963 and another version in the Belfast *Protestant Telegraph* in 1967. The best example of Joseph's anti-Catholic convictions, *The Jesuit*, was first published in 1911, though it saw many reprints, well into the latter half of the twentieth century. The foremost Methodist magazines such as the *Methodist Recorder* and *Christian World* continued to serialise Joseph's novels into the 1940s. In fact, the 1932 novel, *The Eternal Challenge*, appeared as a serialisation in the *Christian Herald* in 1948, under the title of *Strange Inheritance*.[85]

However, the aftermath of the Second World War brought about the true decline in interest in the work of Joseph. Mass media provided new entertainment other than reading. Britain entered a more secular age, which would witness a vast decline in Christianity and church and chapel attendance undreamed of by the Hockings.[86] Could Joseph ever have anticipated a conference in 2001 which attempted to explore the best use for listed Methodist chapels in Cornwall?[87] This had become the time of Ken Phillipps' father's disparaging comments when the once popular author's books met with, "Tis only an old Joseph Hocking.'

Harman records a brief revival in 1958. The 1898 novel *Mistress Nancy Molesworth*, argued by some observers to be one of Joseph's finest works, and maybe the nearest he ever truly came to the growing genre of historical romance, was adapted for television by David Goddard. The story was renamed *The Rebel Heiress* and was broadcast on BBC television in six parts, shown on Sunday afternoon at 5.25pm, from 15th November to 20th December 1958. Described as a 'Cornish adventure', it was among the first of a kind of historical drama that is now emblematic of the BBC. The role of Nancy was taken by Mary Holland, Roger Trevanion by Patrick Troughton (later to become the second television *Dr Who*) and Daniel by Richard Statman.[88] This was the only media adaptation of any Joseph Hocking story, and sadly, like the film *Her Benny*, no print of it remains.

Having now dealt with the two writing brothers – Silas, and Joseph – and their literary revolt against the restrictions of the Methodist Ministry, I now turn our account to tell of Salome, their sister. Her story will be different, but in many ways just as radical and revolutionary.

Notes

1. K.C. Phillipps, 'A Calling Sacrificed to Writing Novels' in *Western Morning News*, July (1976), p.5. Article found in the Thomas Shaw Cornish Methodism archive in the Courtney Library, Royal Institution of Cornwall.
2. See Alan M. Kent (2000) *The Literature of Cornwall: Continuity, Identity, Difference 1000-2000*, Bristol: Redcliffe, p.161-3.
3. Norman Truscott in *Cornish Guardian*, 11th March 1937, p.13.
4. The early manifestation of this institution may well have been a Dame School.
5. *St Stephen-in-Brannel Methodist Church Sunday School Minute Books*, cited in St Stephen Methodist Church (1970), *St. Stephen Methodist Church Centenary 1870-1970*, St Stephen-in-Brannel: St Stephen-in-Brannel Methodist Church, p.7.
6. *Cornish Guardian*, op.cit. Norman Truscott comments 'Joseph would have been a child of six or seven at that time, but the year was to come when he, too, appeared 'on the plan' as being on trial'.
7. John Dunnerdale 'Joseph Hocking: The Man and His Books' in David Lyall (ed.) (1903) *The Secrets of Upland Farm*, London: United Methodist Free Church, p.273.
8. Andrew C. Symons, 'She, 'Er and 'Un: Study II in Language and History' in *An Baner Kernewek / The Cornish Banner* No. 94 (1998), pp.6-7.
9. A comment attributed to Joseph Hocking in Michael Dorey 'Joseph Hocking' in *Cornish Scene: New Series* No.15 (1992), p.58.
10. Ibid.
11. *Cornish Guardian*, op.cit.
12. Sir Walter Scott (1771-1832) was an enormously successful writer, his medieval and Tudor romances enjoying huge popularity. He established the form of the historical novel. *Kenilworth* is set in the court of Elizabeth I and is based on the tragedy of Amy Robsart, who was enticed into a marriage with the Earl of Leicester, Queen Elizabeth's favourite, rejecting the worthy Edmund Tressilian, a Cornish gentleman.

    Harriet Beecher Stowe (1811-96) was born in Connecticut, and her anti-slavery novel *Uncle Tom's Cabin* had great success, being first published in serial form in the *National Era*. She was rapturously received by Queen Victoria on several visits to Britain, but later alienated British opinion regarding Byron's incestuous relations with his half-sister in *Lady Byron Vindicated* (1870).
13. Quoted in Dorey, op.cit.
14. Dunnerdale, op.cit.
15. Dorey, op.cit.
16. *Cornish Guardian*, op.cit.
17. Ibid. See also Ordnance Survey of England (1880) *Book of Reference to the Plan of the Parish of St Stephen-in-Brannel (Hundred of Powder)*, London: George M. Eyre and William Spottiswoode. A copy of this is held in the Cornwall Records Office, Truro.
18. Ibid.
19. A view argued in Alan M. Kent, 'The Cornish Alps: Resisting Romance in the Clay Country' in Ella Westland (ed.) (1997) *Cornwall: The Cultural Construction of Place*. Penzance: The Patten Press, p.60. See also Bernard Deacon. 'Proto-Industrialization and Potatoes: A Revised Narrative for Nineteenth-Century Cornwall' in Philip Payton (ed.) (1997) *Cornish Studies: Five*, University of Exeter: University of Exeter Press, pp.60-84.
20. Dorey, op.cit. Despite research no more details of the Prize can be found.
21. Ibid.
22. For an interesting critique of these, see George Orwell 'Boys' Weeklies' in George Bott (ed.) (1958) *George Orwell: Selected Essays*, London: Heinemann, pp.116-144.
23. For a response to this 'control', see Bill Ashcroft, Gareth Griffiths and Helen Tiffin (1989) *The Empire Writes Back: Theory and Practice in Post-Colonial Literatures*, London and New York: Routledge. Orwell notes some of the stereotypes offered: - 'Frenchman: Excitable. Wears beard, gesticulates wildly. Spaniard, Mexican, etc.: Sinister, treacherous. Arab, Afghan, etc.: Sinister,

treacherous. Chinese: Sinister, treacherous. Wears pigtail. Italian: Excitable, Grinds barrel-organ or carries stiletto. Swede, Dane, etc: Kind-hearted, stupid. Negro: Comic, very faithful'. See Bott, ibid., p.129.

24. Peter Ackroyd (2000) *London: The Biography,* London: Chatto and Windus, p.599-605
25. Joseph Hocking (1890) *Jabez Easterbrook: A Religious Novel,* London: Ward, Lock and Company.
26. Joseph Hocking (1887) *Harry Penhale: The Trial of His Faith.* London: Andrew Crombie, (1888) *Gideon Strong: Plebeian.* London: Andrew Crombie, (1889) *From London to Damascus.* London: Ward, Lock and Company, (1890) *Elrad the Hic.* London: Ward, Lock and Company.
27. George A. Greenwood, 'Daughter of famous Cornish novelist writers her 40th book: Anne Hocking's West Reminiscences' in *Western Morning News,* 2nd December (1953), p.7
28. The history of the town is considered in Michael Townsend (1999) *Burnley,* Stroud: Tempus Publishing.
29. For a flavour of discontent in northern England during this period, see Christopher Hampton (ed.) (1984) *A Radical Reader: The Struggle for Change in England 1381-1914.* Harmondsworth: Penguin, pp.507-603.
30. John Rowe (1993 [1953]) *Cornwall in the Age of the Industrial Revolution,* St Austell: Cornish Hillside Publications.
31. For a history of Brunswick Chapel, see Brunswick Chapel (1959) *Brunswick Chapel 1869-1959 and the original Mount "Pleasant",* Burnley: Brunswick Chapel. I am indebted to James Howell for bringing this document to my attention.
32. Joseph Hocking (1928) *The Eternal Challenge,* London: Hodder and Stoughton.
33. Detailed in Brunswick Chapel, op.cit., pp.11-12.
34. Information supplied by James Howell.
35. For detail on the life of William Burnett (c.1808-1900) see Oliver A. Beckerlegge (1968) *United Methodist Ministers and their Circuits 1797-1932,* London: Epworth Press, p.36. Burnett starts as a Wesleyan but becomes a Wesleyan Reformer.
36. R.L. Galley (n.d.) *The History of Woodford Union Church,* London: Woodford Union Church, p.61.
37. Ibid.
38. Cited in ibid.
39. This property was also known as Higham Lodge. It was demolished in 1931, and is now covered by Lodge Villas and Harman Avenue.
40. Galley, op.cit.
41. Ibid., p.62. Galley records that some wag named it 'Hocking's Folly'.
42. Ibid., p.63. It is unclear precisely why oak should be any more comfortable than deal. However, deal probably needed more upkeep and varnishing than oak.
43. Ibid., p.64.
44. A talk first published in *Methodist Monthly* (1894), pp.302-5 as 'Novels and Novel Writers'.
45. H. M. Creswell Payne 'Pages from Book of Memory: Joseph Hocking' in *Cornish Guardian,* 20 May (1954), p.5. This useful article summarises much about Joseph Hocking's work as a novelist. The visit to Rome was a hugely controversial event, which is dealt with in Chapter Five in more detail. Interestingly Payne makes much of Joseph Hocking's Celticity – ironic when every indication was that the Cornish-Celtic Revivalist movement had aligned itself with Catholicism, rather than Methodism. As a point of clarification here 'Trevannion' is spelt with a double 'n' by Payne – whereas Joseph and Annie's residence had only one. Presumably one of Joseph Hocking's well-wishers was the shadowy *West Briton* columnist 'Argus' who argued for the promotion of 'a Cornish school of writing'. See Kent (2000) op.cit., p.148.
46. Galley, op.cit., p.66.
47. Ibid.
48. The minutes of the United Methodist Conference of 1910 were revisited in *West Briton and Cornish Advertiser,* 11 March (1937), p.3.
49. Cited in Galley, op.cit. p.67.
50. Greenwood, op.cit. Beckerlegge notes that Joseph 'resigned due to ill health'. See Oliver A. Beckerlegge *United Methodist Ministers and their Circuits 1797-1932.* London: Epworth Press, p.113.

51. 'Joseph Hocking's Stories: Amusing Yarns at Cornish Gathering in London' in *Cornish Guardian,* 23rd December (1921), p.6. Comparable humour to this is interestingly found in Salome Hocking Fifield (1903) *Some Old Cornish Folk.* London: Charles H. Kelly, 1903. For similar humour, see the work of John Tabois Tregellas, William Bentinck Forfar and Joseph Thomas in Alan M. Kent (ed.) (2000) *Voices from West Barbary: An Anthology of Anglo-Cornish Poetry 1549-1928.* London: Francis Boutle, pp. 85-90, pp.121-4 and pp.153-4 respectively.
52. *West Briton and Cornish Advertiser,* op.cit.. Here, as well as details of electoral success, Joseph is labelled 'Distinguished Son' and 'Outstanding Figure'. A friend of Cedric J. Appleby remembers that as a boy he felt the Hockings were reclusive while at Penmare. Charles Thomas (whose grandfather knew Joseph Hocking) visited Penmare as boy. He recollects that the Hocking family kept a pet owl which could be seen in an upstairs window, and which sat on Joseph' hand.
53. *The Cornish Gorsedd at Boscawen Ün Stone Circle, near St Buryan, September 21st, 1928* from Cornishman, Penzance. Booklet, p.8. This booklet was a pull-out feature. For background to the emergence and development of the Cornish Gorseth, see Amy Hale 'Rethinking Celtic Cornwall: An Ethnographic Approach' and 'Genesis of the Celto-Cornish Revival? L.C. Duncombe-Jewell and the Cowethas Kelto-Kernuack' in Philip Payton (ed.) (1997) *Cornish Studies: Five,* University of Exeter: University of Exeter Press, pp.85-99 and pp.100-111. Henry Jenner was trying to convince the Cornish Methodists that they actually had more in common with Breton Catholicism than Protestantism. See Henry Jenner (1904) *A Handbook of the Cornish Language,* London: David Nutt.
54. For background on the Liberal cause in Cornwall, see Garry Tregidga (2000) *The Liberal Party in South-West Britain Since 1918,* Exeter: University of Exeter Press, pp.23-86.
55. 'Illness of Mr Joseph Hocking: All-Night ambulance journey to Cornwall' in *Cornish Guardian,* 19th September (1935), p.9.
56. Ibid.
57. Truscott, op.cit.
58. See Kent (2000) op.cit., p.163.
59. Joseph Hocking (1933) *Not One in Ten.* London: Hodder and Stoughton.
60. Joseph Hocking (1932) *The Eternal Choice.* London: Hodder and Stoughton, (1934) *No Other Name.* London: Ward, Lock and Company.
61. Noted by Greenwood, op.cit. Joseph regularly preached at the Carbis Bay Wesleyan Church. In 1937 he was watched by a Mr Charles Baker – the Proprietor of *Newspaper World* – who admits to be impressed with his performance. See *Cornishman,* 10th March (1937).
62. Michael Tooby (1993) *Tate St Ives: An Illustrated Companion,* London: Tate Gallery Publications, pp.14-17
63. Joseph Hocking (1936) *Davey's Ambition.* London, Ward, Lock and Company. This novel was still being reprinted in 1970.
64. *Cornish Guardian,* 11th March (1937), p.13. Joseph's Will is far less complex than Silas's. He bequeathed all his real and personal estate to his wife. It would appear the Joseph and Annie had, like most families of their status, a domestic servant – one Ethel Bagot. See *Last Will and Testament of Joseph Hocking,* Probate Registry, Bodmin.
65. *West Briton and Cornish Advertiser,* op.cit..
66. See Kent (2000) op.cit., pp.174-5.
67. D.H. Lawrence (1975 [1923]) *Kangaroo,* Harmondsworth: Penguin, pp.262-4.
68. D.H. Lawrence (1960 [1928]) *Lady Chatterley's Lover,* Harmondsworth: Penguin..
69. Dorey, op.cit, pp.58-9.
70. Ibid., p.59.
71. Dorey and Phillipps agree on this. See ibid., and K.C. Phillipps, op.cit.
72. A view deconstructed in the Introduction to this book, and also by their non-inclusion in many anthologies, companions and even histories of Cornwall.
73. Dorey, op.cit. For a useful history of the the realistic novel, see Ian Williams (1974) *The Realist Novel in England: A Study in Development,* London and Basingstoke: Macmillan.
74. Dunnerdale, op.cit., p.274. Optimism was a feature of the Enlightenment.
75. For a useful overview of Britain, see Allan Massie (1990) *The Novel Today,* Harlow: Longman. For Cornwall, see Kent (2000) op.cit., pp.221-3 and pp.252-8.

76. For comment and examples, see Judy Giles and Tim Middleton (eds.) (1995) *Writing Englishness 1900-1950: An Introductory Sourcebook on National Identity,* London and New York.
77. This is from *In Tenebris II*. See David Wright (ed.) (1978) *Thomas Hardy: Selected Poetry,* Harmondsworth: Penguin, p.292
78. Dunnerdale (1903) op.cit., p.274.
79. Ibid., pp.273-4.
80. For a representative example, see Arthur Quiller Couch (1995 [1916]) *On the Art of Writing,* Fowey: Fowey Rare Books. Arthur Quiller Couch (1863-1944), known better as 'Q', was a Professor of English at the University of Cambridge. The influential *Cornish Magazine* which 'Q' edited also contains notable examples of literary and cultural criticism.
81. See *Methodist Monthly,* op.cit., p.303. William Black (1841-98) was a Scottish novelist helping to establish the Kailyard School with its emphasis on the vernacular and small-town life. Thomas Carlyle (1795-1881) is now regarded as an important historian, social prophet and critic. For a perspective on the social impact of novels, see Louis Gazamian (1973 [1903]) *The Social Novel in England,* London and Boston: Routledge and Kegan Paul.
82. See John Carey (1992) *The Intellectuals and the Masses: Pride and Prejudice among the Literary Intelligentsia, 1880-1939,* London: Faber and Faber, p.250.
83. *Methodist Monthly,* op.cit., p.305.
84. New Cornish Studies pays particular attention to the nineteenth century, often to the exclusion of contemporary culture or other centuries. Considerable academic energy has been spent on showing how the Cornish Celtic Revival failed to connect with Cornish society still based on Mining and Methodism. Much of the energy of Cornish publishing is devoted to these time periods. Many novelists, such as E.V. Thompson and Daniel Mason, and playwrights such as Nick Darke set material in this age. See E.V. Thompson (1977) *Chase the Wind,* London: Macmillan,. Daniel Mason (1996) *Cousin Jack,* Fowey: Alexander Associates, and Nick Darke (1999) *Plays: 1,* London: Methuen.
85. Information contained in the Leonard W. Harman MS. in possession of the author. These magazines, though once popular, have not been possible to trace.
86. For a useful summary of these changes, see Alan Sinfield (1989) *Literature, Politics and Culture in Postwar Britain,* Oxford: Blackwell.
87. See English Heritage (2001) 'Historic Methodist Chapels in Cornwall: Bane or Blessing?' Conference, held at Truro School, Conference Programme, 16th-18th July.
88. Harman MS.

A photograph of Salome Hocking taken in 1894 in the summer before her marriage.

Chapter Four

Romancing Idealism:
Salome Hocking Fifield, 1859-1927

> *"What a peculiar thing the feminine mind is? What queer little nooks and crannies there are if anyone will take the trouble to explore it? How few of us can argue a question straightforwardly. Our minds are like country lanes – which have been likened to cork-screws, and have many turnings."*
>
> Salome Hocking Fifield, from 'Chats with Girls' in *Methodist Monthly*, 1894[1]

Of the trio of Hocking authors, the most interesting and mysterious of them all is Salome. There is no doubt that Salome Hocking Fifield was an enigma. She was also a progressive thinker, a Socialist, a feminist, a supporter of a Tolstoyan community and as I have argued elsewhere, Cornwall's most important, early, female Anglo-Cornish novelist.[2] These associations and movements alone would make her worthy of investigation, and yet in addition to the above, she was also a successful folklorist and anthropologist, as well as being one of the finest recorders of Cornu-English 'dialect' in the modern era. Salome probably faced much prejudice in becoming the writer she did – much of it from her brothers, and some from general nineteenth-century society – and yet the fact that she did succeed, shows her tenacity and determination. Salome was a modern idealist. Society needed to change for the better and she wanted the Tolstoyan message of equality to sweep across Britain. It was the combination of her Methodist upbringing with Tolstoyan idealism which informed all her romances. The mixture was powerful; the message uncompromising.

Salome Hocking was born in April 1859, and like the other Hocking siblings, given a biblical name (probably from the hellenisation of the Hebrew Shalom ['Peace']); this name appearing in the Bible twice: Salome was the wife of Zebedee and the mother of James and John. She was also of course, the daughter of Herodias (thought to be a witches' deity), who asked for the head of John the Baptist. Her mother and father's reasoning is impossible to deduce, yet even so, the name was fairly uncommon, and somewhat unusual for a mid-Cornwall parish. Named so, it already seemed Salome was set for an unusual life. Being born after Mahala Mary and Thirza, Salome was the third and youngest daughter in the family, and the closest in age to Joseph. If we are to believe in folklore, then the much considered 'gift' which ran in the Kitto line (and as mentioned earlier, recognised in her mother Eliza), was to pass to the last born girl – Salome.

By the time Salome was born, mining around the River Fal's head waters had declined markedly and so Cap'n Jimmy Hocking had turned his mind more fully to farming, leasing the 'new-take' holding at Broadmoor. However, this did not stop Salome learning much about the extractive processes of winning by stamping and dressing tin when she was still a girl. Indeed, in many ways, this was not unusual. All across Cornwall, and further afield, many girls and women knew much about such processes; they had to, in order to earn a living.[3] However, it seems that Salome in particular, enjoyed her father's company and hearing his stories about his more prosperous mining days. Indeed, in reviewing Salome's fiction, it is easy to see this knowledge put to use. Even in her later work, the influence is marked.[4]

The transition to farm work for the Hocking family was to have a dramatic impact on Salome's future life however. It came one morning in summer. The event is well documented in Arthur C. Fifield's *In Memoriam*,[5] which forms our principal source of knowledge concerning Salome's life. Salome, and presumably the other family members had been helping to load corn sheaves with pitch forks in fields beside the River Fal. Extra help at this time of year was difficult to obtain and mechanisation had not arrived, so anyone who could potentially lend a hand was engaged. While pitching the corn sheaves, somehow Salome injured her back. Fifield tells how 'she was too proud to mention the injury to her father, lest he should decline her further aid'.[6]

What is clear is that her shoulder and hip were permanently thrown in opposite directions, and her spine was put into permanent curvature. She never recovered from the injury, despite treatment in later life. In order to disguise the disability, Salome grew her hair very long. As well as the physical difficulties this gave her, it provided many psychological ones too – issues which later formed core aspects of her writing. Many of her texts consider characters with disabilities: stock Victorian cripples, hunchbacks – like herself, or those more explicitly disabled. The trauma of this event did not affect her determination. She remained stoic about her disability, despite confessing later on how it sometimes sapped her strength and vitality. Sadly, it also led to her sometimes wishing to keep out of public sight. This must have been painful, for Salome was clearly a gregarious and talented young woman.

Being female of course, restricted Salome's ambitions. She was not afforded the opportunities of her brothers. Indeed, familial and social expectations were taking her in an opposite direction – towards established family life,[7] yet her thoughts obviously turned towards a literary career when she saw how well her two brothers were doing. She, of course, did not require the revolt against the established norms of non-conformity and Methodism that both her brothers had already shaped. Indeed, other writers, such as Mark Guy Pearse, were by now, blazing an exciting and well-established trail of pulp Methodism across these islands.[8] Salome's revolt and interest would be longer coming and more frustrating. Besides dealing with the inevitable sexism of her brothers, and of the publishing industry itself, her themes were to be, in a way, far less manufactured and, to use a contemporary expression, 'more edgy'.

It was actually only after the death of her father that Salome began to write seriously. An initial flurry of activity gave rise to five novels: *Granny's Hero: A Tale of Country Life* (n.d.), *The Fortunes of Riverside or Waiting and Winning* (1885), *Norah Lang: The Mine Girl* (1886), *Jacky: A Story of Everyday Life* (1887) and *Chronicles of a Quiet Family: A Temperance Story* (1888).[9] If we view the first undated novel here as being published

Plate from *The Fortunes of Riverside*, 1885.

in 1884, then we see that by her late twenties, Salome had become a very productive novelist. There are two ways of considering these texts. Either we see them as simple, unassuming stories for girls, set in the mining, farming and seafaring settings so familiar to her, or we regard them more productively as popular, subversive texts – which when read against the grain – show a writer, trying to develop a female perspective on mid-Cornwall life in the later part of the nineteenth century. There will be more analysis of Salome's literary achievement in Chapter Five. What is evident though, is that Salome – still writing in Cornwall – was producing popular works of fiction for a Britain-wide audience.

While she was writing, Salome also worked as a teacher at the Dame School in the village of Coombe, and was honorary organist and sub-choir leader of the United Methodist Free Church in St Stephen-in-Brannel. For a number of her teenage years and twenties, she sang contralto in a Chapel Quartet, of the kind that was once very popular in Cornwall.[10] Much of this was to form the background for *Norah Lang: The Mine Girl,* which will be considered in more detail later. Despite growing success in the world of publishing, when her mother died in 1891, Salome was left as the last of her family in Cornwall, and according to Fifield, almost totally 'robbed her of ambition'.[11] Salome's life spiralled out of control – unsure of her direction. Terras and Trelion would have to be left behind. She moved to England.

According to Fifield, during the period in which 'Joseph Hocking was a religious and social force at Thornton Heath in Surrey, and Silas Kitto Hocking the most popular preacher in Southport,'[12] Salome lived for three years alternatively with one and then the other, housekeeping for them when they travelled (both brothers were regularly speakers in many countries and could also afford to travel now). For the modern reader, such a move may seem somewhat baffling; though during this period, such a position would have been well-paid and secure. Besides, Salome knew she might become 'an old maid': provision needed to be made. In these years, she published only one novel – *A Conquered Self* (n.d.) which was not published under her own name but written under the pseudonym of S. Moore Carew – who was an ancestor of the Kitto family.[13] From all accounts, the novel did not sell particularly well and economic slowdown in the Cornish mining industry meant that her earlier works were already becoming romantic, dropping out of fashion. These must have been frustrating years for Salome. After being dislocated from the ideological base of her narratives, she had to gaze longingly upon the success of her brothers, who were bringing out new novels, most often at the rate of two each, per year. Salome's pulp Methodism and pulp idealism had to take a back seat.

In the front seat however, was a man who was about to change Salome's life forever. It was while staying with one of her brothers that she met her future husband – Arthur C. Fifield. Fifield was handsome and a powerful publisher. He was a rich and ambitious socialist, who foremost was to care deeply for her, but additionally enabled Salome's social circle to increase, so finding a wider readership for her work. Fifield was well-connected, but also knew many radical thinkers and writers of the age. Among those that Salome met were George Bernard Shaw (1856-1950). Best known now as a dramatist, writing over fifty plays,[14] during this period, he was writing music, drama and book reviews for *The Star* (1888-90) and *The Saturday Review* (1895-8). Shaw, like Fifield, was an active Socialist – a freethinker, a supporter of women's rights, an advocate of equality of income, the abolition of private property and radical change in the voting system. These were views not antithetical to Salome. Her nonconformist heritage had given her much of this radical ideology. After her family's experiences of land law in St Stephen-in-Brannel, she was also sympathetic to those idealistic enough to imagine the abolition of private property.

Frontispiece from *Chronicles of a Quiet Family*, 1888.

As well as Shaw, Salome was also introduced to Samuel Butler (1835-1902). Perhaps best remembered now as a novelist and critic of Darwinism, as well as numerous works on art and travel, Butler had outspoken views on religion and on the importance of money and property.[15] Indeed, Shaw was to later praise Butler in his preface to *Major Barbara* (1907). It had been Shaw's wife – Charlotte – who had suggested to Butler that when his publisher Grant Richard's firm folded, he should use Arthur C. Fifield. Fifield eventually reissued Shaw's *Major Barbara*, as well as a reprint of Butler's satirical novel *Erewhon* (about a traveller who comes across an undiscovered country) – first published anonymously in 1872. Ford Madox Brown in *The Daily News* praised Fifield for making the works of 'this rare and inestimable writer' available.[16]

Clearly this scene engaged Salome's mind. In many ways, it was a more sophisticated and progressive scene than that of her brothers, who had 'lapsed' from religious radicalism into pot-boiler production and travel. Meanwhile, Salome and Arthur's courtship continued happily and they were married on Christmas Eve in 1894.[17] Salome was aged thirty-five, a relatively old age then to become married. They did not have any children; a further indication of their modern views on marriage. Earlier that year, she had published a series of articles titled 'Chats with Girls' in *Methodist Monthly*. The articles were witty pieces of moral – yet progressive instruction for young women, in many ways forerunners of the modern women's magazine market. Silas's approach to such articles was far more didactic – and though temptation in general and in the specific case of young women and their relations with men was similar to her brothers, Salome opted for a more discursive style. The example given at the beginning of this chapter asserts (albeit gently) a growing feminist perspective.

After her marriage, Salome became further acquainted with a group of Russian and Continental Tolstoyan exiles and English followers; in the main friends and associates of Fifield. The groups followed the system of living espoused by Count Lev Nikolaevich Tolstoy (1828-1910). He was a Russian prose writer, who had served in the army during the Crimean War and is best known now for the novels *War and Peace* (1863-9) (his epic of the Napoleonic invasion of Russia) and *Anna Karenina* (1873-7).[18] From about 1880, Tolstoy began to wrestle with many moral questions causing him a spiritual crisis. This led to radical changes in his life and the writing of works such as *A Confession* (1879-82), *What Men Live By* (1882), *What I Believe* (1883) and *What is Art?* (1898)[19] – books and positions promoted by Shaw and Fifield, who were crucial in establishing Tolstoy's reputation in Britain. Once Tolstoy had begun to work through his crisis and moral position he more openly promoted non-resistance to evil, the renunciation of property, the abolition of churches and governments, but a belief in God and love of human beings. It was this Christian anarchist position which led to the banning of many of his works and to his excommunication by the Orthodox Church in 1901.[20] However, Tolstoy's moral authority began to be extremely influential all across Europe, and his place of birth – Yasnaya Polyana – became a place of pilgrimage for many intellectuals of the age. Tolstoy's fashionable position also encouraged numerous individuals to begin communities based on his position.

Dennis Hardy has drawn attention to the proliferation of such 'Utopian communities' across these islands during the late nineteenth and early twentieth centuries, as a response to social and spiritual change, but also the genuine quest for alternative lifestyles. One of the earliest was the community at Whiteway in the Cotswolds, which Salome and Arthur joined and supported. Hardy notes that...

...the first settlers, who came from Purleigh and Croydon, were undaunted by what they found. They knew that the Kingdom of God, perfection on Earth could only be achieved by hard climbing. In spite of difficult material conditions, in their first years they tried to avoid compromise, living together in the house and working the land communally on the basis of voluntary cooperation. One of the pioneers Nellie Shaw, records, that women could enjoy more freedom than in conventional society. She spoke of women doing the same work as the men (though not of the men undertaking domestic tasks), of the wearing of what was termed 'rational dress', and of the choice of entering into free union in preference to marriage – whereby 'according to law, a woman became a chattel, being ringed and labelled as a man's property, losing even her name in marriage'.[21]

One can see how this would appeal to Salome. Hardy describes Whiteway as 'the most significant Tolstoyan experiment in England',[22] a fact well-known by Joy Thacker, who has spent much time documenting and recording the history of the community at Whiteway:

Appalled by the terrible living conditions endured by the poor in our cities at the end of the nineteenth century, concerned middle-class people were inspired by the Tolstoyan message of equality among all men which was sweeping the country. Brotherhood Churches were formed where freedom for all mankind was discussed and practised. From these came land schemes, which it was envisaged would cause others to see the errors of capitalism that kept the poor in a situation from which it was almost impossible to escape.[23]

As Thacker demonstrates the Colony was one of the most radical movements in Europe at the time. It went against all the conventions of Queen Victoria's reign and made young men and women forsake common sense and established assumptions of how to live.[24] As well as this effect on families and communities, perhaps for the establishment, more worryingly, the Colony's idealism collided head-on with British Imperialism and the Industrial Revolution. That said, the Colony was also incredibly naïve in thinking that it could change centuries of oppression overnight. Thacker describes why problems emerged and how these were overcome:

> It 'failed' the first year when it was thought to be immoral, with 'free-union' relationships projecting the wrong image, and again the following year when the 'no-money' phase was discontinued. The year after that communal living was dispensed with and individual homes were introduced. But in reality these were the 'settling in' years, a time of discovery, a time of trial.[25]

Interestingly, Fifield records that despite her commitment to the community, Salome often teased many of the Tolstoyan followers with urban origins, about their almost abysmal ignorance of the realities of country living[26] – which she had known could be very harsh. This has interesting parallels with the New Age Traveller movement of the late twentieth century, who visit Cornwall for the very same principles outlined by the Whiteway Community.[27]

The precise amount of time that Salome and Arthur Fifield spent at the Colony is open to conjecture. Hardy and Thacker remain silent on this issue since Fifield moved in high circles. Two possibilities exist. As Shaw has shown, Fifield was one of those original organisers from the Croydon Brotherhood Church who helped raise money and put the Colony into action. The Church had witnessed something of a decline due to the emergence of a Labour Church in Croydon as well, but it was Fifield (and presumably Salome) who kept the Brotherhood's aims and objectives in focus.[28] In addition, he was running the Free Age Press from Christchurch in Hampshire, so maybe Arthur and Salome had a number of properties they stayed in, perhaps, as Thacker views, being hosted by early colonists.[29] Certainly, as Hardy notes, one Vladimir Chertkov, 'who set himself the task of disseminating Tolstoy's ideas to a wider audience', formed one community in Christchurch.[30] This happened a good deal at the start of the community.

Detailed records of the Colony are kept at Whiteway, but some of the early records have not survived. Therefore, Salome and Arthur may have taken a property, but no details remain. Either way, considering Fifield's publishing interests, it would seem unlikely that these would have been completely run out of Whiteway. Perhaps Arthur and Salome were ideologically committed to the project, but could not give their full time to it. Besides, Arthur had other politically minded projects in mind in his publishing career and there was the vexed question of Salome's disability and growing infirmity. In the end, by World War One, the Colony went into a decline, but the village itself had become well-established. Some of those following the Community's ideals stayed, bringing up their families there. Others moved on to new movements and places. What is clear is that the Colony still has impact today. Thacker describes how Colonists of today and their ancestors still regularly meet.[31]

The Tolstoyan association produced two novels: *Beginnings* (n.d.) and *Belinda the Backward: A Romance of Modern Idealism* (1905).[32] The former book starts to explore the ideals which the community ascribed to, though the latter is a more sophisticated exploration of Tolstoyan idealism. In the 1905 novel, the setting is Dorset, the colony renamed 'Strangeways'[33] rather than Whiteways – yet the narrator is a Cornish woman – Belinda Annette Tremayne. The Colony is fictionally described as being 'five miles from Seadown'.[34] In reality, this was Stroud. Salome also shows how radical this group must have been in terms of their appearance, perhaps having the same shock value to early twentieth-century Britain as the hippie movement in post-war Europe and America:

> *Just then her husband came in from the fields. A fine, stalwart fellow, with his hair worn long, which I thought gave him a rather fantastic appearance.*[35]

Belinda continues by showing how 'novel' and 'strange' the Colony was to visitors and how radical their views were:

> *Like every other, so-called new movement, our Colony has called forth a great deal of curiosity. Journalists have come to interview us, photographers to photograph us, and artists to sketch us; but there are others who probe deeper, and they want to know the reasons which have led us to abandon the ordinary forms of livelihood and take up with a life which to many appears devoid of all that makes life worth living. For the majority of people, to have no ambition to acquire wealth, or power, or luxury, is to deprive life of its only incentives. But we think differently. It is our desire to live in good relations with all mankind, to feel that no man, woman, or child can look at us with reproach, and say, 'You live in luxury, while we starve.' If we cannot do much to help people, we will at least do nothing to keep them in degradation.*[36]

One of the fictional characters in the novel is a representation of M.F. Vestamis, who in 1927 became the Latvian Minister in London, and later the first Judge of the High Court of the Republic of Latvia, but in Salome's time at Whiteway he was a refugee from Russia. Another member of the group became the President of the Polish Republic from 1925-6.[37] Despite, and maybe even because of her encounters with wider European multi-culturalism, while living at Whiteway, Salome kept her Methodist associations. It seems strange that her brothers fail to comment on Salome's time with the Tolstoyan Community. Reading between the lines, it is thought that they would not have approved of the association – and the paucity of correspondence between them during this phase – seems to indicate as such. Even after her death, Silas – admittedly less close to Salome than his younger brother – seems to offer a distanced respect, with his patriarchal and establishment eye on her 'cranky' views:

> *She was a keen observer, and a shrewd judge of character. She hated*

> *shame and pretence as she hated vulgarity, and had small respect for many of the conventions of modern life, but her love of sincerity was almost a passion and to the last hour of her life she remained faithful to her ideals.*[38]

Joseph meanwhile – closer in age to his sister – seems more accepting of this radicalism, acknowledging the importance of her idealism:

> *After my mother died Salome came to live with me at Thornton Heath, Surrey. It was at my house that she met with her husband, and from my house that she married. By that time long years had rolled on since our childhood, and I was able to realise her qualities with a more mature mind. A more honest woman I never met, a more intense hater of shams of all sorts never lived, while loyalty to what she believed right and true was almost a religion to her.*[39]

Towards the end of her life, it appears that Salome had progressed beyond the pulp Methodism of her brothers, and yet she did keep former linkages. Around 1900 she was commissioned by the Reverend S. Telford, editor of the Wesleyan *Church Record*, to write a serial story, which was eventually issued under the title of *Before the Year is Out*.[40] This was followed in 1903 by her most successful, if not her most characteristic book, *Some Old Cornish Folk*.[41] The volume follows hot on the heels of much of the Cornish folklore collected in the nineteenth century,[42] and is effectively a kind of anthropological portrait of mid-Cornwall characters she recalled from her childhood. They were in many ways stereotypes that were already fading, but which presumably could be identified by the local readership who knew them. As the tourism industry began to emerge in Cornwall, the book also provided readers further afield with a picture of who the Cornish were. Considering much of the book was written from memory, and not from research in St Stephen-in-Brannel, it is testament to how important her Cornish background was. The volume now remains one of the finest documentations of Cornish ethnicity to exist, and will be considered in more detail in a Chapter Five.

In 1909, after the success of *Some Old Cornish Folk*, Arthur and Salome (now aged fifty) settled permanently in a small house he had built high up on the Smitham Downs at Coulsdon, Surrey. Salome named the house Trenowth, after the woods above her old home on the River Fal.[43] Though there is no source that records the reason for this move, it is easily related to their age and health. Salome could not cope with the kind of conditions at Whiteway. Her spine was now giving her great trouble causing her constant lassitude and headaches, although she continued to lead an active life, still campaigning for the kind of principles of living established by her Socialist and Tolstoyan communities twenty-five years earlier. Fifield captures how Salome dealt with her final illness when she was also ill with cancer:

> *Her will-power over herself (it was a first principle with her never to*

attempt to govern others) was almost complete; she simply would not given in to minor ailments or take drugs of any sort; not an aspirin ever passed her lips; when her head was too bad she just took went into a quiet room by herself or wrung out a cloth in hot water; and she would not let others do her domestic work while she had any strength left unless she could treat them as equals and friends. This made her life hard, but it preserved the unity between inward profession and outward practice, which was, without talk, more to her than bodily wariness.[44]

During World War One, she was one of the most constant workers of the Coulsdon Women War-Work Party, knitting no less than seventy-nine mufflers for Tommies at the front.[45] To the outside world, her literary career had almost finished and she herself was becoming more and more reclusive. However, she managed to contribute a commissioned series of sketches of World War One characters to the *Wesleyan Magazine*. Her literary career was not over however. Despite declining health, after the war, Salome completed an ambitious full-length Cornish-themed novel, titled *Pensweeta*. According to Fifield, the manuscript was completed in draft, but it never saw publication and the only copy has been long since lost.[46] *Pensweeta* certainly sounds interesting – and may perhaps be the crucial 'historical romance' link between the novels of the nineteenth century and those which would emerge from the pen of Daphne du Maurier – only a decade later.[47] Salome died in her bed at Trenowth cottage after a swift collapse, on April 10th 1927. She was aged sixty-eight. Fifield describes her as 'a wit and a stoic to the end'.[48] Her body was cremated at Golders Green on April 13th. In line with their beliefs, no flowers or mourning were asked for. The cremation and lack of mourning were a sign of radicalism during at this time.

In the same year, Fifield, still recovering from the loss (and perhaps looking towards Tennyson as inspiration[49]) published *In Memoriam*. In this small but useful volume, Fifield makes pertinent and very personal observations about Salome's life and work. Some of these observations are worth considering here to gain a fuller picture of the writer. For instance, Salome's shrewdness in financial matters is recalled. Fifield explains how he joined her name with his own on his bank account, partly because she believed in marital equality, but Salome also keep a Post Office account for her own earnings from her writing. At the end of her life, she had a considerable sum saved. Out of this, she begged him to let her pay her spinal specialist's fee, but then if Fifield did not want the rest he was to divide it between two people whom Salome loved. In the will of Arthur Fifield there is a bequest to a local orphange at Purley and another to assist Cornish girls in their education. Both of these were associated with the name of Salome Hocking Fifield. Salome, it appears, had made her own Thoreau's phrase, 'Let your affairs be as one or two and not as a hundred'. Fifield genuinely believed that her mind instinctively moved in a Thoreauvian groove, busied with realities and indifferent to luxuries, with simple living for mental freedom. To demonstrate her concerns, Fifield writes of one particular incident:

> *In all her life she drew one cheque only on our banking account, and then I had to stand over her with a humorous threat to force her to learn how to do it, to fill in the counterfoil and post it in the account book. At the close, with a smile but with forehead and upper lip bedewed with moisture, she declared she would never draw another and never did.*[50]

It seems Salome was always shrewd in expenditure as in all else, always disliking shoddy goods of any sort, especially after she realised the social evil of 'sweated goods' – produced by child labour in these islands or elsewhere. These were vestigial Methodist traits: Salome felt that money was earned with effort and should be spent with care; though she hated what was termed 'cheapening' – the process of going from shop to shop and place to place, to buy 'bargains'. In this, Fifield capture perhaps more the social etiquette of early twentieth-century urban Britain, rather any particular qualities of his wife. However he does state that 'she never changed a tradesman if he treated her honestly, and was not to be tempted by offers of rivals'.[51] Loyalty it appears, was a fundamental part of Salome's character, and that loyalty extended into the smallest details. All this helps us to build up a picture of Salome. Only two photographs remain of Salome, both proving her beauty, though the second image (p.126) apparently shows her characteristic expression when in pain. Fifield describes her as...

> *...physically and mentally wholesome, she preserved a fine complexion and sweet natural aroma to the last, and never in her life used powder or scent. Her voice was quiet, strong and pleasing, and her hand-clasp, not freely offered, very firm, yet soft. When she wanted to caress or thank me it was generally with a firm wordless handshake.*[52]

In attempting to document Salome's life, what strikes us the most is her belief in the value and importance of women. That the world was kept going by the good sense and moral character of women was her creed. She believed that fine buildings, cities and empires were the natural work of men, but women's work was character-building and character-living, and they alone, had kept communities together from the beginning of time. Women, she felt, brought human society out of barbarism. Men, left alone, would soon revert to savagery and fighting. Many of these views can be related back to her childhood in Cornwall: 'Father was a saint; but mother was the business women... I was lost in dreams as a girl, and was neither'.[53] Apparently, Salome would sometimes repeat with quiet pleasure and pride a remark of her mother's: 'Salome is a true Parkin; she has the Cornish granite'.[54] Another saying of her mothers of headstrong or foolishly extravagant people always pleased her: 'If they won't be ruled by the rudder, they will be hit by the rock'.[55]

Such phrases somehow bring us to Salome's Cornish identity. Fifield explains how some Cornish boys, sons of her old home comrades and other Cornish people that she knew could come to visit her, and she always made an effort to see them and conceal her fatigue and weakness. Yet he also tells us that when he asked her to return to Cornwall for holiday, or to accept an invitation from Joseph, recently resettled there in Hayle, or even to settle there themselves, she declined. She had, it appears, become an exile who could not return, telling her husband that 'Cornwall for me is now only a place of sad memories'.[56] It is hard to assess this statement, given the period of time she was away from Cornwall. However, it may be that Salome felt that with her natural family now removed from St Stephen-in-Brannel, that there was nothing left for her there. The parish itself had also altered dramatically in the time she was away with the expansion of the china clay extractive industry.[57] This is not however, to say that she was dismissive of her Cornish identity. Indeed, it is celebrated continually in her writing, as well as in family folklore. She used to tell with enjoyment a Cornu-English story she had heard from her widowed mother, who had employed a local labourer named Seth to 'teel'[58] their potato field:

When the job was done [Seth] was called in and asked what he would like for tea, with some dishes named. Without the least intentional impoliteness he replied: Ef you've got a bit o' maate, 'aive 'n up 'pon taable, en doant stand gab gabbin' 'bout et'. I kept her alive the last week on two tablespoonsful of Panopepton a day, recommended by a specialist, which she could keep down and assimilate when all else had failed. I asked her fancy for a meal one day before a dose, running through a list of twenty absurd dishes, from baked elephant's feet to toad-in-the hole. She heard me through with a little smile and twinkle (perhaps it was only kindness to me) and replied in a gentle slow voice: 'Ef you've got a bit o' maate, 'aive 'n up 'pon taable; but let's have the old panopep first.[59]

The connection with her origins was never lost in her writing. It was never lost in the parish of her birth either. The bequest in Arthur C. Fifield's will has been set aside for the further education of girls in the parish. Originally these funds allowed them to travel to the then Grammar School in St Austell. Presently, the fund is used to help female students in funding their further and higher education.[60] In the village of St Stephen-in-Brannel, there is in Dabryn Way a block of flatlets for the elderly, appropriately named 'Fifield House',[61] to perpetuate her memory.

Having considered the lives of the three writers, I now move to examine their literary legacy.

Notes

1. Salome Hocking Fifield, 'Chats with Girls' in *Methodist Monthly* (1894), p.30.
2. Alan M, Kent (1998) *Wives, Mothers and Sisters: Feminism, Literature and Women Writers of Cornwall,* Penzance: The Jamieson Library, pp.16-23, (2000) *The Literature of Cornwall: Continuity, Identity, Difference 1000-2000,* Bristol: Redcliffe, pp.163-4.
3. Sharron P. Schwartz, 'No Place for a Woman: Gender at Work in Cornwall's Metalliferous Mining Industry' in Philip Payton (ed.) (2000) *Cornish Studies: Eight,* University of Exeter: University of Exeter Press, pp. 68-96.
4. See Salome Hocking Fifield (1905) *Belinda the Backward: A Romance of Modern Idealism.* London: Arthur C. Fifield, p.69. She writes, 'Beliefs which I had never before heard questioned were pushed to one side with the careless indifference with which an expert tin miner will wash away the sand that is gathered around the ore, even while to the uninitiated it all appears of equal value'.
5. Arthur C. Fifield (1927) *Salome Hocking Fifield: In Memoriam.* Coulsdon: Arthur C. Fifield.
6. Ibid., p.7.
7. Cf. the life of Mary May in Jack Gillespie (ed.) (1988) *Our Cornwall: The Stories of Cornish Men and Women,* Padstow: Tabb House, pp.104-7. For the rise of the women's rights movement in Cornwall, see Katherine Bradley (2000) *Friends and Visitors: A History of the Woman's Suffrage Movement in Cornwall 1870-1914,* Penzance: The Hypatia Trust.
8. See, for example Mark Guy Pearse (1902) *West Country Songs,* London: Horace Marshall and Son. See also Charles Thomas 'The Reflection of Methodism in Cornwall's Literature' in Sarah Foot (ed.) (1988) *Methodist Celebration: A Cornish Contribution,* Redruth: Dyllansow Truran, pp.48-58.
9. Salome Hocking Fifield (n.d.) *Granny's Hero: A Tale of Country Life,* London: Publisher unknown, (1885) *The Fortunes of Riverside or Waiting and Winning,* London: Partridge, (1886) *Norah Lang: The Mine Girl,* London: Andrew Crombie, (1887) *Jacky: A Story of Everyday Life,* London: Andrew Crombie, (1888) *Chronicles of a Quiet Family: A Temperance Story,* London: Andrew Crombie.
10. A musical culture alluded to in Herbert Julian, 'Music in Cornish Methodism: The First 250 Years' in Foot, op.cit., pp.61-7.
11. Fifield, op.cit., p.8.
12. Ibid., p.8.
13. S. Moore Carew, (n.d.) *A Conquered Self.* London: Publisher unknown.
14. See, for example, Dan H. Laurence (ed.) (1946) *Bernard Shaw: Plays Pleasant,* Harmondsworth: Penguin.
15. See Christopher Hampton (ed.) (1984) *A Radical Reader: The Struggle for Change in England 1381-1914,* Harmonsworth: Penguin, pp.561-2.
16. P. Raley (ed.) (1993) *Samuel Butler: The Way of All Flesh,* London: Dent, pp.388-9. This edition contains much useful introductory material.
17. Fifield, op.cit., p.9.
18. Rosemary Edmunds (ed. and tr.) (1957 [1863-9]) *Leo Tolstoy: War and Peace,* 2 vols, Harmonsworth: Penguin, (ed. and tr.) (1973 [1873-7]) *Anna Karenina,* Harmondsworth: Penguin.
19. For useful commentaries on these works, see Jane Kentish, (ed. and tr.) (1987) *Leo Tolstoy: A Confession and Other Religious Writings,* Harmondsworth: Penguin, Richard Pevear (ed. and tr.) (1995) *Leo Tolstoy: What is Art?* Harmondsworth: Penguin.
20. For detail of Tolstoy's excommunication from the Russian Orthodox Church, see William Shirer (1994) *Love and Hatred: The Stormy Marriage of Leo and Sonya Tolstoy,* London: Aurum Press, pp.205-8. For Tolstoy's life, see A.N. Wilson (1988) *Tolstoy: A Biography,* New York: Norton.
21. Dennis Hardy (2000) *Utopian England: Community Experiments 1900-1945,* London: E & F. N. Spon, p.176.
22. Ibid.

Chapter 4 – Notes

23. Joy Thacker (1993) *Whiteway Colony: The Social History of a Tolstoyan Community,* Stroud: Joy Thacker, p.i.
24. Ibid., p.1.
25. Ibid., p.i. Another history of Whiteway was written. See Nellie Shaw (1935) *A Colony on the Cotswolds.* London: C.W. Daniel. See earlier citation in Hardy.
26. Fifield, op.cit., p.10.
27. See Kent (2000), op.cit., p.243.
28. Shaw (1935) op.cit., pp.35-6. This would have been around 1896.
29. Discussion with Thacker on 11/8/01.
30. Hardy (2000) op.cit.
31. Thacker, op.cit., pp.191-213.
32. Salome Hocking Fifield (n.d.) *Beginnings.* London: Andrew Crombie, (1905), op.cit.
33. Hocking Fifield (1905), op.cit., p.8.
34. Ibid., p.43.
35. Ibid., p.114.
36. Ibid., p.114-5.
37. For mention of this, see Fifield, op.cit., p.9.
38. Ibid., p.3.
39. Ibid., p.4.
40. Ibid., p.9. Though this is mentioned by Fifield, I have been unable to trace this publication. The title seems remarkably Hocking-like however.
41. Salome Hocking Fifield (1903) *Some Old Cornish Folk,* London: Charles H. Kelly.
42. See for example, Margaret Courtney (1989 [1890]) *Folklore and Legends of Cornwall [Cornish Feasts and Folklore],* Exeter: Cornwall Books.
43. See Fifield, op.cit., p.9.
44. Ibid., p.16. The likely medical diagnosis for Salome's disability is *scoliosis.* Hers was, of course, *traumatic,* resulting from the harvesting accident. When the bones become fixed in this double curvature, treatment in Salome's day would have been impossible. Today, the injury is possible to correct, requiring a wedge resection of some vertebrae. I am indebted to Roger Winslade and Rosemary Thurlow for this information. There is reference to Salome's final illness in the 1945 will of Arthur Fifield when he made a substantial bequest for research into cancer 'from which my wife died.'
45. This was a popular activity during the conflict.
46. Fifield, op.cit., p.10. 'Pensweeta' may be based on Pennance and Tresweeta farms near the family home at Terras.
47. A position argued in more depth, in Kent (2000), pp.147-94.
48. Fifield, op.cit., p.1.
49. Alfred Lord Tennyson wrote *In Memoriam* as an epic poetic elegy on the death of his friend Arthur Henry Hallam. Tennyson set much of the trend for this kind of elegiac writing in late nineteenth- and early twentieth-century Britain. See John D. Jump (ed.) (1974) *Tennyson: In Memoriam, Maud and Other Poems,* London: J.M. Dent, pp.75-153.
50. Fifield, op.cit., p.14. Henry David Thoreau (1817-62) was an American author and philosopher who writes with a deeply challenging directness, questioning materialism. He fought hard for the abolition of slavery.
51. Ibid., p.15. Further commentary on shopping is found in Hocking (1905) op.cit., pp.15-17.
52. Ibid.
53. Ibid., p.17.
54. Ibid., p.19. A *Parkin* is a tough, hard biscuit, or may refer to her grandmother.
55. Ibid.
56. Ibid., p.20
57. See R. M. Barton (1966) *A History of the Cornish China Clay Industry,* Truro: Bradford Barton.
58. Cornu-English: 'till'

59. Fifield, ibid., p.21.
60. The author's Primary School-teacher – Mary Hacker – benefited from one of these bursaries.
61. See P. Behenna and Kathleen Caddy, 'Our Village – St Stephen-in-Brannel' in Peter Bishop, Susan Morcom, Babs Bennett, Liz Toms, (eds.) (1994) *A Century of Change: One Hundred Years of St Stephen-in-Brannel Parish Council 1894-1994*. St Stephen-in-Brannel: St Stephen-in-Brannel Parish Council, p.71.

Chapter Five

From 'Pot Boiler Methodys' to 'Revolution': The Literature of the Hockings 1878-1937

> 'Intimate pictures of Methodism are far from rare in Cornish fiction. If the novelists are themselves Cornish, and especially if they are Methodists, the scenes and characters will have grown out of their own knowledge and personal experiences.'
>
> H.M. Cresswell Payne, 'Cornish Methodism in Fiction', 1958[1]

In many ways, the novel is a Protestant genre. It has its origins in the Reformation and its immediate aftermath. Prior to the Reformation, Catholic literary energies broadly had to make do with either drama or poetry, but while these forms continued, they were also, in some respects, to become outmoded. Therefore the novel matches the move away from an essentially religious view of life to an interest in the complexities of everyday experience. Collectively, the Hockings, however, do not quite fit this hypothesis. While they believed in the novel as a genre, they were convinced by a Protestant way of life. It is this factor which caused their novels to be both incredibly popular, reflecting as they did, Cornwall, and a wider Britain, quickly industrialising, but inevitably their still religious view on life, was the cause of their eventual fall from grace.

It is this paradox which is at the heart of understanding the literature of the Hockings. Put simply, on the one hand, they were a modernising influence in nonconformity, at the didactic end of the genre; on the other they laced the novel too thickly with Methodism for their works to eventually become canonized. By the end of their careers however, their works had interestingly moved in revolutionary new directions – actually, as we shall see, patterning Semmel's observations upon nonconformity as the 'Methodist revolution'.[2] It is a fascinating dichotomy – one running at the heart of Cornish and British society during the eighteenth and nineteenth century, yet having repercussions in both the twentieth and twenty-first centuries as well.

Initially, the Hockings were pot-boiler Methodys. They wrote novels the way most people eat hot dinners. This has major implications in this chapter. Clearly, with both Silas and Joseph, each writing over one hundred texts, and Salome writing nine books, it would be impossible in a work of this kind, to examine every novel, deconstructing each book in the light of the social, economic and political events surrounding its writing. Even a cursory look at every work would be an impossible task. Purposely, in the biographical sections of this book, I have avoided, for the most part, telling where and when particular works were written. This is for two reasons. First of all, a glance at the bibliography will tell the reader when particular books emerged. Secondly, the Hockings were so prolific that the biographies would dissolve into a mere list. In the biographies, I only alluded to texts which had a very specific effect on the writers' life-stories; for example, the dramatic effects surrounding the publication of *Meadowsweet and Rue*.

I shall begin by outlining the characteristics of the Hockings' novels throughout different phases of their careers, alluding to those texts which had particular reverberations throughout nineteenth- and twentieth-century society, but also those which are of most interest and relevance to the contemporary reader. Like most academic enquiry, particular phases of history and culture become fashionable and unfashionable, and it is clear that the Hocking novels could be read from a variety of perspectives all with different agendas – feminist, Marxist, historicist – and so on. Each agenda could find alternative and contradictory explanations, even sometimes from the same text. But I am referring to the future here. Those kinds of readings of the Hockings need to be completed, as well as specific enquiries into each of the three writers at specific times in their careers. Happily, this process, seen in the work of Appleby and others,[3] is beginning to happen. That said, I do not wish this chapter to be slight. My hope is that I can range widely through the Hockings' works, offering the reader a degree of completeness, mixed with some specific enquiry into those texts, which I feel are most significant. There are enough paradigms emerging from these for the reader to follow his or her own interests.

Silas Kitto Hocking

Let us begin like most critics of the Hockings' novels: negatively. It is arguable that the chief problem with Silas's achievement in his writing was that even from outset, he was out of step with the literary establishment. The new period emerging was the golden age of the realistic novel and the prose essay, not moral fiction. Heavy-handed symbolism was simply out of kilter with literary fashion; then, when in the second half of his career, Silas was effectively denied an official pulpit because of his unorthodoxy, he became even more self-consciously didactic. However, we could turn this reasoning around. We might argue that Silas's achievement included some masterpieces of symbolic literature, a genre to which didacticism is perfectly suited.

Added to this, useful perspective on Silas's work is offered by the critic Raymond Williams. Sympathetic to our analysis here, Williams in all his literary and cultural studies, has been at pains to show how important popular culture is, while explaining the importance of the impact of industrialism and industrial capitalism on nineteenth-century Britain. Crucially, Williams argues that this formed an ideological and spiritual crisis in the nineteenth century, to which writers such as Silas reacted. This crisis became a 'general crisis, because of the interconnections of urban and rural poverty, industrial and agricultural production, and industrial and agricultural labour and settlement'.[4] This has obvious implications, considering Silas's background, as well as what he was to encounter as a minister. Williams demonstrates the many forms this crisis took:

The long struggle over rents and leases, between owners and tenants, the long struggle over prices, and the relations of home production to exports, in a developing trade economy; the long struggle between employers and workers, on wages and the right to form unions; the long struggle between the demand for cheap labour and the rights of men,

Silas Kitto Hocking in later life.

> women and children and specifically right of education... By the middle
> of the nineteenth century the urban population of England exceeded the
> rural population: the first time in human history that this had ever been
> so, anywhere. As a mark of the change to a new kind of civilisation [this]
> has unforgettable significance.[5]

We may therefore argue, that Silas was documenting this 'crisis', what Williams called earlier 'the long revolution'.[6] But this offers us but one perspective on Silas's work. As this volume has shown, the second crisis that he was documenting was that of the Enlightenment's effect on the Reformation: nonconformity's reaction against the Church of England, and Anglo-Catholicism, in effect, a double polarisation. Finally, related to this, was a sociological phenomenon. Methodists were rising socially, but this brought with it a feeling of unease and insecurity. Maybe the Hockings' fictions could negate that unease. These three critical moments therefore underpin all of Silas's writing: the aim for social justice in the midst of the social crisis, alongside the best theological way of dealing with the modernisation process – nonconformity. Pot-boiler production would facilitate more opportunities of confronting these two inextricably linked events. The politics of Liberalism, the Empire, Cornishness at home, and overseas, would all, at various points, contribute to the complexity of this crisis and its telling.

Her Benny carries much of the early phase of this crisis. It is Silas's most famous work, but it is a special case because it is perhaps the only Hocking text that is still popular. It is a slice of popular literature which has worked culturally in the opposite direction that history tells us it should. Such texts, like the other Silas novels, are usually defined by their immediacy, their consumption quick and normally not long lasting. In Liverpool, however, *Her Benny* has been re-read and passed down through successive generations, its blend of hardship and injustice marshalling its endurance, religious tract and sentimental novel merging. Modern editions are marked as 'A Tale of Victorian Liverpool'.[7] Despite this, the novel contains all the contextualising aspects of the crisis. Poverty abounds, and there is abject child abuse and neglect. Benny and Nell make a living selling matches and carrying the bags of gentlemen, but they are regularly beaten by their father, Dick Bates. Such an atmosphere is vividly described in the opening of the novel:

> On the Western side of Scotland Road – that is to say, between it and
> the Docks – there is a regular network of streets, inhabited mostly by the
> lowest class of the Liverpool poor. And those who have occasion to penetrate their dark and filthy recesses are generally thankful when they find
> themselves safe out again. In the winter those streets and courts are kept
> comparatively clean by the heavy rain; but in summer the air fairly reeks
> with the stench of decayed fish, rotting vegetables, and every other conceivable kind of filth.[8]

In these conditions, the doubting Christian, Joe Wragg, the night-watchman, is concerned that Nell will end up as a prostitute and that Benny will turn to crime. Reflecting the nonconformist agenda, the stories of the Bible are the one place where Benny and Nell escape from the traumas of day-to-day living, and marvel at Betty Barker's reading of the Christmas story. This was the direct appeal to the emergent industrial workers of Britain: that despite the difficulties and hardship, despite wrongful accusation, despite illiteracy, Benny lives by his wits, and in the end, finds happiness. The wish-fulfilment of the readers is developing in Benny, but the strongest character of the novel is Joe Wragg. Here is where Silas and Joe, reality and fiction, connect from Silas's time in the Liverpool docklands:

> [He] had been for many years a complete enigma to a number of well-meaning people, who had become much interested in this silent and thoughtful man, and were anxious to know more about him than he cared to reveal. Several "town missionaries" had tried to make something out of him, but had utterly failed. He had never been known to enter a house of prayer and whether in the matter of religious knowledge and belief he was a heathen or a Christian was an open question; and yet notwithstanding this, he lived a life that in many respects was worthy of the imitation of many who made greater professions.[9]

In the end, it is Joe who finds accommodation and care for Nell and Benny when they run away from home. Silas presents Joe as a good man, but one who does not apparently, need the label of Christianity. The text never lets go of this issue, since the children, having found faith, question him. His reply is curt, strong-willed and realist. Like the nonconformist author, Joe Wragg works at his own 'nonconformity', showing Silas's emergent, and even unorthodox concern for social change:

> All this pain and suffering for His glory. What kind of glory can it be, to bring folks into the world doomed aforehand to eternal misery? to give 'en no chance o' repentance, an' then damn them for ever 'cause they don't repent! O Lord a mercy, excuse me, but I canna see no justice in it anywhere.[10]

The concern for justice in times of crisis, is a prevailing theme in many of the early novels. *Ivy: A Tale of Cottage Life,* for example, was published two years after *Her Benny* but retains many aspects of the earlier novel. The central character this time is female, Ivy, who is forced to live a life of fear, poverty and repression in the fishing village of Northhaven, after her father, James Stewart is lost at sea. The Cornish ideological context is strong; this reflected much real heartache for fishing communities. The novel develops her battle against the local landlord, one Jeremiah Swift, an Anglican, who wishes Ivy to enter service, in so doing, losing her non-conformist freedom, and for her younger brother Ned, to enter the workhouse. Ned and Ivy have a similar relationship to Benny and Nell; though the most interesting character is Ivy's older brother Fred, who bullies Ivy, and has no time for children or religion, but plenty of time for gambling and drinking, and wasting the money their father saved. Fred is the warning to young male readers of how not to live:

> He generally endeavoured to spend his evenings by tacking himself on to a set of foolish young fellows a good deal older than himself, who were highly amused at his upstart ways, and who used him for the butt of most of their jokes. In their company he learned to talk slang and to smoke cheap cigars, in which articles most of his pocket-money went. He could even embellish his sentences with an oath occasionally, though he was careful never to swear in his father's hearing.[11]

Ivy: A Tale of Cottage Life therefore establishes the ground rules of much of Silas's fiction which followed in the late nineteenth century. A moral order is encoded onto the fiction, where, in this case, Fred is pitted against the careful and responsible Captain Jack. Ned eventually dies, though Ivy becomes a nurse to those affected by cholera in the town. Cholera was actually rife in Cornwall during this phase. Captain Jack, being the non-conformist Cornish philanthropic engineer of his day, devises a water and sewage scheme which is a great success, while Fred returns and is found near dead in the gutter. Wiser and older, he sees the errors of his ways – adopting the creed of Methodism – and leaves for a new life in Nebraska.

This sets up another important theme in Silas's work – and eventually also in the fiction of Joseph and Salome. With a background of Cornish emigration, characters leave, often for North America, or South Africa, and the journey brings about, or contributes towards their spiritual reform. The journey – sometimes by walking, sometimes covering wider distances, form Pilgrim's Progress-like, a central metaphor for change and development. This is the usual point in many novels for conversion. The other device established by *Ivy: A Tale of Cottage Life* is that of marriage. Obviously here, it is between Jack and Ivy – the model being Shakespearean comedy; the old world is long since passed, the green world of chaos defeated with order (via Methodism) in the new world returning – 'after all the storms that had beaten the years of her childhood, Ivy had come at length to the green pastures and to the still waters'.[12]

The crisis of the nineteenth century is not only therefore in the urban context, but also in rural settings, most obviously, of course, Cornwall. In *Sea Waif: A Tale of the Cornish Cliffs*, Ezekiel Blight and his wife Mary, find a baby boy washed up on the beach after a ship-wreck.[13] Unable to find anything of his parentage, they raise him as their own, but the boy Tom, proves to be a handful. The prevalent theme of tenancy comes to the fore again. He is accused of poaching on Squire Newlyn's plantation, and has a set of trials to pass to redeem himself.

Here, Silas demonstrates many of the qualities that make up his standard novel. Aside from characters taking Biblical, often Old Testament names, another of the techniques – also coincidentally used by Hardy[14] – is the renaming of people and places with other Cornish words – something the Introduction to this book alluded to. It is an important technique because it allows a fictionalisation of the landscape, but which keeps immediate focus on Cornishness: Newlyn, the fishing port, becomes the Squire's name, while Treviscoe, now a 'china-clay village', near St Stephen-in-Brannel, becomes mutated into the coastal Cornu-English of Trevisca Bay.

Eventually Tom ingratiates himself with both his father and the Squire and is allowed to marry his local sweetheart, Sophy. This is not, however, until he had undergone a conversion to the Methodist faith. Broadly and bluntly, upright Methodism leads to getting the girl; a persuasive device in terms of converting adolescent boys, which Silas uses frequently. Tom is to become a missionary, while even old Ezekiel says 'If I ever become religious, I will join the Methodys'.[15]

By now, we are starting to understand the response to the crisis. Typically, the Silas plot runs as follows: the scene is often Cornwall, unspecified and generic, or the north of England. The male protagonist is in love with a female, who is usually inaccessible. This may be because of class or religious differences (she is Anglican, or the local squire's daughter, or both), finance (he has no money or wastes it on drinking and gambling) or simply because initially, the two put on a front that they are not interested in each other. Despite this, the male hero, swears that he will travel and make his fortune 'Dick Whittington-style' and will return within a given time to claim her as his bride, sometimes undergoing non-

Frontispiece from *Sea Waif: A Tale of the Cornish Cliffs*, 1882.

conformist and temperance reform along the way.

If he is lucky, or if fortune or God is on his side, he will become successful. If he is not, fortune not finding him, he will still return; importantly, a better and more Methodist a man for the hardship he had endured. Meanwhile, the female character is left feeling uncertain of her direction. She is generally courted by another male, often a swarthy factory owner, or rich squire, or the bitterest rival of the man who left to seek his fortune. Upon the male hero's return, the plot usually moves in two ways. He will claim her as his bride having proven himself, or she will reject the engagement of the rich suitor to marry her childhood sweetheart. Destiny of this kind is important. It binds the characters to 'age-old' affiliations and ties, the link often ethnically attributed.

Fairy-tale forms an important construct of all the fiction. The novels tell

Plate from *Tregeagle's Head: A Romance of the Cornish Cliffs*, 1890.

us that good will eventually triumph over evil, though characters need to face adversity for the value of that 'goodness' to be recognised. Evil figures always lurk in the background. They are more materialist – leaders of industry or the aforementioned squires or landlords – whose greed is put above every other value in their lives. These were very real concerns of the working-class readers of this kind of fiction, both in serial form and in the hardback books. It showed them that it was possible to beat the system they found themselves working in. Such elements form the core subject matter of several of the remaining novels of the nineteenth century; among them, *Caleb Carthew: A Life Story* (1884), *For Such is Life* (1887), *Tregeagle's Head: A Romance of the Cornish Cliffs* (1890), *Where Duty Lies* (1892), *The Blindness of Madge Tyndall* (1894) and *Tales of a Tin Mine* (1898).[16]

The format had been well-established by the opening years of the twentieth century, and to a certain degree, highly refined. As the crisis of social justice came upon Silas at the turn of the century, his fiction followed these strands and interests; the sincere nonconformity of the earlier works taking a less obvious position in the narrative. The theme of fortune matches that of justice, and this is perhaps best played out in the 1909 novel *A Desperate Hope*. Here, the ambitious farm labourer, Jack Penguire, is in love with Agnes Drew, the daughter of the local veterinary surgeon. The novel thus opens with this statement:

> He was going to seek his fortune, and not only to seek it, but to find it. That he might fail did not occur to him. He was young and strong, and full of enthusiasm. Failure was not for the man of will and determination. Only the idle and worthless failed, or the men who had no ambition and hope.[17]

His intention is to return in three years time as a successful man, and marry Agnes. During the time he is away, fortune does not smile upon him however, since Agnes is pursued by one Eric Percival, and on Jack's journey home, he is dropped down a mineshaft by a gang of thieves he had heard talking about a recently committed robbery. Coupled with earlier wonderful description of the mine shaft ('The darkness fell suddenly. The patch of light went out of the sky as though some one had closed a window-shutter'[18]), the call is again to fortune and fate, key words in Hocking ideology:

> For a while he cursed the evil fortune that had landed him on the "sollar", cursed the villains that let him down the shaft, cursed the storm that drove him for shelter to the disused boiler-house, cursed the fate that brought him back penniless, cursed himself for being a failure.[19]

The themes of fortune and fate are repeated in numerous other titles and storylines. Interestingly, as part of the crisis, the Hockings were witnessing a transition in the world-view of most people. The Reformation and its aftermath had already seen a move to a more secular world, which

Chapter 5

revealed that individuals were responsible for their own actions, and yet in such Hocking texts, there remains a residual notion that another force controls the way people led their lives. Thus, Silas and Joseph invoke a believability about fortune and fate – based either on blind fate or a more benevolent providence. Interconnected with fortune and fate, however, is the secondary issue of ambition. If we hold with the notion that Silas's fiction is the product of a point of crisis in mass industrialization and its effects on humanity, then we have to place more scrutiny on the characters striking out in life. While the previous age tolerated ambition, industrialization permitted it in wholly new ways and methods. Silas's characters thus refuse to accept roles and aim for new goals – a concept reasonable within nonconformity and its reforming ideals. The contrast is best

Frontispiece from *A Desperate Hope*, 1909.

seen in the old and new attitudes embodied in Jack Penguire's uncle:
> His uncle was an old man, steeped in the prejudices of a bygone generation. He believed that people should remain where Providence had placed them, and be content with their lot, whatever it might be.
>
> "Ambition," he would say, "is a snare of the Evil one; it leads to discontent and unrest. It burns men's eyes and men's hearts from the humble duties of life, and leads them into the quagmires of adventure and speculation – ay, and sometimes into dishonesty. Take warning, boy, and be content to remain where you are."[20]

But this is not an ideology to which Silas himself ascribed, or the message that the whole novel gives to the reader. Indeed, it actually matches Wesley's own ambitious 'self-help' ideology – popularly 'to gain some, save some and give some'. Presumably, however, it was such passages, as we shall see in chapter six, that began to cause some observers to doubt the earnestness of the Hockings' texts.[21] Indeed, Silas might have argued that one needed both ambition to confront outmoded religious practice as well as the confrontation of injustice. This happens on a micro- and macro- scale in the novels. Here, on the micro-scale Jack Penguire is then himself accused of being a villain because of his dishevelled state after escaping the mine-shaft, but on a macro-scale, it is the limitations imposed upon the average man by the class systems in place; an issue redolent of the fate of James Hocking.[22]

This macro-scale is best explored in the fairly late novel, *The Broken Fence* (1928). Land ownership is again the novel's core theme. The local squire, Sir John Tregunna, decides to enclose some common grazing land that the villagers traditionally had access to on Carloggas Downs. In the opening chapter, the squire's fence is broken down by Cambridge student Paul Pendean and an angry mob of villagers; the story complicated since Paul is in love with the squire's daughter, Cathy. At first, the injustice causes this love to pale by comparison:
> That night about eleven o'clock a crowd gathered in the Fore Street of Carloggas. Each man came silently and fell into line, and each man was armed with a pick or an axe or a sledgehammer. No one spoke. They waited in close formation till the church clock had finished striking eleven. Then they began to march towards the "downs". Tramp, tramp, tramp, they went to the tune of:
>
> "And shall Trelawney die,
> Then thirty thousand Cornish men
> Will know the reason why."[23]

Clearly Silas knew that such writing would immediately call to mind not only earlier Cornish rebellions,[24] but more recent historical events, such as the China Clay Strikes of the previous decade, as well as the 1896 riots in Newlyn over Sabbath-breaking fishing crews.[25] All three siblings had also started to incorporate more explicitly Cornish revivalist icons and symbols into their writing, of which 'The Song of the Western Men' was but one.[26] The conflict cannot be sorted out by violence, however. It must be completed by legal processes, but justice, it appears, favours the rich. Again, this is the social commentary which Silas was so keen on incorporating; Judges usually being of Anglican persuasion and who by association knew the landowners. Then, not only do we have an Anglican/nonconformist divide, but also an English/Cornish split:

> It if were a matter of going to law, [the villagers] feared they had no chance. The law they regarded as being one-sided. It favoured the rich; the longest purse generally won. Sir John was rich and influential. He had friends at court. Moreover many of the laws relating to the land were out of date. They were made centuries ago by the landowners in their own interests. Judges had to pronounce according to the law irrespective of the merits of the case.[27]

However, once the land issue has been resolved, Paul (like Silas), pursues a career in politics as a Liberal. In these sequences, Silas is able to make the kind of speeches he wishes he had been able to do as a politician. The effect is to link several themes together: Silas's concern for land-reform, his wish for World Peace, and the formation of the League of Nations. Like Silas, Paul's beliefs are founded metaphorically on mending 'broken fences' through justice:

> "We stand," he said, "not for revolution but for evolution, not for violent methods but for ordered progress, not for reactions but for steady, patient advance."
>
> Much remains to be accomplished. There were wrongs to be righted, evils to be redressed. Large measures of reform were needed. Land-law reform, temperance reform, educational reform, electoral reform. Retrenchment was also urgently needed, especially in armaments and engines of destruction. Peace never came through preparation for war.
>
> As a nation we should set an example, practise what we preached, lead the van in the arts of peace. He closed with an earnest and passionate appeal for the League of Nations.
>
> There was a moment's pause when he finished, then followed a prolonged roar of applause such as had been rarely heard in that hall.[28]

We have now established some of the wider trends and thematic concerns of Silas's writing, a move away from works like *Her Benny* where the crisis was specific: the poverty of industrialization, but as the effects of modernisation occurred, this crisis opened into new avenues to explore, so although Silas's central plots remained rigid, the subject-matter did alter and develop, as witnessed by the above call for the League of Nations. Silas integrated the themes and effects on his own life into his fiction.

Emigration is one such theme which had pervaded his own youth. Both his father and brother spent considerable time working in California. As both Rowse, and later Payton have argued, in the late nineteenth and early twentieth century, there was probably no Cornish family that did not have at least one member of their family who was 'away' working.[29] Thus all Cornish writers have had to take this theme into account since it left complex social and cultural traces on the Cornish homeland. As James-Korany has argued, 'Emigration [was] a naturally accepted and on-going phenomenon' forming 'an integral part of the Cornish psyche'.[30] This psyche was something that Silas was to allude to again and again in his work, forming the context for much of the theological and moral debate, not to mention instruction.

Much previous scholarship on emigration has been couched in terms of statistics and mining engineering,[31] rather than the social effect. It is here that the Hockings become of greater interest. One text that typifies this kind of construct and examines the social effect of emigration, in Silas's writing, is the 1923 novel, *The Lost Lode*. Jasper Blake, the novel's protagonist, has returned to Cornwall from Canada. He has slept rough there, had hard times, but also made money:

> He recalled his landing at Quebec half dead from sea-sickness, and then his steady drift westward – ever westward. It took him eleven years to reach the Yukon, and during these years he had tried his hand at nearly everything. He had worked on railroads and on farms and in lumber mills. He had been tram conductor and cowboy. He had hunted for pelts in the great forests, and trapped salmon in the rivers. He had slept in the open and wintered in wooden shacks. Had listened to stories by camp fires and fallen asleep to dreams of home. He had suffered from frost-bite and hunger and blistered feet. He had tramped day on end over mountain passes and through interminable forests. He had given up hope more than once and lain down to die.[32]

The Cornwall he returns to is Hocking archetype – a 'projected' Cornwall of the 'unreal' – a fictional space; put another way – an imagined Cornish landscape. The place is Pengowan, where he arrives at the town's inn and is quizzed by the landlord as if he were a stranger. The morality is set up early on; if he had not left his childhood love, then Susie Barett would not now be married to the irresponsible farmer, Jim Soper, with more children than she can cope with. The returnee therefore has his illusions shattered. Before reality hits home, Blake dreams:

> To other fortunate ones gold has spelt Seattle, or 'Frisco, or Los Angeles, or the cities back east; Toronto, or Chicago, or Washington, or New York. To him, it spelt Pengowan. There was only one thought in his mind, one desire in his heart – he must get back home. His Cornish hills called to him across ocean and mountain and plain; the lure of his native land was in his blood; it had never left him during all the years of his absence. Nothing would ever satisfy him until he had seen again the little grey town lying in the lap of the hills; it was a homesickness that only the sight of home would cure.[33]

Not only is his sweetheart married but other illusions are shattered. The lost lode of the title is a tin lode which runs under the estate of Sir Wilfred, a squire, who, after repeated attempts to locate the lode, has run into debt. He and his daughter Enid let the sett to Blake, who after a struggle, manages to locate the lode, at Wheal Tilley and work begins. In the meantime, the squire's daughter, who Jasper is now in love with, is pursued by the villain, Mr Strauss, to whom Sir Wilfred owes money. Strauss even tries to kill Blake, for he is aware of his intentions, but fails in his plan. Jasper Blake is an interesting role-model; he is both the Cornish boy made good – redolent of many other Silas texts; but he also prefigures the later twentieth-century fictional Cornish heroes, like Ross Poldark and Ben Retallick.[34] What remains of interest in such novels of emigration, is not only the projected fate of the characters abroad, but also the return back home.

Another slightly earlier novel, *Nancy* (1919) also develops this theme. Put together these two books – *Nancy* and *The Lost Lode*, define the changes noticed by the returnee, as well as the projected future for Cornwall. The novel is set in Quayporth – probably an amalgam of Newquay and Perranporth, just as the Great Western Railway begins marketing Cornwall in earnest.[35] Hugh Martyn, who left Cornwall aged thirteen, returns home, now in his mid-twenties. In his dreams he imagines 'the sight of the cliffs, the smell of the sea, the tang of the gorse and ling, the quiet of crooked lanes, the perfume of the hedgerows, the musical lilt of the vernacular...,'[36] but all this is disrupted by his actual findings when he meets Dr Musgrave and understands the changes which have taken place:

> "As a lad I rambled all over this countryside. Quayporth, by the bye, is a blot on the landscape. The glorious cliffs have been spoiled by jerry-builders."
>
> "Quayporth is not beautiful certainly," Musgrave admitted.
>
> "Beautiful? I think the town is positively hideous. I could have wept when I arrived after twelve years' absence and wandered down the long, narrow street looking in vain for the sea."
>
> "You see, the town was never planned. It just 'grow'd', like Topsy. The newer parts are being properly laid out..." and he looked at Hugh with the light of dawning comprehension in his eyes.[37]

As a consequence of the tourist industry, other changes are noted in the same novel. Hugh used to think 'Quayporth was the centre of the universe'[38] but now finds a Cornwall driven by new values. As I have argued elsewhere, part of this response is the wider realisation that by this phase, Cornwall was no longer industrial cock-of-the-walk,[39] and in the face of serious economic and industrial decline, rapidly had to reinvent itself:

> "You see, we are awfully stagnant here," the doctor went on, "except during what we call 'the season'. For three months of the year I am pretty

well run off my feet. The other nine months – I'm not idle mind you. I'm a county magistrate for one thing, then there are committees galore. Still, we are at the world's end, as you know."[40]

These novels both arose as an additional response to changes in Cornish and British culture in the aftermath of the First World War. Silas, as Appleby notes, wrote a good deal less fiction on the First World War than his younger brother.[41] When he did turn his attention to this theme, it was generally with a pacifist agenda, whereas Joseph spends more energy on narrating the conflict in the trenches and elsewhere. The novel which is most representative of this phase of Silas's writing is *The Crooked Road* (1925) which looks at the experiences of the demobbed Tommy returning to Cornwall. He is posted by his employers to another town named Poldulo, and there falls in love with a Miss Lawrence. In the opening sequences of the novel, he manages to save her from being killed by a runaway horse and carriage, allowing Silas to develop the respect given to the ex-soldier:

"I mean," he went on a little hurriedly, "that we never know when a bullet will come along and get us."

"You have been a soldier?" she questioned.

"For my sins," he laughed. He was beginning to feel much more at his ease.

"And you have become indifferent to danger?"

"Not a bit. I am anxious to keep alive as most men – more anxious than a good many."[42]

The response here is a good deal less jingoistic than as we shall see in the fiction of his younger brother, Joseph. Throughout the novel, Silas is at pains to show the reader the true repercussions of war, and how the best intentions can often be misinterpreted. To the uninitiated, it may appear as if many of the novels of Silas and Joseph were carbon copies of each other. Silas in general, kept to more contemporary themes, whereas Joseph moved to more historical material. In general then, the earlier Silas novels have the heavier overlay of nonconformity, though there are some notable exceptions. Even as late as 1910 with *Who Shall Judge?* and 1917's *His Own Accuser*,[43] the overlay could be explicit; more tract still, than novel. One of the most interesting studies of this theme however, comes in his 1907 novel *St Gwynifer*. Here the religious construct is to the fore. St Gwynifer is an imagined parish in Cornwall, where we follow the progress of two brothers, George and Robert Pengowan. Robert is presented as a hard-working, though unqualified new teacher, whom the new rector wishes to Anglicize.

George, after making a name for himself as a dynamic preacher in the Midlands, returns home, first to Truro, and then to the parish, where he receives a tremendous welcome. Fame as a preacher has brought him (like Silas) into money, and adoration from village sweetheart, Doris. The section however, concerning Robert's meeting with the rector is full of tension. It is explicitly where the differences between Methodism and Anglicanism are debated in a pulp format, where religious difference is seen in very polarised terms:

> "I don't know what you mean by a schismatic," Robert said mildly. "I hope it is nothing offensive. But might I remind you that five-sixths of the children come out of Methodist homes?"
>
> "I am aware of that. John Wesley was a good churchman. He never ought to have been lost to us. That was the fault of our forefathers. It is our business now to get the rising generation of Methodists back again into the true fold."
>
> "Is that necessary, sir?" Robert questioned timidly. "Are not the Methodists doing God's work? And is there not work enough for all the churches?"
>
> "There is only one true Church." was the quick reply.[44]

Here we see the embattled position of the unestablished Methodists and the proselytising, if ineffective tactics of the Church of England. The debate within the novel patterns this. George is dismissive of his background, scathing of Cornwall, a man later identified by Doris as having 'fine manners and glib tongue'.[45] Eventually, Doris and George marry since she has always carried a candle for him, despite his ego. Robert meanwhile, holds true to his faith, and follows an initially less spectacular, but eventually equally successful career as a writer. Psychologically, it seems George was the man Silas tried to resist becoming; Robert was the man he hoped he was. When Doris and George divorce, Robert has to be patient with Doris, for she feels she will never trust another man again. Yet, in time, and with patience and love, Robert wins her and the two are married. It is precisely at this point that Silas's novels became radical. He was writing in a society where divorce was still frowned upon, yet he was progressive enough to see the need for it.

Occasionally Silas will set his fiction back in time, though perhaps less often than his brother. The preaching of Wesley forms the turning point of one of the best examples of his historical fiction, *The Strange Adventures of Israel Pendray* (1899). Israel is greatly impressed by John Wesley and his two lay-preachers, Mr Shepheard and John Nelson, when he acts as pilot to the Mayor of St Ives' boat 'The Nautilus', in which the Methodys made a visit to Scilly in 1743. A storm erupts and so during the terrible passage, landsmen as they were, they sang to keep faith:

> I saw when we got a few leagues from land that my passengers were beginning to get alarmed, especially when great waves rose up and curled almost over our heads; but I assured them there was no real danger, and after a while (perhaps to keep their courage up) they began to sing most lustily the following lines:-
>
> "When passing through the watery deep,

I ask in faith His promised aid
The waves an awful distance keep,
And shrink from my devoted head.
Fearless their violence I dare,
They cannot harm – for God is there."[46]

The fictional Israel Pendray is a well-drawn example of those many Cornish men, who answered Wesley's call to preach, but has to contend with strong opposition and fierce persecution. Early in the novel, Pendray has to deal with the smugglers of Porthliddy. The theological debate is then given imagining:

I saw now that all solemnity had departed from the gathering, and any further words of mine would only add fuel to the fire of levity which was now in full blaze. Then someone began to sing a piece of doggerel common enough in these days throughout the county –

"Wesley he is come to town
For to pull the churches down.
Let'n mind our passon Jack,
We'll scat his face and send'n back."

Fortunately for me the darkness deepened rapidly, so that I was able at length to slink away through the crowd without attracting much attention. An old fisherman named Peter Hunkin – who had stood near me all the time, and who, since he had heard Mr Wesley preach on Hilary Downs, a year before, had been trying to live a new life – followed me, and took me to his house and gave me supper. Yet was I too depressed to eat...[47]

The picture then is one of the struggling Methodist trying to right wrongs, and whether this was completed in fictional eighteenth, nineteenth or twentieth centuries, the ideological stance was the same. In each of his novels, both before his spiritual crisis, and after, Silas confronts and writes of the wider crisis facing Cornish, British and World society. The fiction, as shown above, could be highly repetitive – even in phases where Silas's altered his ideological or theological position, for instance, in the aftermath of 1899-1900, or following the First World War.

Despite these changes, the overall repetitive nature of the novels had two purposes: to reinforce the values of nonconformity and to encode onto the next generation what it was morally correct to do. Silas wrote by example. Many of his own mental and spiritual debates are explored in the fiction: crisis in society inspiring his own theological crisis, eventually finding its way into the narrative. It is, as should be clear by now, no longer good enough to move to a reductive view of Silas's fiction, since he was documenting social and spiritual change on a massive time scale. Most novelists are able to deal with twenty years of upheaval and transition. The fact that Silas wrote more or less continually from 1878 until 1936 underpins his importance.

Joseph Hocking

Although starting to write some nine years after Silas, Joseph Hocking was also to write his response to this crisis, and it is his fiction that I will now consider. He began his career as a novelist with three novels which are not much more than religious tracts: *Harry Penhale: The Trial of His Faith* (1887), *Gideon Strong: Plebeian* (1888), and *Elrad the Hic* (1890)[48] but these texts went more or less unrecognised, as did an account of a Christian pilgrimage, *From London to Damascas* (1889).[49]

It is however, with *Jabez Easterbrook*[50] that the pubic started to take notice of Silas's younger brother. When *Jabez Easterbrook* was published in 1891, Joseph had just turned thirty. As a novelist, he saw his chief purpose, like the Monarch, as a defender of the faith, and he choose a Protestant genre to do so. Protestantism could only be preserved, in his view, by a fresh probing into the word of God and the whole personality of the human race. As a nonconformist, this task suited him, and in the course of his career his overriding aim was to try to strengthen the faith of his readers. Joseph never had any illusions about his books and their literary stature. He knew they were pulp Methodism.

If we are critical, then like Silas, the superficiality of Joseph's work is most obvious to us when he attempts to 'slay the giant of impurity' or Catholicism in an all too clumsy way. However, Joseph took much note of the success of his brother's writing, since he incorporates many of the narrative techniques and devices into his work, that had been developed by his brother. Joseph, however, gave them his own stamp, and whereas Silas kept broadly within the confines of symbolic religious tracts, Joseph, writing slightly later, realised the potential of developing the form into historical romance. In that lies Joseph's significance. Whereas Silas understood the way that the novel might be mobilised into a champion of nonconformity, Joseph knew he could develop the genre and its message to new heights; eventually producing a format which would come to dominate not only religious novelisation throughout Britain, but also the twentieth-century romance of Cornwall

Like most early works of all writers, the religious novel, *Jabez Easterbrook* drew on much of Joseph's own experiences. Why *Jabez Easterbrook* breaks the mould of the earlier tracts is because its narrative was both refreshing and its themes more questioning. Put another way, Joseph's early achievement was to 'hot up' such tracts. *Jabez Easterbrook* tells the story of a young minister in Yorkshire, and of his fight to create that deeper religious commitment to his own Christian ideal, amidst mounting opposition from society. Clearly it drew much out of Joseph's experiences in Manchester and at Burnley. Those battled against include the owner of large, local cotton mill, and those supported include colliers, all rising against the crisis of industrialization. Jabez manages to overcome the trials of his faith, culminating in his own spiritual life being enriched, yet there is much pain and growth along the way. The novel's structure allows the reader to witness the enrichment process in action:

> [The young minister] was intelligent, yet bigoted, sympathetic, yet narrow; while the people among whom he had come to labour were rugged, yet honest, settled in their opinions, at the same time possessed of a large amount of common-sense. What will be the effect of his sojourn among them? What effect will his labours have? What will be the consequence of his being brought into contact with them? Who will be the greatest teacher, the preacher or the people? Who will receive the greatest benefit, he or they?[51]

Unfortunately for Jabez, things do not go to plan, and despite being a first-class scholar, it is the people who become the 'greatest teacher', the young minister having to adapt and develop. At one point Jabez debates evolutionary theory with Margaret, an atheist, whom Jabez has difficulty in talking round. Later, Hetty and Margaret talk about him; the agenda being didactic. Readers are meant to see the right path to take:

> "Laugh at that young minister, Hetty, but he has something which you have not, and which I have not. Life is far more to him than it is to you and me."
>
> "Why, Margaret, what has come over you?"
>
> "Come over me! I don't know. I disbelieve in his religion as much as I ever did, and to-night I came out with some strong statements. I told him I was a disbeliever in the Christian faith."
>
> "And he, what did he say?"
>
> "He tried to defend his belief."
>
> "Well?"
>
> "He succeeded badly. His arguments were unsound, he championed his cause in anything but a masterly way, until he seemed fairly mystified."[52]

Very often, in all Hocking fiction, the narrative will suddenly slow down, like the above section, to allow a piece of theology to be debated. For the modern reader, the concertina effect is both somewhat dislocating and frustrating, since it seems the narrative is artificially on pause; the omniscient narrator stepping in a little too clumsily to get the point across. Yet, when one considers the sermon, it is actually this method which is employed: the narrative slows down so as the teaching point can be made. Thus, each of the novels can perhaps be more productively read on occasions as extended sermons. Yet despite all the sermonising in the early part of the novel, events change, as does Jabez's technique, and the community and minister grow spiritually. At the end of the text, a Mr Bowman and Mr Graysteel discuss the merits of Jabez, where we witness the 'mythic' effects of Methodist conversion:

> When he went there four months ago, all the public houses were full, and people were almost afraid to pass through it. Now a better state of

things exists; the public houses are not nearly so full, and some of the worst of characters have been reformed.[53]

The last word here is crucial to understanding the core ideology of Joseph's fiction: the on-going reformation of Christian belief in general, but also the reformation of individuals in specific societies. The reformation is positioned as a response to the various crises set on an historical time line. Whereas Silas tended to set his fiction in a contemporary context, Joseph could return to the Renaissance, the War of the Five Peoples, the nineteenth century or in the present day. In many ways this is what makes him more interesting as a writer, how he used his contemporary nonconformity to illuminate historical events and peoples. Very

Frontispiece *O'er Moor and Fen*, 1901.

often the background was of course, religious upheaval, although Joseph attaches to these prevalent ethnicities, identities and nationalisms. Clearly he was well-read in the history of religious crisis in Cornwall, yet also understood the wider, pan-European dimension of such crisis points.

Jabez Easterbrook, like Silas's *Her Benny*, formed a blueprint for all the successive early 'novels of purpose': *The Weapons of Mystery* (1890), *Ishmael Pengelly: An Outcast* (1893), *The Story of Andrew Fairfax* (1893) and *The Monk of Mar-Saba* (1894).[54] In the latter novel, Joseph begins to assert his Protestant attack more readily. There follows a phase of Joseph actively integrating Cornish historical themes into the books – exemplified by *And Shall Trelawney Die?* (1897), *The Romance of Michael Trevail* (1900) and *Greater Love: A Cornish Romance?* (1902).[55] At the same time, works such as *O'er Moor and Fen: A Tale of Methodist Life in Lancashire*, (1901) allowed for a re-telling of his earlier experiences in Burnley,[56] creating his more explicitly autobiographical novel, while property, class and land-law form the background to *All Men are Liars* (1895).[57]

Like Silas's less frequent forays into the past, a central historical location was of course, the period of evangelical revival in the middle decades of the eighteenth century. Here, wider pulp Methodism could merge with real 'Methodys'. One of the best examples is *The Birthright*, written in 1897.[58] The chief character here is Jasper Pennington, whose father had been robbed of his inheritance of valuable lands and property, yet because of his faith, later wins through. His success means that he is eventually able to buy back the Pennington Estates and win the hand of Naomi Penryn in marriage. The frontispiece of the novel is unusual, since it outlines the narrative to the potential reader, using a device to convince us that the manuscript was not written by Joseph, but by Jasper, and that Joseph only acted as the 'agent' in passing on the story. In so doing, however, it does much to summarise the typical Joseph narrative of this phase, incorporating much Cornish adventure and folklore, presented as if a broadsheet ballad heading:

> *The Birthright, being the adventurous history of Jasper Pennington of Pennington in the County of Cornwall. How he was robbed of his Birthright, and how he tried to regain it. His sufferings in the pillory at Falmouth Town; his experiences with smugglers and wreckers at Kynance Cove and the Lizard; his imprisonment at Trevose Head; his dealings with Betsey Fraddam the witch, and her son Eli; his search for a buried treasure, together with the true history of his love for Mistress Naomi Penryn, and of his successes in winning back what was rightfully his own. Written by his own hand in the year 1758, and now placed before the public by Joseph Hocking.*[59]

The clever part of this narrative is that Joseph engineers a meeting with John Wesley, whom Jasper has rescued from the mob ("Laive us git to un! Laive us git to un!"[60]). The great 'riot' in Falmouth in 1745, was also introduced into fiction by the Anglican Arthur Quiller Couch, in *Sir John Constantine* (1906),[61] but what is clever about this section is not only the Cornu-English realism, but the way present Cornwall meets past Cornwall head on:

> *For a moment there was quiet, and the friends of Mr Wesley took heart: for although it seems like boasting to say so, I think the sight of one strong courageous man, as I thank God I have ever been, always has a tendency to quell the anger of an unreasoning mob.*
>
> *"He's not a friend to the people," they cried. "He's destroyed the trade of Jimmy Crowle, who do kip a kiddley wink over to Zennor. (Tedn' no use kippin' a public 'ouse after he've bin to a plaace. He do turn people maazed. He do convert 'em and then they waan't zing songs, nor git drunk, nor do a bit of smugglin', nor nothin'."*
>
> *Others shouted, "If we can git to un, we'll kill un. We doan't want no canorums; we doan't want no new sort ov religion. We like our beer and wrastlin', we do."*[62]

Having saved Wesley, the preacher gives a benediction to Jasper, which in the fullness of time is brought to fruition. It is at this moment and others like them in Joseph's fiction, that the didacticism is in full operation. The benefit of the preaching is not only to Jasper, but to the reader, and if read aloud, as many were, to those listening as well:

> *"What is your name, young man?"*
>
> *"Jasper Pennington," I replied. "It is an old Cornish Name."*
>
> *And then, looking into my eyes, he said, "Is your heart at peace with God and man; especially with Man?"*
>
> *This he asked me, meaningly.*
>
> *"Trust in the Lord and do good, Jasper Pennington," he said quietly, "so shalt thou dwell in the land, and verily thou shalt be fed. Delight thyself also in the Lord, and He shall give thee the desires of thine heart."*[63]

This is an ambitious text, actually of the kind of biographical-novel which emerged popularly in the late twentieth century.[64] Joseph was unafraid of using complex narrative techniques within his fiction. These come to the fore in the period between 1894 and 1914 when Joseph developed his true forte: the proto-historical novel. Creatively he was generally balancing one historical work with another novel which had a more contemporary theme. It was a highly successful technique, so that historical novels depicting the War of Five Peoples, such as *Follow the Gleam: A Tale of the Time of Oliver Cromwell* (1903), and *Roger Trevanion* (1905) – a tale of Cornwall in the 1750s[65] – were interspersed with more contemporary work – like the legal novel, *The Madness of David Baring* (1900) and the pro-Protestant fiction, *The Scarlet Woman* (1899).[66] Probably his most famous work in the proto-historical genre was *Mistress Nancy Molesworth* (1898), the only Hocking novel to be turned into a television series.[67] It is set during the Jacobite rebellion of 1745. Roger Trevanion, the hero, endeavours to free Nancy from the clutches of the pro-Stuart loyalists, the Killigrews, a wealthy and influential family, who secretly plan to overthrow King George II. The text concludes with a special honour being bestowed upon Trevanion by the King himself, and the hand of Nancy in marriage. The novel covers much ground in Cornwall, and very often real locations are used. K.C. Phillipps has praised the swashbuckling action of this work, though there remains, he notes, vestigial elements of Joseph's original calling, 'when a group of fugitives fleeing what I can only suppose was a very roundabout route from St Kew to Polperro come upon "the shadow of a great rock in a weary land"'.[68] The rock is presumably Roche Rock in mid-Cornwall.

Like *Mistress Nancy Molesworth*, with its thread of religious conflict, *The Sword of the Lord* (1909) takes us into the heart of the Reformation.[69] It is

Plate from *Mistress Nancy Molesworth* showing Roche Rock. 1898.

set in the time of the reformer, Martin Luther, in the dual locations of England and Germany. The narrative is of obvious appeal to Joseph. The novel opens as Brian Hamilton, of Protestant background, finds favour with the Earl of Devonshire. His task is to free one Lady Elfrida and convey her safely back to England, and to assist him he takes young David Grenville, a trusted friend, from an old Cornish family. In their travels, they come face to face with Martin Luther at his home in Wittenburg, and learn of the false doctrines that abound, and the way the great reformer encourages them in their difficult task. Another interesting historical novel is *A Flame of Fire* (1903) which is set in the period of the Spanish Armada.[70] It has three Protestant heroes, Rupert Hamstead, John Trenoweth and Mawgan Killigrew, and follows their journey on a secret mission to Catholic Spain, culminating in their capture and imprisonment in the dungeons of Alcazar. However, they escape, and after gaining valuable information about the movements of the Armada, eventually make their journey back to Britain, granting them, as is typical, an audience with Sir Francis Drake.

These three novels embody the ideals of much of Joseph's historical work. Usually, they had a Cornish dimension to them – though not exclusively. In many ways, this factor is interesting, since Joseph correctly saw Cornwall as a pan-European power throughout history, very much at the cutting edge of conflict, the empire and religious change. Protestantism, as ever, forms much of the background to the historical texts, and wherever possible, Joseph tries to get one over on the opposition – generally Catholics, though sometimes other creeds.[71] Characteristically, real historical figures are also integrated into the narrative, so that what we, as readers, witness, is a background story in the wider telling of the arrival and development of British Protestantism. Put together, and read in sequence the novels form an important popular imagining of British history, from the Renaissance, through the War of the Five Peoples, into the development of nonconformity and the industrial revolution. There are few novelists who have covered such a span of history, nor any who have understood it with such peculiarly Cornish eyes.

Joseph's fiction turned away from the proto-historical novel towards Catholicism in the early 1900s. This theme had always been prevalent, but now seemed to occupy more of his creative energy up until the start of the First World War, where his fiction detailed events in that conflict. The last novel which was to fully capture 'Cornish romance' was *The Spirit of the West* (1913).[72] War narratives then occupied his creative energies until the earlier 1920s. Cornwall remained a crucial space within the fiction, but always linked with the First World War. It was only then that Joseph returned to the historical romance of the first phase of his career, in truth, when there was no more to write about the conflict.

No consideration of Joseph's fiction during this pre-First World War phase however, would be complete without dealing with his anti-Catholic stance. Though there are many other publications, including *The Chariots of the Lord* (1905), *The Woman of Babylon* (1906), *Rosaleen O'Hara* (1912)[73] the novel which encapsulates his position is the 1911 text, *The Jesuit*.[74] The text begins with another enquiry into spiritual crisis. The Jesuits have apparently taken the recently converted Eva Gascoigne into their clutches. The situation is eventually resolved by Kerry Trevanion Killigrew, who by unlikely parentage, is half-Cornish (a Puritan father), and half-Irish (a Catholic mother). Kerry is a self-made man, who through success in agriculture and mining, has gained a seat in Parliament. The religious divide is made clear from outset though; this, the only time Kerry's parents argue:

> *In only one matter did he disagree with her, and that was at my birth, when she desired a priest to come and baptise me. But my father would not have it. What passed between them I do not know, but I do know that I was christened in the old parish church, and that the vicar came to dine with my father afterwards.*[75]

On entering Parliament, Kerry encounters the liberal Mr Binton who explains his view of the situation, and warns Kerry (if his name were not clue enough) never to mention anything of his tolerance towards the Catholic faith in front of Mr Gascoigne, the hardline Protestant, and father of Eva:

> "For heaven's sake, don't say anything about it. Personally, I'm very tolerant about the matter. Of course, I'm a member of the Church of England, and naturally I want to see England kept a Protestant country. Moreover, I do think we are giving the papists a good deal of rope; but I don't hold with these ultra-Protestants. Many Roman Catholics are good people..."[76]

When Eva becomes involved in Catholicism, and is whisked away from Mr Gascoigne, he reveals his true colours – colours which underpin much of Joseph's own religious views:

> *God help us if popery or priestcraft ever come back in power. Our strength would be gone, our right to think would be gone, our manhood would be destroyed and we should become even as Spain and other nations have become who have not thrown off the papal yoke.*[77]

Kerry makes enquiries to find out what has become of Eva and traces her to Ireland. Accusations hit him from both sides. Gabriel O'Hara tells him that 'if you are half Irish you must love Ireland, you must be on her side' and 'you must be of the old faith',[78] yet he is bombarded with Protestant propaganda elsewhere. Kerry is led to trace a mysterious priest, the symbolically, yet clumsily-named Father Halloween. While there is even some degree of balance in the early part of the novel, Joseph is unable to resist revealing his true ideological stance, when it comes to an attack on Catholic society in Ireland:

> *I only stayed a few hours in Virgin's Dell, but even in that short time I felt the atmosphere was utterly difference from that of an English village. In spite of the natural beauty of the place, ignorance, squalor, and thriftlessness prevailed everywhere. It seemed to me as though the hands of the clock of life were placed back hundreds of years. Education was discouraged, reading was practically unknown, the free play of ideas was something unheard of, the people's lives were stagnant, and, to a very large extent, degraded.*[79]

The novel continues in this manner, ignoring the real issues of why poverty abounded in Ireland at this time (much of it usually levelled at the mismanagement of Ireland from Britain, although there is a growing tide of scholarship proving this position to be incorrect[80]) until Eva is rescued of her fate and indoctrination. Were such a text published today, it would be frightening to consider the consequences. Joseph's racism and religious intolerance are utterly distasteful to us now, yet we must understand that it was part of his full ideological position, which is inseparable from his fiction. To him, his views were without challenge. Anti-Romanism and fear of an Anglo-Catholic revival were the central pillars in a progressive world view; the Papacy worked as a bulwark against revolution across Europe.

In view of such novels, throughout his career, Joseph faced much opposition. He and his sometime co-author Dr Robert Forman Horton,[81] were attacked by pro-Catholic organisations, and these were later collated and published as a collection by the Catholic Truth Society.[82] Roger Thorne has completed an initial study of Joseph's anti-Catholic tendencies.[83] He explains how the editor of the volume, Father Keating, was a Jesuit. As we have seen, this was the group for which Joseph reserved what Thorne calls 'his bitterest attack'.[84] Keating commented that…

> *…Dr Horton and Mr Hocking have in their several ways been bent on robbing Catholics of their good names. They cannot be surprised if Catholics exert themselves to defend it with at least equal vigour.*[85]

As Thorne details 'one pamphlet indignantly repudiates an accusation by Horton that Catholics could tell other than the truth if it was expedient. The carefully argued case in the pamphlet is well put, but to a mere Methodist it seems to prove that there are indeed times when a Catholic may disguise the truth, when a questioner has no right to know, for example'.[86] Thorne also details how Joseph treated the Anglo-Catholics badly in *The Soul of Dominic Wildthorne* (1908)[87]:

> *The Catholic Truth Society again came to their rescue in a pamphlet, and in case the reader has not understood fully Joseph's agenda, the pamphlet adds as a foot-note: "…Meremeadows and the Community of the Incarnation' can hardly be anything but Mirfield and the Community of the Resurrection." The pamphlet concludes charitably enough that, "Only a threat of legal proceedings will bring them to their*

knees and it is matter for regret that this means is not more frequently employed."[88]

Despite this request, just as he was writing *The Jesuit* in 1910, Joseph, with Dr R. F. Horton, published *Shall Rome Reconquer England?* The chapter titles alone were enough of a declaration of war: 'Why Romanism ruins a Country' and 'The Determination of Rome to Reconquer Great Britain'.[89]

The most notorious example of Joseph's anti-Catholic stance came after Joseph had made an attack on Roman Catholicism at the Free Church Conference in Swansea in 1909. Events at the conference were reported by the *Cornubian* newspaper. The conference was 'aroused to a considerable pitch of excitement and tumult by an address by the Rev. Joseph Hocking on "The Alarming Development of Modern Romanism"'. Among Joseph's observations were that 'the story of monastic institutions was the blackest in history', that 'Romanist pressmen were imported to British newspaper offices' and that 'a number of the clergymen of the church of England are betraying the Protestants of that country'.[90] A Dr Henry S. Lunn wrote to the newspaper and pointed out that he had personally introduced Joseph to Cardinal Merry Del Val and others. Joseph apparently, had travelled to Rome, and was received with great courtesy by the Cardinals. One of the younger clergy – Father Whitmee – was set aside as his cicerone in Rome. To Lunn's 'horrified amazement', Joseph produced the first of his sensational *Scarlet Woman* novels and comments on how Joseph had 'broken every canon of friendship to find out information to attack his hosts'.[91] It was this behaviour which was later satirised by *Vanity Fair*,[92] and brought him into a good deal of conflict with the Methodist authorities. Joseph was as unorthodox as his brother. While considering the dangers of Roman Catholicism, Joseph also attacked spiritualism and theosophy in *Zillah* (1892), and materialism and big business in *God and Mammon* (1912).[93] Sometimes, in his crusading zeal he countered two anti-Christian forces in the same text, as in the serial *Strange Inheritance,* later published as *The Eternal Challenge*[94] where he takes the central characters to Palestine in order to refute their cultured scepticism, then brings them swiftly back to the Midlands of England, to meet the apparent menace of Communism among factory workers there. This kind of dash from one ideological battlefield to another is very characteristic of the late-period Joseph Hocking novel.

However, by 1914, it was to real battlefields that Joseph took his fiction. Joseph Hocking's fictional examination of the First World War forms a considerable thematic concern in the developing of his writing. Joseph was aged fifty four when hostilities were declared, already having shaped many successful novels. So far, both his historicised vision of Protestantism and fictional fight against Catholicism had formed the basis of his work. This was now about to change. Joseph saw his fiction of the conflict as literary weapons designed to support the cause. It was in his view, a holy war. As Appleby perceptively notes, Joseph 'saw his production of novels as a positive contribution to the struggle against Germany, and they were clearly written to provide moral justification for active participation in hostilities, especially among those who would have felt uneasy in the light of Christian teaching and to encourage recruiting'.[95] It was a position that diverged considerably from that of Silas, whose son Arthur died in 1919. Having put so much energy into the war effort, and having seen his own son Cuthbert killed in the War, was a bitter blow, and probably contributed to Joseph's decline in health.

There is not the space here to enter into a full survey of Joseph's fiction of this phase, and since Appleby has completed an excellent analysis, it would also be redundant. That said, a few contextual and thematic observations are helpful. Initially the novels were written to match contemporary events, but texts like *The Kaiser's Investments* continued to deal with the aftermath of the War as late as 1920.[96] Most often, Joseph's war heroes were of Cornish extraction, from middle-class families, who are offered commissions on the nod, but who often choose to join the rest of the 'Tommies' in the thick of the action.[97] The novels detail the conditions in the trenches as well as broader issues surrounding the conflict, often culminating in a spell in a segregation or prisoner of war camp. Joseph integrates his usual technique however, whereby the characters come, by fate and circumstance to meet 'real' figures; for example in *All For a Scrap of Paper: A Romance of the Great War* (1915), the protagonist, Bob Nancarrow gains a face to face interview with the Kaiser after being captured by the Germans.[98] Crucially, novels like *The Curtain of Fire* (1916) and *The Pomp of Yesterday* (1918) express the vast scale of the conflict, as well as the human cost.[99] Despite this, Joseph was not moved in the way other now more famous writers and poets of the period were.[100] Blind patriotism is the overwhelming concern. The core novel of the period is *Tommy: A War Story* (1916), which has a different construct from the outset.[101] The 'Tommy' hero is a young man from a working-class background in Lancashire, who goes on to have a distinguished battle career and on the way, exposes a spy. Joseph was also keen to make sure his military writing was accurate. As a disclaimer in *The Pomp of Yesterday*, he notes in his forward:

> Neither are the descriptions of the Battle of the Somme the result of the writer's imagination, but transcripts from the experiences of some who passed through it. Added to this, I have, since writing the story, paid a second visit to the front during which I transversed the country on which Thiepval, Groomecourt, La Boiselle, Contelmaison and a score of other towns and villages once stood. Because of this, while doubtless a military authority could point out technical errors in any description, I have been able to visualise the scenes of battle and correct such mistakes as I made at the time of writing.[102]

Joseph drew on much real experience in such novels. He had travelled widely with Europe, so knew the landscape and settings of the Western Front, as well as those in the Middle East. He had also been heavily involved with the recruitment campaigns of the early part of the War, visiting a training camp on the Sussex Downs in 1915. In this, he seems to have been 'wheeled in' as one of those respected figures who could paint an attractive and heroic picture of life at the front, even at one point coming back to Cornwall when the War Office felt they were not making the desired impact there. In an interview in the *Daily Chronicle* quoted in the *Cornish Guardian,* Joseph claims this how his task was described to him:

> *The Cornish are a very clannish people and are suspicious of strangers. But you are a Cornishman. You know the people and they know you. You are acquainted with their history, their characteristics, their language. They have not done well as far as recruiting is concerned; won't you go and arouse their Celtic fire?*[103]

Joseph took a hardline with 'shirkers', showing wherever possible in his fictions either the results of not enlisting, or the glory that could be obtained. Joseph's hope was that Cornishmen would be as persuaded by his rhetoric as they were in Wesley's day, but after addressing meetings elsewhere in Britain, he found the Cornwall he had returned to was very different than the one he had left, commenting that 'the people instead of being easy to move are adamant. Young men laugh at appeals to the emotions, flights of oratory leave them cold... They are not stolid; they are stony. They will listen keenly, intelligently, critically and show no sign'.[104] This frustration is given different spin in *All For a Scrap of Paper*:

> *Events have moved so rapidly in our little town of St Ia, that it is difficult to set them down with the clearness they deserve. We Cornish people are an imaginative race, just as all people of Celtic origins are, but we never dreamed of what has taken place. One week we were sitting idly in our boats in the bay, the next our lads had heard the call of their country, and had hurried away in its defence. One day we were at peace with the world, the next we were at war with one of the greatest fighting nations in the world.*[105]

Despite his concern that not enough young Cornishmen were enlisting, Joseph maintained his stance throughout the conflict. Appleby, following Thorne, makes a useful summary of the ideological, not to mention propagandist, themes of the novels:

> 1. The Germans are a good people misled by the Kaiser who is sincere but mad.
>
> 2. Germany was responsible for the war. It was not a war she had drifted into because of her alliances but the war had been planned by her in advance.
>
> 3. It was a religious war because the rulers of Germany were under the

influence of such writers as Trieshke and Neitzsche who advocated a philosophy that might was right.

4. Britain was riddled with German spies, most of whom spoke good English and could display impeccable loyalty to this country to the extent that they could even join the armed forces of this nation and play a double role. Their names could be Anglicised.[106]

These attitudes were reinforced by a deliberate imagining of British heroism. In *All for a Scrap of Paper,* the novel's epilogue is an imaginary letter, with Joseph attesting the virtues of joining up:

When I have time to write properly, I shall have some wonderful things to tell you concerning the heroism of our army... If only we had more men, we could put them to rout and that right quickly. That is our great need. More men like the London Scottish who have simply covered themselves with glory... You should hear what the men at the front are saying about the shirkers who are hanging back. They are a disgrace to the country and deserve to be flogged... If ever God called volunteers to fight in a Holy War, it is now.[107]

The conflict had long lasting reverberations in Joseph's novels. The naïvety which had accompanied some earlier narratives dropped out, once statistics of the numbers of dead started to reach Britain. When the reality of this hit the British public, Joseph's jingoism became decidedly more low key.[108] In the postwar period he had to reinvent himself again. This reinvention took several paths. Joseph's attacks on Roman Catholicism lessened after the War, when Britain drew on support from many Roman Catholic countries. It seems that Joseph realised there were more important enemies. His writing returned now to more historical themes, with a gentler pro-Protestant stance.

The fiction returned to explicitly Cornish subject-matter, retreating from the grander European themes, ideologically letting his brother Silas, pick up the pieces. Once the post-war discussion was over, Joseph eased back to write some of his most famous texts: *Andrew Boconnoc's Will: The Story of a Crisis* (1926),[109] *Bevil Granville's Handicap* (1926), *The Tenant of Cromlech Cottage* (1927), *Felicity Treverbyn: A Love Story* (1928), *Nancy Trevanion's Legacy* (1928) and *The Secret of Trescobel* (1931).[110] Many of these novels were set in the present day, but relied on Cornish Celticity for their inspiration and resolution. *The Tenant of Cromlech Cottage* stands out in this respect, not only with its tongue-twisting protagonist 'Gwithian Trewithen', but because of its association of the Cromlech (or quoit) with Cornwall's Celtic past (misplaced, since most chamber tombs date from much earlier, yet as Chapman has observed, intrinsically connected with Celtic peoples[111]):

In the direction opposite to that of the Hall, a high hill rose, rock-covered, grim, almost forbidding. On its summit huge stones rose, stones which looked as though they had been placed there by human hands.

> "That'll be the Cromlech after which the cottage is called," he reflected. "I expect there are legends about those old stones. Probably some of the old Cornish kings were buried under them."[112]

Not only was Joseph here prefiguring much of the later fiction which would look at such features in the Cornish landscape, at the same time alluding to the Celtic Revival in Cornwall, he was also using the pathetic fallacy of projecting emotions onto the Cornish landscape, which would become so central a component of later writing.[113] This emergent technique, as Westland puts it, allowed for a convenient imagining of Cornwall, since it was 'a mentally manageable region... offering Celtic depth without inconvenient breadth'.[114] By the end of his career, Joseph had fully understood this paradox. The crises of industrialization, of religion, and of the Great War had been negated and this realisation met with Joseph's only possible option: to return to the landscape and culture that had first constructed who he was. This of course, patterns his own life, as by now, he had returned to Cornwall.

At this point a short diversion into semantics is important. Four of the titles of Joseph's most successful novels commence with the words 'The Man Who...' indicating a personal wrong or failing that will eventually be righted; the instruction explicit and unwavering. Chronologically, these were *The Man Who Rose Again* (1906), *The Man Who Almost Lost* (1922), *The Man Who was Sure* (1931) and *The Man Who Found Out* (1933).[115] These titles do not form a quartet in the conventional sense, though structurally they have some similarities. The best example is the first, *The Man Who Rose Again*. This is an archetypal mid-period Joseph Hocking novel, the tale of an alcoholic, who gambles freely, endeavouring yet to win the hand of the daughter of a wealthy man. As the narrative unfolds, he receives Faustian temptations and plummets the depths of despair with disastrous results. However, we finally see the true and worthy man who has been redeemed and who triumphs over his deleterious and sordid past. Such a novel forms the template of Joseph's fictional sermonising. There were many more of similar ilk.

In *The Man Who was Sure*, the setting switches back and forth between Cornwall and Yorkshire, the story revolving around a minister who faces battles against modernist doctrines and materialism. *The Man Who Found Out* is located in Cornwall. The humble dwellings of the Cornish working classes are juxtaposed with the Squire of Pendarsick Hall in another conflict over land use. *The Man Who Almost Lost* is a post- First World War text concerning Marcus Baron, who returns to Britain in 1919, a very sick man. Even worse, it has been reported in the press that he was presumed dead. He finds all his hopes shattered. He is now penniless and his former lover has proved herself faithless to him. Marcus finds his way up to Yorkshire, and meets up with an old friend, Dick Barraclough, who is also finding the rehabilitation after trench warfare no easy task. Working amongst the colliers, Marcus soon finds both good and bad influences in evidence, with growing dissension from a section of miners, led by Harry Mitchell, a Bolshevik Left-winger, who stirs up trouble. It is some time before Marcus can show the Colliery Manager that he does have the interest of both management and workers at heart. In doing so, he also marries the Colliery Manager's daughter. In this sense, Marcus Baron is

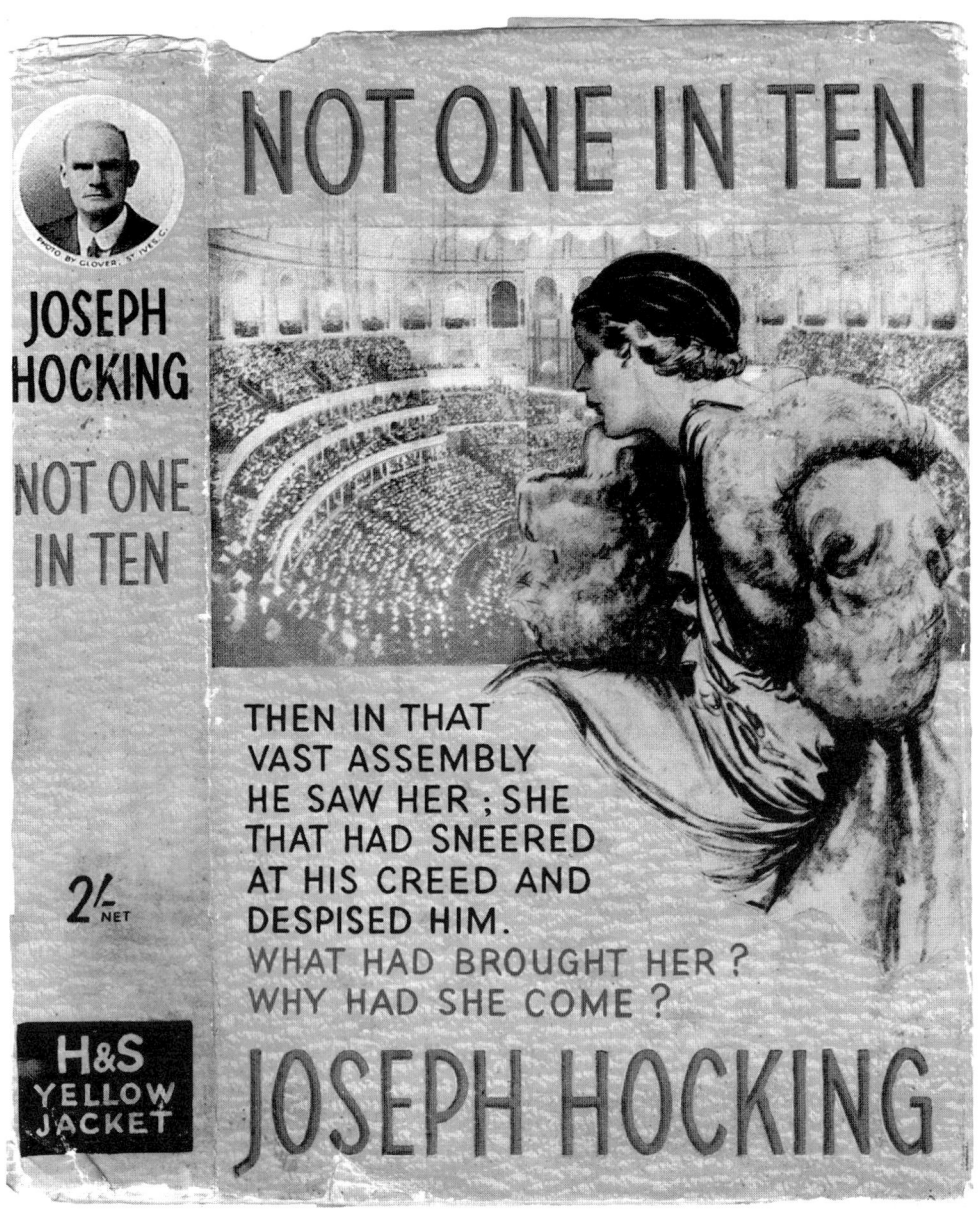

Jacket for *Not One in Ten*, 1933.

Joseph's response to the crisis of industrial change as well as the War. As theorised by Moody, like Ross Poldark, who, though fictionally set in the eighteenth century, is actually a post-war settlement hero in the aftermath of the Second World War,[116] Baron, though not historical, is his equivalent, a post-war settlement hero after the 1914-18 conflict.

Although it was not as to the fore as it was in Silas's novels, for Joseph, nothing could dispel his faith in Methodism. Joseph records one of the most interesting twentieth-century moments of Methodism in his 1933 text *Not One in Ten*, which has, as its central theme, the union of the three Methodist churches (Wesleyan, United and Primitive), which took place a year earlier at the Royal Albert Hall in London. The protagonist here is the Reverend Robert Penhale. To accentuate the importance of the union, Joseph takes Penhale and the other characters to the Hall on the 20th September 1932, blending again the real with the fictional:

And yet the young man felt that what was happening was right. The Hall in which they met was called the Albert Hall, named after the husband of Queen Victoria, and who was in a way for some time the King of England. He was also great-grandfather of the young man who represented his father, King George V of England.

Then the great organ pealed out, and it seemed to Penhale as though every man and woman in the whole assembly were following the tune which the organ was playing, and when presently the vast multitude stood up and sang:-

"We come unto our fathers' God;
Their Rock is our Salvation;
The eternal arms, their dear abode,
We make our habitation."

Penhale thought surely the roof would lift.
"Great God!" he found himself saying...[117]

Thorne is of the opinion that although the intention was positive, it actually forms 'salutary reading for modern ecumenists',[118] for there are restrictions placed on Penhale; among them not permitting 'him winning the woman he loved for his wife'.[119] However, by the end of the novel, even that restriction appears to have been lifted. *Not One in Ten's* other strength as a work of fiction is its more realistic depiction of chapel life in Cornwall in the first third of the twentieth century; in particular the social conventions that had to be followed in order to move up the social scale. The Methodist community wanted to be more accepted socially, yet at the same time, this work was radical. Girls have no chaperones and are put in compromising positions. Though Joseph was trying to be progressive, no doubt it was not everyone's cup of tea.

Jack Clemo is critical of Joseph's construction of Cornwall in his fiction both along nationalist lines, and in his capturing of Cornwall as a whole.[120] I am not with Jack Clemo on this, for in very many ways, Joseph intimately understood the need for the Cornish to assert their identity against the processes of globalization. While Joseph championed the English cause in wider conflict, he also understood both the residual nationalism of old Cornwall, and that which was newly emerging in tandem with the Cornish Revival of the early twentieth century. The following section from *The Sign of the Triangle* (1929), written just after the first Cornish Gorseth, refutes Clemo's criticism:

> *He started to his feet and began pacing the room. Everything connected with Cornwall was of interest to him. It was true he had never visited the county in his life. Yet he always regarded it as his home county. He was a Cornishman both on his father's side and on his mother's. He bore a Cornish name, and Cornwall was like no other county in England. Up to a few centuries before, Cornwall had practically been a nation, and had been far removed from the life of England. Perhaps that is why Cornwall was as much a country as Scotland or Ireland or Wales, and why the true Cornishman was always so proud of his county.*[121]

Many other Joseph novels have similar sequences. A second description from *The Sign of the Triangle* provides another refutation of Clemo's criticism. Joseph knew St Ives intimately, and understood the social processes occurring in Cornwall:

> *Ten minutes later, he found his way through the woods and came down to the Malakoff. After that he went down Tregunna Place, passed Smith's Bookshop; noted the road which led down to Land's End, and then, passing Barclay's Bank, he came down to the Town Hall – the Town Hall!*
>
> *"But this is beautiful! beautiful!" he said aloud. "It's just as it should be!"*
>
> *Up above the hillside yonder were large villas, many of them occupied by "foreigners", who having discovered the beauty of St Ives came there to live. There the people spoke English with hardly a suggestion of the Cornish accent, but down here in the old town it was Cornish all compact.*[122]

Such sections allow us to see how intimately Joseph understood Cornish Celticity, and as can be seen from all his novels, how he considered Protestantism the natural religious progression for the Celtic peoples. It is at such a point one can see the overall structure of Joseph's fiction. Whilst it is right and proper to be ambitious, this should not be compromised for the nonconformist values taught at home. Overambition will inevitably lead to a fall, and a return to one's roots to reassess one's life. Quite often, Celtic Cornwall operates as a Methodist safety net, catching those who dare to venture, then desire to return to the very things they most wanted to escape from.[123] Again and again, this message is taught.

This brings us to what I consider to be one of Joseph's best and most interesting novels, *What Shall it Profit a Man?* (1924). Directly inspired from his own childhood experiences at Terras and Trelion, the novel is an intimate portrait of a tin-mining community in the early years of the twentieth century. The novel opens with the death of Gabriel Poldu who had belonged 'to an old order which is fast dying'.[124] His son, Michael, is left to sort out a debt Gabriel had run up with the local squire, Richard Tremaine, meaning that he will lose everything. Michael swears that one day he will rise above the pompous Tremaines and have the kind of power they have.

The narrative is then recast twenty-two years later, as Michael is to meet his ambitious son, Granville, who has studied at the School of Mines in Redruth, and left for South Africa, 'where he worked under one of the ablest mining engineers in that continent'.[125] Michael has worked and saved hard, risking 'a goodish bit on clay works... but it turned out well',[126] and reveals his plans to the returning Granville to mine a sett known locally as Pisky Gully. The two set out to explore the Gully, but are watched by Paul Trefusis, whose father, Jethro owns the land. The Trefusises are duped of the their land, yet Michael is heading the same way as the Squire who once duped his father. History is repeating itself. However, the mine – clearly based on the Terras Tin Mine at Trelion – is doing well:

> *The heaps of tin ore grew in size every day, and Granville's reports became increasingly glowing. Poverty Downs and Pisky's Gully, instead of being lonely and desolate, had become a very hive of industry. The engine-house was nearing completion, while machinery was daily arriving. Men were talking about drags, buddles, recks, mine floors, vanning, trunks, cobbing hammers, and a number of hitherto unfamiliar terms. No longer was there any unemployment in the district, and strangers were constantly coming who found employment.*[127]

Jethro Trefusis comes to Michael in an appeal to the good side of his nature, but this falls on stony ground. Defeated, he has no choice but to bad-mouth the Poldhus throughout the community. Paul Trefusis tries a different approach, talking over the problem with the Methodist Minister, Mr Lovejoy, who confronts Michael and appeals to his good side:

> *"Sophistry, sophistry," replied the old preacher, "in the eyes of God it would be the same deed."*
>
> *"Then what will you have me do?"*
>
> *"I would have you obey the law of Christ, 'Do ye unto others as ye would they should do unto you'."*[128]

It is Methodism which rings the changes and Granville's conscience takes the right turn. He knows he has taken advantage of Jethro Trefusis's ignorance. He even goes so far to offer the Trefusis family a thousand pounds of mining royalties, but after the revelation of the evil machinations he used to obtain the land, Granville now knows the profit he has made is meaningless to him. Michael falls into a decline, a sadder, wiser man, though this is not before he has seen Granville take Eve Trefusis to be his wife. With this, a reconciliation is achieved and Michael feels he 'can sleep a bit now'.[129] Thus runs one Joseph's most powerful novels, which in all fairness, has dated better than some other works, since it prefigures much of the historical fiction of the post-war period, dealing with the same issues of mining control.[130] Despite Joseph's wide panorama of fiction, in this author's view, it is actually those texts closest to home which have distilled the finest fiction. Clearly the memory of the landscape and culture of St Stephen-in-Brannel were having an effect late in his life.

Salome Hocking Fifield

Though less prolific than her brothers, early experiences also shaped the written world of Salome's Hocking Fifield's literature, and it is to her, I now turn. Many of the observations upon Silas and Joseph's fiction are just as applicable to Salome; yet compared to both brothers, the nonconformity is less explicit, and the overt preaching absent. What Salome makes up for in this area, and in her observations on Cornish people and emergent Socialism, she perhaps loses, in being over-sentimental and romantic. Despite this, Salome is Cornwall's first Anglo-Cornish female novelist, and her writing remains of great importance to anyone interested in the field of literature produced in Cornwall. A comparatively short novel, *Norah Lang: The Mine Girl* is representative of Salome's ability to develop both characterisation and narrative to an accomplished level.[131] The story itself concerns a woman who finds her loyalties divided between two men, both with character flaws. Cap'n's Phil's flaw is his tendency to indulge in alcohol, while Frank Newton is haunted by the way his late first wife treated him. Despite a 'teetotal' sermonising effect from the outset, a lively Cornish narrative is assembled, clearly based on Salome's knowledge of her father's activities, and life around Terras and Trelion: a mining disaster leaves Norah's father trapped underground, to which Cap'n Phil responds. For this task, Phil asks that she should marry him. Norah herself works at the mine, at the 'recks',[132] because the family needs a second wage; this itself patterning much nineteenth-century experience for Cornish women.

The setting is St Orme, clearly a fictional imagining of St Stephen-in-Brannel. More striking however, is the character of Phillippa, or, as she is nick-named 'Flipsy'.[133] Flipsy is a projection of Salome herself: the stock Victorian deformity, a cripple whose action is always contrasted with Norah's 'swan-like motion'.[134] Flipsy even spends her time growing her hair long, so that the curvature of her spine is hidden. The most impressive section of the novel is Flipsy's dream, where the local children take

Salome Hocking Fifield in the summer of 1894 at Marazion.

her to the top of Prospect Hill so that...

> ...she forgot that she was an invalid. The wood which she was in grew into a city, the trees were people who talked to her, and praised her for her beauty and accomplishments and offered her a place among them. Her carriage was turned into a palace which ran on wheels, and she, beautiful and rich, felt like a princess in a fairy tale.[135]

For Flipsy, this magical-realist sequence ultimately leads to a fairy-tale ending and wish-fulfilment for the sentimental Victorian readership. She marries her step-brother George. Norah's 'happy ever after' comes later, but only after much agony. After a row with the mine management, following an evening's drinking, Cap'n Phil decides to leave St Orme and travel to California. He asks Norah to wait five years for him to return a rich man who will have conquered his drinking problem by becoming a Methodist. Norah promises, yet finds that this is broken, when Frank Newton; initially a sarcastic, abusive outsider, arrives as the new parson. In so doing, the Anglican/Nonconformist dichotomy is constructed. Frank and Norah's relationship develops, but their progression towards marriage is fraught with difficulties. Their eventual union comes about in a scene strangely reminiscent of the meeting of Garth and Irma in Jack Clemo's *Wilding Graft*.[136] A longing in Norah for 'the touch of a vanished hand'[137] comes when she hears the sound of the church organ. The music

Frontispiece from *Norah Lang: The Mine Girl*, 1886.

symbolically unites them, and Frank is able to take her away from working at the mine. At this moment, Cap'n Phil returns from California, just after the five year promise, declaring his love for another to Flipsy, though cynically admitting he will still marry Norah. Once revelation occurs, Norah is able to bless his marriage to another. From a feminist critical position, the text is littered with difficulties: Norah's life revolves around three men: her father, Phil and Frank, and she, at various points, finds herself rejected by all three. She does not have an identity beyond them. The text asserts frequently that women 'belong' to men, and the proverbial problem of the old, unmarried maid, is raised frequently. Norah tests these boundaries however. In this sense, it may stand as the earliest Anglo-Cornish novel written by a woman, and in itself, that is a notable achievement.

Like Silas and Joseph, although *Norah Lang: The Mine Girl* was her

Frontispiece from *Jacky: A Story of Everyday Life*, 1887.

breakthrough novel, a couple of earlier texts had already seen some limited success. These were *Granny's Hero: A Tale of Country Life* (c.1884) and *The Fortunes of Riverside* or *Waiting and Winning* (1885).[138] These were naïve, sentimental romances for female readers of the day, but with less morality than those fictions of her brothers. *Jacky: A Story of Everyday Life* (1887) is of greater interest since it takes for its theme again mining – this time based on events in the village of Treggonoweth, at Great Louisa Tin mine, where two unscrupulous miners plan their own raising of a vein of tin, without the Cap'n knowing. They are overheard by the boy Jacky, a hunchback, aged fifteen who we are told is a 'strange mixture of innocence and cunning, good and evil'.[139] Much of the atmosphere of the novel is based on St Stephen-in-Brannel and also changing working conditions for tributing.[140] It is this which causes the initial unrest in the mine. Jacky comes to be placed, like many Hocking characters in an untenable situation because of what he knew: 'Poor Jacky! his conscience was growing as crooked as his back'.[141] Importantly this is why the novel is subtitled, 'a story of everyday life' since these were the moral choices people had to make in real life. Here, this ranges from becoming teetotal to operating mining equipment safely. The novel, like contemporary soap opera, allowed Salome's readership to project themselves into the narrative, and imagine what they would do in similar circumstances. This is best seen in the sequence where the scheming miner Nicky Green does not return to grass:

> *Those who have never been underground when danger was nigh, never know what it is like to feel that next minute your body might be lifeless clay, while your soul was drifting into the unknown, cannot realise with what feelings of thankfulness and joy John Williams and Bob Trethewey hailed the daylight, nor with what a close grasp they clasped the hands of the men who helped them on firm ground.*
>
> *"All the men are up now, I believe," said the Captain, as his gaze wandered over the little group of miners standing by the shaft.*
>
> *The men looked around at each other as Captain spoke, and one said hurriedly, "Where's Nicky Green? Has anyone seen him?"*
>
> *Each man looked at his neighbour, but no one spoke.*
>
> *"What!" said the Captain. "Do you mean to say he has not come up?"*
>
> *A silence as of death fell on the men.*[142]

Nicky Green does not make it. In many of the Hocking novels death is common, as it was during the period of their writing. Industrial injury, infant mortality and disease were much more rife. Salome revisits the teetotal theme in *Chronicles of a Quiet Family: A Temperance Story* (1888),[143] which while a fashionable cause then, is rather more limited now. Another novel, *Beginnings* (c.1890) follows,[144] but from both of these texts, one feels Salome's fiction is becoming dated. Another problem was that her obsession with deformities did not provide all readers the role models nor empathy needed. Salome knew this herself, which prompted her reinvention as S. Moore Carew with *A Conquered Self* around 1892.[145] However, despite considerable effort, I have been unable to trace this novel, so its subject matter remains conjecture. Its success was limited since sadly Salome stopped writing for ten years. Her energies were employed in other ways, and the process was to pay literary dividends at the end of her career.

Published a number of years after her main period of creativity, *Some Old Cornish Folk* is now Salome's most remembered text. This is partly because of its more explicitly Cornish theme, but also because, being anthropological and folkloric, the material is less dated. The book works by being a collection of portraits; some real, some fictionalised, of characters and individuals whom Salome remembered from childhood; in many ways a kind of proto-*Under Milk Wood* of Cornwall. The work begins with an explanation of her endeavour. She writes how only after she had left Cornwall, did she realise how 'quaint' some of the characters were.[146] Her task is therefore to preserve 'zum ov the ould people'.[147] She begins with an impressive, yet grotesque vision of the little Shoemaker of the village – Old Elias Polkinhorne, his attempts to cut his own hair, get drunk and take a wife. Much projection of the fairy tale is at work. This is her description of his shop, which, though romanticised does capture a pre-modern Cornwall:

> The walls were built of cob; and when the old man's back was turned, we used to enjoy scratching with a nail, and seeing the dust trickle down. The roof was thatched and we liked to look up at the places where it had bulged in, and wonder how many more coats of thatch those bent rafters would stand without breaking. But this was only on sunshiny days, when the door and hatch were both open; then we had a fine view of the black rafters, and the hundreds of spiders' webs that hung in festoons in all directions.[148]

While Polkinghorne is comic, the most entertaining portrait comes mid-way through the volume, in the form of 'Cap'n and Missus Treleaze'. This pair own the small village shop, though the premises are run according to the Cap'n's strict ways and mannerisms. In addition to owning the village shop, he was Cap'n at a local mine, and therefore expected his employees to spend their wages at his shop, or else they would be out of work. Salome tells us how 'he spoke much better English than the majority' and that he was 'pompous and overbearing'.[149] Such pretentious English sensibilities therefore, make him the receiver of much Cornish practical joking. At one point, he is conned into providing a new pair of boots for an employee, much to his wife's amusement. Clearly Cap'n Treleaze is of a particular type at this point in Cornish history, looking to England for advancement and progression – making allegiances there both linguistically and economically. The catalogue of goods available in the shop forms another piece of social history:

> To make your way from the door, which was in the end, to the one seat (a chair without a back) by the counter, you passed on your left a ladder, a barrel of paraffin, a box of soap, a bag of dried peas, a stack of dried codfish, and a box of herrings. On the counter, mingling their perfumes with the other conglomeration of smells, were a can of treacle, a tub of lard, and a few pieces of bacon. Rows of candles, brushes, boots, and tinware hung from the beams; and if you could steer your way safely through without knocking any of these things down, you might consider yourself lucky.[150]

A sadder portrait is given of Joshua Endean, who Salome describes as the 'village artist'.[151] His story is a desperate one, in which he runs away from debt and his family to be found by the police, being employed as a decorative artist near Monmouth. At the time of his arrest, to be taken back to Cornwall, he is singing a plaintive lovesong to the accompaniment of the piano before a female audience. His protest to the police is 'For God's sake don't handcuff me before the ladies!'[152] The picture given is of a frustrated artist on the periphery, who aside from one fashionable painting – 'Mount Vesuvius in Flames' – is unable to make the centre notice his achievement.

Another story shows further changes in Cornish society, perhaps even the end of Methodism itself. There is Aunt Betty Rowse, a woman, who is so saddened by the death of her first husband, that she devotes her life to chapel, but a realisation later in life, that nonconformity has failed her, make her refuse to go to chapel for six months. Initially the portrait is comic, with Aunt Betty being able to sing higher than anyone else in the chapel and being a general village busy-body, but Salome subverts this, showing how nonconformity (perhaps patterning her own shift to Christian socialist anarchy) was 'a rather poor and narrow conception'.[153] It is this kind of observation which shows how towards the end of her career, how far Salome had moved from her earlier pulp Methodism to a new realisation of the modern world.

This realisation is continued in the sections on Ferrel's Van, a symbol of progress as a reflection of identity and community. Here, Salome selects both the driver and various passengers who travel in the horse-drawn van towards market (probably at St Austell), rather than in their own open traps. The van itself, we are told, is not particularly comfortable, but this did not stop it being popular. Indeed, Mrs Treleaze remarks that she would "Ave luved to ride to 'Merica in Ferrel's Van'.[154] What Salome achieves is an imagining of the effect of the tales and jokes inside the van being more important that the actual journey:

> There was one topic which seemed of never-failing interest to both old and young, and was a prime favourite of Jobber's, and that was love, or, as he termed it, "coortin'". Sometimes, if there happened to be an old

> *maid among the passengers, the jokes, to an outsider, might seem a little pointed; but as the victim seldom ever showed that she felt it, the topic rolled on merrily.*[155]

Chiefly however, the book is of most interest now for Salome's definitions of Cornishness. Considering the current debate on Cornish identity, there are relatively few studies which have attempted to define the group.[156] However, in the section titled 'Some Cornish Characteristics', she does just that, making the work, in this author's view, one of the most sophisticated anthropological observations on the Cornish ever completed. She begins by tellingly describing how the Cornish Methodist 'will patiently sit out the lengthiest and prosiest sermon' but 'it must not be dry' for that is a deadly fault.[157] Secondly, she understands that the ordinary Cornish person is not a good debater, but achieves success in other ways:

> *Flashes of wit, bursts of eloquence, quaint and picturesque language, often characterise his speech; but as a rule, he cannot stand what a Londoner would term "heckling". To have his most carefully thought out sentences met with smiling derision, his facts questioned and put to naught, his passionate eloquence received with cold silence, is more than he can bear calmly; hence it is that Cornwall has sent out so many more preachers than politicians. But he has a nimble wit, and often scores a point by the use of it...*[158]

Identities are difficult to define, and in many ways, it is even dangerous to do so. However, Salome seems to have captured something, however nebulous and indefinable, of the Cornish spirit here. Likewise, there is some truth is this observation:

> *There is no-one who loves a humorous, well-told story better than a Cornishman. It does not matter even if the story tells against him; if it is kindly done, he will enjoy it. But once let him think (if you are a stranger) that you are laughing at him, and he will withdraw himself inside his shell as completely as a snail when his horns are touched. With his own countrymen, however, he will hit back without mercy...*[159]

Salome continues this well-observed section by identifying other qualities which make up the Cornish; among them diversions on hospitality and thrift, paying attention along the way to their 'Celtic nature', concluding that in Cornwall 'faith was more a matter of custom than of thought and reason'.[160] There is much sentimentalising in Salome's work, but we cannot fail to be struck by the accuracy of her remarks. Indeed, maybe it was the distance from which she was writing, that allowed the depth of reflection:

> *Sometimes, when I grow a little tired of the flat, tuneless voice of the "Cockneys" on their native 'eath, I close my eyes and dream that I am down in old Cornwall, with the smell of the salt sea mingled with the perfume of dog-roses and new-mown hay all around me; and gathered*

together to hear some famous preacher in a great crowd, and among them are Cornish miners – miners from South Africa, Colorado and California – and they all join in singing their favourite hymn:

>*Oh God, our help in ages past,*
>*Our hope for years to come,*
>*Our shelter from the stormy blast,*
>*And our eternal home;*

>*Time, like an ever-rolling stream,*
>*Bears all its sons away;*
>*They fly forgotten, as a dream*
>*Dies at the opening day.*[161]

This reflection, and others like it within Salome's work prove the importance of her literature in the overall continuum of writing produced from Cornwall. As Chapter Four explained, Salome's final book *Belinda the Backward: A Romance of Modern Idealism* (1905) was a fictional recreation of her experiences with the Whiteway Community.[162] By 'backward', Salome appears to be commenting on the anti-materialist ethos of the community she and her husband idealised and help form. It is as radical a text as any Cornishwoman might write in her age, championing causes which would have met mostly with ignorance and derision in Cornwall. But then, by this phase in her life, Salome had become part of a very radical group, who she knew would never be accepted or understood by the bulk of the Cornish people. Nevertheless, it is important that Salome chooses a Cornish heroine – Belinda Annette Tremayne, to describe her experiences, since they are more or less autobiographical, words which both Silas and Joseph would have some sympathy with:

>*As I look back I can see that the night when my mother died, and I with that stony calmness which is the outcome of despair watched the terrible battle which was fought between life and death, and instead of submitting with resignation to the Divine decree, repudiated with bitterness all belief in a personal prayer-answering God, that I then took the first step away from the peaceful paths of orthodoxy. And as I look back over the road I have travelled since that night, I see how one by one my hitherto unquestioned beliefs were subjected and exposed to the burning light of rational criticism, until one after another they shrivelled and died, dropping by the way like autumn leaves.*[163]

The sophistication of this work surpasses any of Salome's earlier novels, as it veers a balanced path between Socialism, land reform and alternative living. There are residual elements of earlier writing (Belinda's Uncle Seth 'had come to believe that nonconformity rather than the Established Church represented the true Protestant faith of England'[164]) though this is tempered by the novel's progressive utopian and anarchic vision, even controversially embracing 'cranks' and vegan living, concepts that would only be considered mainstream towards the end of the century:

> "That is Frank Mordaunt, our hut-and-nut man."
> "How do you mean? Does he live in a hut and eat nuts?"
> "Something of that. He holds the theory that food is spoilt by cooking, and thinks it a pity that fire was ever invented. He believes that fruit and nuts are the proper diet of man, and that as soon as the body grows accustomed to this diet it will become so strong and healthy that there is really no reason why it should ever die."[165]

The novel continues by showing the radical attitudes of the Colony, with one of the Russian colonists speaking a 'breathless torrent' against Christianity, which clearly by this phase in her career, Salome had much empathy with, and which paradoxically would offer the very reasoning for the decline in the reception of all the earlier Hocking literature. It is a telling place to end this chapter:

> Why! how can you call yourself a Christian and object to bloodshed? Do you not go out to convert the heathen wid a Bible in one hand and a sword in de oder? You say to dem take our Jesus or we will take your life. I tink your Jesus would be very much ashamed of His disciples... Go and live in one of your stinking slums in London, work in a sweater's den as I did when I came to England first, and den say if you dare 'Blessed are ze poo.' Why! if all who say dey are followers of Jesus acted up to His teaching, there would be no need for revolutionists. It is because you do not believe it, that we revolutionists have to take up the work which ze Christians profess to do.[166]

As we have seen then, though sometimes offering us difficulties in its reception, the achievement of all the Hocking siblings has been central in the imagining of Cornwall, and industrial and urban change across Britain. Pulp Methodism it has been, yet it is a pulp fiction which not only has its roots in nonconformity, but also documents a crucial period of the history of these islands. The novel, given its origins as a uniquely Protestant form was the obvious vehicle for that vision, even if it meant sacrificing the canon, for impact and popularity.

That said, time has an interesting effect on literature and writing in general. Only a few years ago, the work of Daphne du Maurier was still considered 'popular'; now she is studied alongside the Brontës, Eliot and Woolf, as part of the British canon of writing.[167] The same holds true for Anglo-Cornish and Cornish literature. It is now being understood by many observers in and outside of Cornwall, as a separate and identifiable continuum that is no longer reliant on nation-state imaginings of a collective literary past.[168] More importantly, texts no longer need to be studied for their greatness, their encapsulation of the human spirit or their part in some misapplied 'English literary tradition'.[169] It is here, as this chapter has shown, that the Hockings become interesting: ethical, moral, wholesome – but also controversial in terms of their political, social and religious affiliations and constructs. They form a central literary imagining of changes in society between 1878 and 1937. Not only this, but there is also substantial evidence of a Hocking legacy on later writers and even the earliest signs of a small, but growing Hocking revival, of which this book forms one part. It is to this legacy and revival of their literature that I now turn.

The Vision of St Ia from *The Bells of St Ia* by Joseph Hocking, 1911.

Notes

1. H. M. Creswell Payne, 'Cornish Methodism in Fiction'. In: *Old Cornwall,* Vol. 5 (1958), p.381.
2. See Bernard Semmel (1974) *The Methodist Revolution,* London: Heinemann.
3. See Cedric J. Appleby (2001) *The Hockings and the First World War.* Unpublished paper; Roger F.S. Thorne, *Hocking: Or the Tales of Two Brothers. A Catalogue of the Works of the Hockings (Joseph, Silas and Salome) in the collection of the late Michael E. Thorne.* Exeter: Heatherdene, 2000 [1978]; Alan M. Kent (2000) *The Literature of Cornwall: Continuity, Identity, Difference 1000-2000,* pp.160-4.
4. Raymond Williams (1975 [1973]) *The Country and the City,* St. Albans: Paladin, p.261.
5. Ibid.
6. Raymond Williams (1961) *The Long Revolution,* Harmondsworth: Penguin.
7. See Silas K. Hocking (1992 [1879]) *Her Benny: A Tale of Victorian Liverpool,* Liverpool: Gallery Press.
8. Silas K. Hocking (1879) *Her Benny: A Story of Street Life,* London: Frederick Warne and Company, p.17.
9. Ibid., p.33. It is interesting that 'hell-fire' had disappeared from literature as early as 1879.
10. Ibid., pp.47-8.
11. Silas K. Hocking (1881) *Ivy: A Tale of Cottage Life,* London: Frederick Warne and Company, p.18.
12. Ibid., p.275.
13. See Silas K. Hocking (1882) *Sea Waif: A Tale of the Cornish Cliffs,* London: Frederick Warne and Company. This, of course, is very similar to Henry Fielding's 1749 'novel' *Tom Jones,* where a mysterious baby boy (later named Tom) is found on a bed.
14. See Roger Ebbatson (ed.) (1986 [1873]) *Thomas Hardy: A Pair of Blue Eyes,* Harmondsworth: Penguin, p.42-3.
15. Hocking (1882) op.cit., p.188.
16. See Silas K. Hocking (1884) *Caleb Carthew: A Life Story,* London: Frederick Warne and Company, (1887) *For Such is Life,* London: Frederick Warne and Company, (1890) *Tregeagle's Head: A Romance of the Cornish Cliffs,* London: Frederick Warne and Company, (1892) *Where Duty Lies,* London: Frederick Warne and Company, (1894) *The Blindness of Madge Tyndall,* London: Frederick Warne and Company, (1898) *Tales of a Tin Mine,* London: Horace Marshall and Son.
17. Silas K. Hocking (1909) *A Desperate Hope,* London: Frederick Warne and Company, p.1.
18. Ibid., p.13.
19. Ibid., p. 63. A "sollar" is a small platform at the end of a ladder, covering the shaft.
20. Ibid., p.2.
21. See the views of Eveline Clemo and the parishioners of St Stephen-in-Brannel in Jack Clemo (1949) *Confession of a Rebel,* London: Chatto and Windus, p.38.
22. See the issues outlined in Chapter One.
23. Silas Kitto Hocking (1928) *The Broken Fence,* London: Sampson Low, Marston and Company, pp.11-12.
24. See Kent (2000) op.cit, p. 44, p.48 and p.107.
25. See 'The Clay Strike – the White County Dispute' in Alan M. Kent (ed.) (2000) *Voices from West Barbary: An Anthology of Anglo-Cornish Poetry 1549-1928,* London: Francis Boutle, pp.206-7, and Simon Parker (1997) *A Star on the Mizzen,* Liskeard: Giss' On Books.
26. See Kent (ed.) (2000) op.cit., p.99.
27. Hocking (1928) op.cit., p.63.
28. Ibid., p.78.
29. A. L. Rowse (1998 [1942]) *A Cornish Childhood,* Mount Hawke: Dyllansow Truran, p.35; Philip Payton (1999) *The Cornish Overseas.* Fowey: Alexander Associates.
30. Margaret James-Korany ''Blue Books' as Sources for Cornish Emigration History' in Philip Payton (ed.) (1993) *Cornish Studies: One,* Exeter: University of Exeter Press, p.31.
31. See, for example, A. L. Rowse (1991 [1961]) *The Cornish in America.* Redruth: Dyllansow Truran,

A.C.Todd, (2000 [1977]) *The Search for Silver: Cornish Miners in Mexico 1824-1947*, St Austell: Cornish Hillside Publications.

32. Silas Kitto Hocking (1923) *The Lost Lode*, London: Sampson Low, Marston and Company, p.12.
33. Ibid., p.13.
34. See Winston Graham (1945) *Ross Poldark 1783-87*, London: Werner Laurie; E.V. Thompson (1977) *Ben Retallick*, London: Macmillan.
35. For background to this, see Chris Thomas 'See Your Own Country First: The Geography of a Railway' in Ella Westland (ed.) (1997) *Cornwall: The Cultural Construction of Place*, Penzance: The Patten Press and the Institute of Cornish Studies, pp.107-28.
36. Silas K. Hocking (1919) *Nancy*, London: Sampson Low, Marston and Company, p.8.
37. Ibid., p.14.
38. Ibid., p.17.
39. Kent (2000) op.cit., p.137.
40. Hocking (1919) op.cit., p.17.
41. Appleby (2001) op.cit., pp.18-21.
42. Silas K. Hocking (1925) *The Crooked Trail*, London: Sampson Low, Marston and Company, p.11.
43. Silas K. Hocking (1910) *Who Shall Judge?* London: Frederick Warne and Company, (1917) *His Own Accuser*, London: Sampson Low, Marston and Company.
44. Silas K. Hocking (1907) *St. Gwynifer*, London: Hodder and Stoughton, p.8.
45. Ibid., p.310.
46. Silas K. Hocking (1899) *The Strange Adventures of Israel Pendray*, London: Frederick Warne and Company, p.13.
47. Ibid., p.30.
48. See Joseph Hocking (1887) *Harry Penhale: The Trial of His Faith*, London: Andrew Crombie, (1888) *Gideon Strong: Plebeian*, London: Andrew Crombie, (1890) *Elrad the Hic*, London: Ward, Lock and Company.
49. Joseph Hocking (1889) *From London to Damascus*, London: Ward, Lock and Company.
50. Joseph Hocking (1890) *Jabez Easterbrook: A Religious Novel*, London: Ward, Lock and Company.
51. Ibid., p.11.
52. Ibid., p.115.
53. Ibid., p.341.
54. Joseph Hocking (1890) *The Weapons of Mystery*, London: Ward, Lock and Company, (1893) *Ishmael Pengelly: An Outcast*, London: Ward, Lock and Company, (1893) *The Story of Andrew Fairfax*, London: Ward, Lock and Company, (1894) *The Monk of Mar-Saba*, London: Ward, Lock and Company.
55. Joseph Hocking (1897) *And Shall Trelawney Die?* London: Ward, Lock and Company, (1900) *The Romance of Michael Trevail*, London: Cassell and Company, (1902) *Greater Love: A Cornish Romance*, London: Ward, Lock and Company.
56. Joseph Hocking (1901) *O'er Moor and Fen: A Tale of Methodist Life in Lancashire*, London: Hodder and Stoughton. This story was printed earlier as a serial in *British Weekly*.
57. Joseph Hocking (1895) *All Men are Liars*, London: Ward, Lock and Company.
58. Joseph Hocking (1897) *The Birthright: Being the Adventurous History of Jaspar Pennington of Pennington in the County of Cornwall*, London: Ward, Lock and Company.
59. Ibid., p.1.
60. Ibid., p.129.
61. See Arthur Quiller Couch (1906) *Sir John Constantine*, London: Smith and Elder. Quiller Couch came from a Methodist family in Polperro and actually originates from the same branch of Methodism as the Hockings. Quiller Couch's position on Methodism is complex. For a discussion, see the Conclusion to this book. He did print articles such as 'Footprints of the Wesleys in Cornwall' and attended many Methodist events. See *Cornish Magazine*, Vol 1 (1898), pp.242-51
62. Hocking (1897) op.cit., p.129.
63. Ibid., p.132.
64. See Allan Massie (1990) *The Novel Today*, Harlow: Longman, p.52.

65. Joseph Hocking (1903) *Follow the Gleam: A Tale of the Time of Oliver Cromwell,* London: Hodder and Stoughton, (1905) *Roger Trevanion,* London: Ward, Lock and Company.
66. Joseph Hocking (1900) *The Madness of David Baring,* London: Hodder and Stoughton, (1899) *The Scarlet Woman,* London: Ward, Lock and Company.
67. Joseph Hocking (1898) *Mistress Nancy Molesworth,* London: Ward, Lock and Company.
68. K.C. Phillipps, 'A Calling Sacrificed to Writing Novels', in *Western Morning News,* July (1976), p.5.
69. Joseph Hocking (1909) *The Sword of the Lord: A Romance of the Time of Martin Luther,* London: Cassell and Company.
70. Joseph Hocking (1903) *A Flame of Fire: Being the History of the Adventures of Three Englishmen at the Time of the Great Armada,* London: Cassell and Company.
71. The Islamic faith is under attack in some of the First World War novels. See for example, Joseph Hocking (1917) *The Path of Glory,* London: Hodder and Stoughton, pp.210-9.
72. Joseph Hocking (1913) *The Spirit of the West,* London: Cassell and Company.
73. Joseph Hocking (1905) *The Chariots of the Lord,* London: The Religious Tract Society, (1906) *The Woman of Babylon,* London: Cassell and Company, (1912) *Rosaleen O'Hara,* Hodder and Stoughton.
74. Joseph Hocking (1911) *The Jesuit,* London: Cassell and Company.
75. Ibid., p.3.
76. Ibid., pp.35-6.
77. Ibid., p.38.
78. Ibid., pp.46-7.
79. Ibid., p.149.
80. See brief history offered by Peter Berresford Ellis (1993) *The Celtic Dawn: A History of Pan Celticism,* London: Constable, pp.31-8. Increasingly, however, many scholars are blaming the Irish for not helping each other. See, for example, the controversial position given by Colm Tóibín (1999) *The Irish Famine.* London: Profile Books.
81. See, for example, Joseph Hocking (1912) *Is Home Rule Rome Rule?* London: Publisher unknown, and Joseph Hocking and R.F. Horton (1910) *And Shall Rome Reconquer England?* London: National Council of Evangelical Free Churches.
82. This is J. Keating (1909) *A Brace of Bigots: Dr Horton and Mr Hocking,* London: Catholic Truth Society, but I have been unable to locate this text.
83. Thorne (2000 [1978]) op.cit., p.5.
84. Ibid.
85. Cited in ibid.
86. Ibid.
87. Joseph Hocking (1908) *The Soul of Dominic Wildthorne,* London: Hodder and Stoughton.
88. Thorne (2000 [1978] op.cit., p.6.
89. See Hocking and Horton (1910) op.cit.
90. *Cornubian,* 18th March (1909), p.3. I am indebted to John C.C. Probert for bringing this to my attention.
91. Ibid. The same edition of *Cornubian* carries Joseph's response to Lunn. Joseph claims that he had planned to write a novel which 'necessitated a visit to Rome', that readers of *The Purple Robe* should decide whether he had 'unfairly used the information' he was given there, and that his attack was not on 'Roman Catholics as individuals', but 'Roman Catholicism as a system'. See Joseph Hocking (1900) *The Purple Robe,* London: Ward, Lock and Company.
92. See 'Men of the Day' No. 1040, in *Vanity Fair* (1906).
93. Joseph Hocking (1912) *God and Mammon,* London: Ward, Lock and Company, (1892) *Zillah: A Romance,* London: Ward, Lock and Company.
94. Joseph Hocking (1928) *The Eternal Challenge,* London: Hodder and Stoughton.
95. Appleby (2001) op.cit., p.1. For useful background here, see Cedric J. Appleby, "Marching as to War': Cornish Methodists and the "Great War"', in *Journal of the Cornish Methodist Historical Association,* No.4 (1994), pp.96-107.
96. Joseph Hocking (1920) *The Kaiser's Investments,* London: Ward, Lock and Company.
97. See, for example, Hocking (1917) op.cit., (1915) *The Day of Judgement.* London: Cassell and

Company, (1920) *In the Sweat of Thy Brow,* London: Hodder and Stoughton.
98. Joseph Hocking (1915) *All for a Scrap of Paper: A Romance of the Present War,* London: Hodder and Stoughton, pp.
99. Joseph Hocking (1916) *The Curtain of Fire,* London: Hodder and Stoughton, (1918) *The Pomp of Yesterday,* London: Hodder and Stoughton.
100. See poetry in Simon Fuller (ed.) (1990) *The Poetry of War 1914-1989,* Harlow: Longman, pp.8-29.
101. Joseph Hocking (1916) *Tommy: A War Story,* London: Hodder and Stoughton. See also (1917) *Tommy and the Maid of Athens,* London: Hodder and Stoughton.
102. Joseph Hocking (1918) op.cit., p.8.
103. *Cornish Guardian,* 21st May (1915), p.5. Joseph makes other observations on the conflict in the same edition. See p.3.
104. Ibid. Probert notes that 'Rev. Booth Coventry… who had supported the clay strike of 1913, had better results than the Rev. Joseph Hocking's effort at his birth place, St. Stephens, in 1915 where there were no recruits despite a rousing speech, and patriotic songs'. Booth Coventry was a United Methodist Minister and an Independent Labour Party Supporter. See John C. C. Probert, 'Recruiting for the 1914-18 War and the 1851 Religious Census Etc', in *Journal of the Cornish Methodist Historical Association,* No.4 (2000), p.130.
105. Hocking (1915) op.cit., p.5.
106. See Appleby (2001) op.cit., p.6. This is a substantially truncated version of Appleby's argument.
107. Hocking (1915) op.cit., p.253.
108. Later obituaries make little of his specific wartime efforts, preferring to praise his public service instead.
109. Joseph Hocking (1926) *Andrew Boconnoc's Will: The Story of a Crisis,* London: Cassell and Company. This novel is interesting since it is a direct exploration of the Boconnoc name and estate (belonging to the Fortescues). Either Joseph has deliberately chosen this to expose this, or perhaps he saw the family as less of a threat now that his father was long dead and that he was in a position of power himself.
110. Joseph Hocking (1926) *Bevil Granville's Handicap,* London: Hodder and Stoughton, (1927) *The Tenant of Cromlech Cottage,* London: Ward, Lock and Company, (1928) *Felicity Treverbyn: A Love Story,* London: Hodder and Stoughton, (1928) *Nancy Trevanion's Legacy,* London: Ward, Lock and Company, (1931) *The Secret of Trescobel,* London: Ward, Lock and Company.
111. See Malcolm Chapman (1992) *The Celts: The Construction of a Myth,* Basingstoke: Macmillan.
112. Hocking (1927) op.cit., p.22. The background story to this novel, concerning wills and their legality, was given to Joseph Hocking by Charles Vivian Thomas (1859-1941) solicitor, alderman and preacher, and Joseph's long-time friend. He is the grandfather of Charles Thomas. The author's foreword to the novel recognises this.
113. See Kent (2000) op.cit., pp.246-52.
114. Ella Westland, 'The Passionate Periphery: Cornwall and Romantic Fiction', in Ian A. Bell (ed.) (1995) *Peripheral Visions: Images of Nationhood in Contemporary British Fiction,* Cardiff: University of Wales Press, p.158.
115. Joseph Hocking (1906) *The Man Who Rose Again,* London: Hodder and Stoughton, (1922) *The Man who Almost Lost,* London: Hodder and Stoughton, (1931) *The Man Who was Sure,* London: Hodder and Stoughton, (1933) *The Man Who Found Out,* London: Ward, Lock and Company. It may be that these novels' titles are derived from the famous 'Bateman' cartoons about social impropriety. They generally began with 'The Man Who…'
116. For this useful perspective on Ross Poldark, see Nickianne Moody 'Poldark Country and National Culture' in Westland (ed.) (1997) op.cit. pp.129-36.
117. Joseph Hocking (1933) *Not One in Ten,* London: Hodder and Stoughton, p.234. The royal genealogy here is not clear.
118. Thorne (2000 [1978]) op.cit., p.16.
119. Hocking (1933) op.cit., p.298.
120. See Jack Clemo 'The Hocking Brothers' in *Cornish Review,* Spring (1969), pp.36-41. It seems Clemo's observations are only based on his reading of a small number of the novels.
121. Joseph Hocking (1929) *The Sign of the Triangle,* London: Ward, Lock and Company, p.38.
122. Ibid., p.41. It is ironic that the reverse of this housing structure is now taking place in St Ives.

Chapter 5 – Notes

123. A narrative structure seen in Joseph Hocking (1936) *Davey's Ambition*. London: Ward, Lock and Company. This was Joseph's final novel.
124. Joseph Hocking (1924) *What Shall it Profit a Man?* London: Hodder and Stoughton, p.1.
125. Ibid., p.21.
126. Ibid., p.39. This is perhaps the exception proving the rule that the Hockings did not refer to china clay.
127. Ibid., p.157.
128. Ibid., p.173.
129. Ibid., p. 320.
130. See Graham (1945) op.cit., and Thompson (1977) op.cit.
131. Salome Hocking (1886) *Norah Lang: The Mine Girl*, London: Andrew Crombie.
132. 'Recks' were inclined frames on which fine ores were washed and separated from gangue.
133. In an interesting parallel, Fifield informs us that Salome's nickname was 'S'lome'. See Arthur C. Fifield (1927) *Salome Hocking Fifield: In Memorium*, Coulsdon: Arthur C. Fifield, p.3.
134. Hocking (1886) op.cit., p.9.
135. Ibid., p.39. Salome also grew long hair to hide her *scoliosis*.
136. See Jack Clemo (1948) *Wilding Graft*, London: Chatto and Windus, pp.232-40.
137. Hocking Fifield (1886) op.cit., p.155.
138. See Salome Hocking (n.d.) *Granny's Hero: A Tale of Country Life*, London: Publisher unknown, (1885) *The Fortunes of Riverside or Waiting and Winning*, London: Partridge. These can usually be compared to J. O. Keen (n.d.) *Midst Mine and Moor and Cornish Folk, or Idylls of Cornwall*, London: Bible Christian Reading Room.
139 Salome Hocking (1887) *Jacky: A Story of Everyday Life*, London: Andrew Crombie, p.11. The reader is asked to consider which trait will dominate.
140. Tributing is the process whereby men are paid by a proportion of the value of ore they raise.
141. Hocking (1887) op.cit., p.32.
142. Ibid., pp.47-8.
143. Salome Hocking (1888) *Chronicles of a Quiet Family: A Temperance Story*, London: Andrew Crombie.
144. Salome Hocking (n.d.) *Beginnings*, London: Andrew Crombie.
145. S. Moore Carew (n.d.) *A Conquered Self*, London: Publisher unknown.
146. Salome Hocking (1903) *Some Old Cornish Folk*, London: Charles H. Kelly, p.9.
147. Ibid.
148. Ibid., pp.11-12. This portrait must clearly have been based on the Truscott family. Norman Truscott, one of the Joseph's schoolfriends, was from a shoemaking family.
149. Ibid., p.60.
150. Ibid., p.62. Inevitably, this description reminds us of Phillipps ironmongers' shop at Roche. See K.C. Phillipps (1994) *Catching Cornwall in Flight*, St Austell: Cornish Hillside Publications, pp.113-26.
151. Ibid., p.79.
152. Ibid., p.86.
153. Ibid., p.37.
154. Ibid., p.101.
155. Ibid., pp.104-5.
156. Exceptions include Kent (2000), op.cit.; Allen E. Ivey and Philip Payton 'Towards a Cornish Identity Theory' in Philip Payton (ed.) (1994) *Cornish Studies: Two*, Exeter: University of Exeter Press, pp.151-163.
157. Hocking (1903) op.cit., p.168.
158. Ibid., p.170.
159. Ibid., p.171.
160. Ibid., p.177.
161. Ibid., pp. 178-9. For Salome's observations on 'Cornish [Methodist] Revivals', see pp.153-64.

162. Salome Hocking (1905) *Belinda the Backward: A Romance of Modern Idealism,* London: Arthur C. Fifield.
163. Ibid., p.12.
164. Ibid., p.20.
165. Ibid., p.46.
166. Ibid., p.67-8
167. See for example, Alison Light (1991) *Forever England: Feminity, Literature and Conservatism between the Wars,* London: Routledge, pp. 156-207. Many university degree courses in literary or cultural studies now feature the work of Daphne du Maurier.
168. See Kent (2000) op.cit.; Westland (ed.) (1997) op.cit.; Alan M. Kent and Tim Saunders (ed.) (2000) *Looking at the Mermaid: A Reader in Cornish Literature 900-1900,* London: Francis Boutle, pp.17-20; *Tim Saunders* (ed.) (1999) *The Wheel: An Anthology of Modern Poetry in Cornish 1850-1980,* London: Francis Boutle, pp.16-18; Amy Hale, Alan M. Kent and Tim Saunders (eds.) (2000), *Inside Merlin's Cave: A Cornish Arthurian Reader 1000-2000.* London: Francis Boutle; Simon Trezise (2000) *The West Country as a Literary Invention: Putting Fiction in its Place.* Exeter: University of Exeter Press.
169. For example, see Bell (ed.) (1995) op.cit., A Robert Lee (ed.) (1995) *Other Britain, Other British: Contemporary Multicultural Fiction,* London: Pluto Press. For a deconstruction of liberal humanist approaches to literary studies, see John Dixon (1991) *A Schooling in 'English': Criticial Episodes to Shape Literary and Cultural Studies,* Buckingham: Open University Press.

Chapter Six

Friends, Relatives and Revivals:
The Hocking Legacy, 1850-2001

> *Genesis mixed: your Terras tap on clean tin*
> *Foreign to me, though your birth-bed*
> *Was only a mile from mine, the hacked hills*
> *Around us carried the white scriptures*
> *Of a sullen trade, the black Bibles were pounded*
> *In Wesley's fold to make us akin,*
> *And your family blood reached me, according to legal files.*
>   Jack Clemo, *Testament*, 1975[1]

As alluded to earlier in this book, the Hocking legacy does have important connections to the visionary Anglo-Cornish poet and novelist, Jack Clemo. Clemo, who later became both deaf and blind, lived for most of life at Goonamarris, near Nanpean, only two miles from the birthplace of the Hockings at Terras.[2] He was also a relative: Clemo's grandmother, Esther Trudgian, was a cousin of Joseph and Silas. In his frank and powerful 1949 autobiography, *Confession of a Rebel,* Clemo details his relationship to the Hocking family and their place in the development of his own writing career.[3] He tells us that the Hocking family was 'respectable and poor',[4] but notes their mental qualities – probably referring to James Hocking. The qualities of sensitivity, a theological bent and a strong subtle intellect, Clemo believes he may have inherited from the Hockings. He comments that...

> ...had not the Clemos been such a rough lot I should probably have become a clever man of the conventional sort, perhaps a writer of genial stories like the Hockings; I might even have entered the ministry.[5]

Clemo was, however, a rebel, just like the Hockings, though perhaps, by the time he was writing, he considered their 'genial stories' a little tame for his tastes. He confesses that it did not occur to him during his childhood that he would become a novelist or a poet of any sort.[6] Even so, the Hockings were well-known in the parish, and so he had thought about their success:

> I knew, of course, that the Hockings were my cousins, but this meant little, as I had never read any of their books. (I have only read one or two of them since) Silas Hocking was a mere name to me – he had settled in

Tree showing relationship of Jack Clemo to the Hocking family

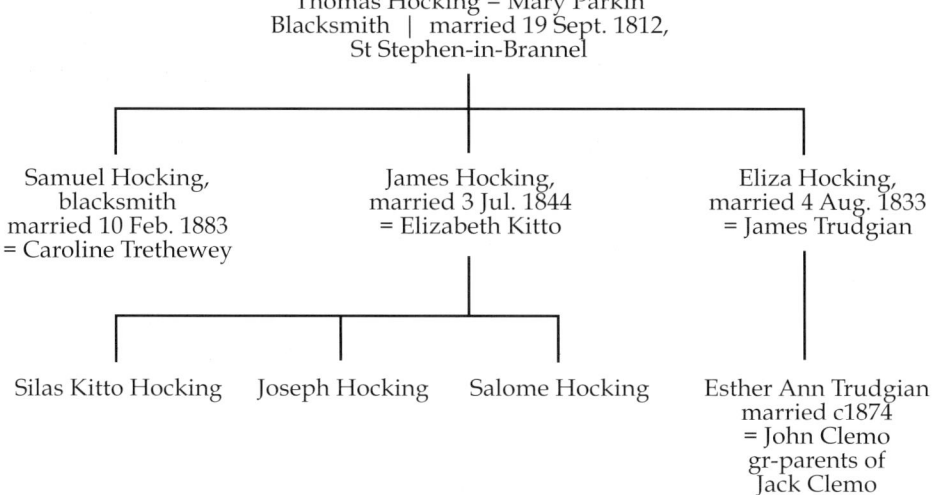

London; and Joseph I saw only twice. I was present when he opened the St Stephen's Recreation Ground in 1924, though I was extremely bored by the ceremony; and on another occasion my mother took me to hear him preach at St Stephen's Methodist chapel. I have completely forgotten the service. I felt no pride or kinship of any kind: it was not the habit of the Clemo's to feel that. None of them attended St Stephen's cemetery when his ashes were buried there in March 1937.[7]

Clemo also explains how they were regarded by local society in Cornwall after their successes:

The inhibition regarding the literary streak in my family was no doubt strengthened by the fact that I so seldom heard the Hockings praised; there grew in me a vague feeling that they had done something to be ashamed of. The local gentry, of course, applauded their success, but I knew nothing of gentry.[8]

To a certain degree, this is vintage Clemo here, at arms length socially, but perhaps not fully understanding the Hockings' earlier struggle, nor the political and social context of their later lives. In Cornwall, the shame that had come to be associated with the Hockings had come out of Silas's stumbling during the Boer War crisis. St Stephen-in-Brannel had been satirised alongside Silas in *Vanity Fair*, and needless to say, the parishioners were aware he had taken the opposite view to the bulk of Cornish people. Silas never returned. Ironically, although the gentry may have applauded Silas, they probably did not read the books. Of course, this division of opinion was very much along class lines: the parishioners sympathising with the miners; the gentry less so.

Secondly, Clemo shows some degree of ignorance with regard to the local gentry. He was possibly unaware of the exact circumstances of James' fate – or otherwise the parish itself felt ashamed of the way 'Jimmy Hocky' had been treated. Either way, the gentry (not necessarily the Fortescues, or any of the controlling clay mining families) would have had a problem with the Hockings by this phase of their literary career. They were among the most famous Cornishmen in Britain. Clemo continues by analysing public opinion further, as well as Silas' changing position in his later years:

> The people who called at my home, and might casually mention the Hockings were uneducated villagers, and the sturdy, chapel-going folks around St Stephen's had never forgiven the Hockings for leaving the ministry in order to write story-books. I remember hearing Silas Hocking denounced from the Trethosa Chapel pulpit when, in his old age, he drifted so far from the Evangelical position as to champion Sunday cinemas and divorce law reforms.[9]

This is of crucial importance to our understanding of the Hockings' life and work. As we have seen, the people of St Stephen-in-Brannel may not have understood nor sympathised with the full picture. Methodism had carried on in the village and at Trethosa[10] in a way more or less unchanged from Silas's youth. He, meanwhile, had seen incredible changes and had been at the very top of the preaching circuit in Britain. The view here, that Silas left to make more money from 'story-books' is not entirely correct. He, of course, had been their nonconformist champion for almost half a century, so they were bound to react in that way. Clemo's word 'drift'

Tennis courts and bowling green, St Stephen Recreation Ground, c.1924.

suggests immorality and decline, whereas we ought instead to insert the work 'progressed'. This attitude towards Silas and his brother and sister may well have been very localised – a case of sour grapes. Elsewhere in Cornwall, for instance, at Dowran Chapel, in St Just-in-Penwith, their books were still seen as 'proper' and circulated widely.[11] Such local opinion would barely affect sales across these islands.

Crucially, Silas, as we have seen, reached several points of spiritual crisis throughout his career, and changed his opinions markedly after the Boer war, and then more particularly after the First World War. Sunday cinemas has a touch of rumour to it, but the divorce law reform seems more grounded in reality. Silas had witnessed some of the suffering of women and children due to outmoded practice. He had to leave behind his original beliefs for wider social reform. However, Silas's position in the newspapers would indicate this more liberal position. Probably, news of Salome's communal and Socialist lifestyle had also reached Cornwall. Clemo concludes that after this time...

> ...*My mother scarcely ever mentioned these brothers: she strongly disapproved of novels, and though she let me borrow them from the school library, she remarked that she would rather I read "good" books.*[12]

This is an intriguing position, since it is difficult to think of novels with more 'ethical' or 'moral' qualities than the fiction of the Hockings, although it would appear that his mother, Eveline Clemo, was referring to other kinds of work. The "good books" were more Biblical texts proper, or canonized Christian literature. By this time, Eveline it would seem, had little time for the 'pulp Methodism' offered by Silas and Joseph, although in her own 1976 autobiography *I Proved Thee at the Waters: The Testimony of a Blind Writer's Mother*, she offers a slightly different testimony on the Hockings from her son Jack:

> *At the early age of twelve, in an evangelical service at our Bethel Chapel, I dedicated my life to Jesus Christ, and this experience gave me a mystical love for devotional reading. These books were written by men of simple faith but with great vision and understanding of the love that redeems and transforms personality. As I developed towards my teens, I became interested in reading good romantic stories. My favourite authors in this field were Silas and Joseph Hocking, who were cousins of the young man I later married. The Christian influence woven into these stories moved me deeply. All of us, as we come into adolescence know that we have reached a new and wonderful stage in the mystery and power of creative love which draws two young people together with the one desire that their love will unite them as one; expressing the wonder and beauty of God's creative love in human lives. The tragedy is that at this age not many of us have the wisdom of discernment. It is so easy to mistake fantasy for reality and human mysticism for divine love and this is especially true for one who had a religious and mystical temperament, as I had.*[13]

What Eveline Clemo appears to be saying here is that the effect of the Hocking's novels on her own life was converse to what they were meant to do. Rather than putting her on the straight and narrow, they paradoxically encouraged her 'romantically'; that it somehow fostered her tragedy; her comment close to the view of the Anglican minister Silas once met on the train to Southport, that 'people were deceived by the poison lurking underneath'[14] and that the pulp Methodism had blinded her, perhaps the reason she later dissuaded Jack from reading their works. This is confirmed by the way she describes her husband, Reginald Clemo:

> It took a few years of suffering before I saw that there was a deceptive beauty in natural mysticism that blinded the inner eye from seeing the need of repentance – that was destructive and so different from the Christian mystic who saw his need and accepted the cleansing of the fire of God's love in the atonement and became aware of being built up into the mystical body of Christ – this was the eternal life Christ was continually speaking about while he was here in human flesh. At the age of fifteen, I fell in love with a young man who was not a Christian. The background of his home-life was very different from my own. He knew nothing of the love and security of Christian parents. I felt very sorry for this young man.[15]

Ironically, of course, these are the very views that the Hockings tried to express in their novels. Depite this, we are left with an impression that the Hockings failed Eveline Clemo on this spiritual level. As Jack's own literary ambitions began to emerge however, he was reminded of them again, but from the Clemo's position, they were also to fail them again. Jack asks his mother, 'What if I was to writes stories like they 'Ockings?' but we are told she 'regarded my ambition as but a passing whim'.[16] Perhaps Eveline tried to put her son off from writing to Joseph, but even so, he eventually seems to have persuaded her, but the result was disappointing:

> Hearing that Joseph Hocking lived at Hayle, thirty miles off, she ventured to write him a letter, telling him of my predicament and mentioning the probable derivation of my talent from his family through Esther. Whether he was irked at the recollection of Esther's marriage I do not know, but a few days later we received a rather curt little note from him, regretting that owning to ill-health he could not help us, and adding: "As to the lad of whom you spoke, he, if he has the real stuff in him, will make his way... He must persist in doing his best and then sending work to what seems the most likely quarters until he succeeds."[17]

Perhaps Eveline and Jack were unaware of the severity of Joseph's ill-health. The letter is encouraging and Clemo certainly had 'the real stuff' Joseph mentions. Even so, Clemo admits throughout his career that he had mixed feelings towards his cousins, a little tinged with regret, as well as sharing their ambition. This ambivalence (referred to as 'mild pattern') is expressed in his poem *Testament* from his 1975 collection *Broad Autumn*, which he dedicates to Joseph:

> *But my craggy and uncouth image*
> *Came another way: Knox-souled and Burns-hearted,*
> *How could I take the sleek service*
> *And the tidy text? My genesis*
> *Was spelled in the scummed saddlebacks*
> *Lolling towards the blasted circle,*
> *The whipped fingers of rock on the pit-floor,*
> *Hoisted hoses making their impress*
> *On rinsed and haggard cliff faces that wore*
> *Slowly away, starting up at smoke-lidded stacks.*
>
> *Brute tools broke me in the riding stillness*
> *Of infancy, then the loping waggons,*
> *Glum and fast on the drummed tracks,*
> *Woke me each morning, along with the brayed*
> *Or shrieked summons of engine-house sirens.*
>
> *My boyhood's dream crossed a mineral stage*
> *Without lark's song or bowing myrtle,*
> *But always with an unbegreyed*
> *Gesture apprehended, God's and woman's*
> *Blood-leap – not in your mild pattern*
> *Of the clean sheet and Victorian climate,*
> *But storming to my unwritten page,*
> *Anguished from all the lost Edens.*[18]

By now, of course, Clemo's own work had been recognised and he is able to understand more intimately the 'Victorian climate' – the pulp Methodism, which they had worked with. Joseph's rebellion is then given sympathy in a nonconformist workout at the poem's conclusion:

> *Neither hint of mineral*
> *Iron nail in the Godhead, nor the shuttle*
> *And prick of moon-change in the bride,*
> *Could check the released heart's witness*
> *That nightmare abate, that the scummed scroll*
> *Spells no legacy where the heaven-eyed*
> *Invader draws love beyond the Fall.*
>
> *My dream drained slowly to the blown trees*
> *And the waking unscourged fingers: wave after wave*
> *Of pleasure would interpret*
> *My opened wealth. So there came to your parish*

> *What old defiant Knox found in Margaret,*
> *What Burns sought with tears at Mary's grave.*[19]

As mentioned in the Introduction to this work, Clemo also considered the achievement of the Hockings in an article for *Cornish Review* in 1969. After initially praising them for their nonconformity and rebellion against the dicta of the Methodist ministry, he reflects on the fact that they never encountered each other:

> *The Hockings I never met, and had I visited either of them I should have felt embarrassed. Despite the fact that they and I are sons of the same parish, and the probable derivation in my talent from them, I feel that I have lived all my life in a Cornwall they never knew and could never have attempted to describe. But they were Christian rebels, and this brings a sense of spiritual kinship across a temperamental gulf.*[20]

This last phrase is interesting. Clemo's spiritual kinship with them is clearly important, yet he find no affinity in them for the landscape that so inspired him. He finds this strange:

> *In My Book of Memory, there are practically no Cornish scenes; he records nothing of those poverty-stricken early years in a dour little cottage on Terras Moor, the narrow flat waste between Meledor and St Stephens. The clayworks, with their powerful symbolism, the idiom of the new, industrial Cornwall, were beginning to scar the hillsides all round when Joseph and Silas left home for college. This fresh land, teeming with craggy and purgatorial images, awaited its interpreter: there was religious mystery in the crossed tip-beams pointing skywards... But the Hockings saw these features as signs of a messy industry with which they had no concern. They turned away to the fashionable world which provided them with material for naïve tales of Society life and for Silas's book of amusing anecdotes about the celebrities he had met.*[21]

This is unfair on a number of levels. The clay industry was still in a relatively early stage of development when Silas and Joseph left Cornwall, aside from the landowning issues surrounding the extractive industry itself. They had been more bound up with the previous generation's mining activity – the search for tin. 'Naïve tales of Society life' is also a little unfair, since here Clemo enters the realms of early 'easy-to-knock' Hocking criticism. He felt that the Hockings only offered but a watered-down statement of the creed held by other nonconformists.

In the Hockings' defence, they did this to make their beliefs more accessible to a wider audience. They allowed the distribution of their nonconformity to be accessed by many more people than both Clemo's poetry and fiction. Finally, Clemo criticises the Hockings for their lack of Celticity. This author would refute that position, as argued against in the previous chapter, but nonetheless Clemo (who himself had many issues with the Celtic Revival in Cornwall considering it pagan and a performance[22]) makes some pertinent observations:

Chapter 6

"Q" [Arthur Quiller Couch] wrote on a far higher intellectual and artistic level than the Hockings, but he was as devoid as they of this elemental mystic awareness, the sense of "mud and Godhead" in the Cornish texture. Did they leave the county too soon before it had really spoken to them? Or was there an innate fastidiousness that made them recoil to the protection of civilised and cultured life? They certainly lacked the Celtic capacity for obsessions which might be expected to show itself in Cornish writers no less than Welsh and Irish ones.[23]

Jacket for *Mediterranean Murder*, 1951

At the end of the day, what Clemo seems to be criticising is not particularly their Celticity but the prevalence towards the popular. Clemo's questions are unanswerable because they are pure conjecture. Circumstances dictated that they left Cornwall early on, in fact, like many Cornish people of the late nineteenth century. If the Hockings were recoiling, then it was away from outdated land law and injustice in their own homeland – best seen in Salome. The recoil and reverberations of the Boer War incident have meant, even a century on, that Silas's name can be vilified. In some senses the above passage tells us more about Clemo than the Hockings. Clemo's own literary ideology was very canonized, and he always found it hard to move or even understand popular cultural trends and their reception. In this sense, he may be a more iconoclastic Christian literary rebel, and on that level he has grounds to criticise the Hockings, though he surely must have been aware of their wider legacy. Regardless, viewing both Silas and Joseph Hocking, and Jack and Eveline Clemo from our twenty-first century position, perhaps we should think less about their differences, but celebrate their unified nonconformist, Cornish heritage. It is a position both sets would surely have found tenable.

Jack Clemo is not the only connection to the Hocking's legacy however. Anne Hocking (1890-1966) is the fourth member of the Hocking family with claim to be a notable Anglo-Cornish author, who during her lifetime wrote a number of highly successful detective and mystery novels in the then very fashionable style of Agatha Christie. Details of her life story are sketchy, and the information here is primarily drawn from an interview with the journalist George A. Greenwood in the *Western Morning News*, in 1953, when she was clearly at the height of her career, celebrating the publication of her fortieth book.[24] When interviewed she was aged sixty-three. Greenwood comments how she is a 'tall woman of striking appearance, looking a good deal younger than her years'.[25] Anne was the daughter of Joseph and Annie Hocking, and thus a niece of Silas and Salome. She was born in 1892, during the time her father and mother lived at Thornton Heath – then a small village south of London. Much of her reflections upon her parents and background have already been covered in this volume, but clearly the Hocking name still rang bells with the reading public as Greenwood questions her about her parents. She comments:

> *Romance was immediate. It was obviously a case of love at first sight. The Brown family frowned on the young couple's intentions, especially as she was only eighteen. But my father was a very determined young man.*[26]

It seems that Joseph was keen for his daughter not to be born in London, but back in Cornwall. Even so, Anne's literary future seemed somewhat assured since her birth was connected with the beginning of her father's publishing career. As she observes:

> *My mother could not get to Cornwall in time. My father often described the circumstances of my arrival during the early hours of an August morning. He was not very well off then, and had, in fact, only just sent off the manuscript of his first novel to the publishers in London. As he was pacing the garden waiting for news of what was happening in the house, the nurse came out to tell him of my arrival, and almost at the same moment the postman arrived with a letter announcing that his story had been accepted.*[27]

Anne spent most of her life living in Hampstead, London, though often travelled to Cornwall and considered herself ethnically Cornish. Greenwood observes, 'I found that she loves everything about Cornwall – its tradition and romance. She herself believes in this inheritance'.[28] Since the Second World War Anne Hocking had been a widow, as her husband H. R. Messer – whom she married when aged eighteen – had died during the War in South Africa. Anne had two married daughters and one son, though their stories and careers are not covered here.[29]

She began writing early – like her famous father and produced small stories and plays when aged just seven, though she was twenty before her first detective novel was published. Anne then stopped serious writing for eight years to raise her daughters and son. She pursued more serious novels for a while, though eventually returned to the detective story, its form appealing to her, and also realising she had found her niche in the market. Perhaps there was some influence at work from knowledge of her father and uncle's writing, since many of their novels also included elements of the detective genre. Critics and Greenwood dubbed Anne Hocking and Agatha Christie 'the two finest living women writers of what is now colloquially called Whodunnit fiction'[30] and though, while the Torquay-born Christie is much celebrated, Anne has passed, like her father and uncle, Silas, into obscurity. Her output similarly, was massive. By the end of her career she had written over fifty novels.

In a telling section of the interview with Greenwood, Anne explains that although her roots were Cornish, she loved travelling, and liked to go by sea, via steamers. She recalls her grandmother Eliza Kitto Hocking here, who came from St Mawes on the south Cornish coast: 'The sea is in my blood. When I am on board I feel as if I am part of the ship'.[31] Like her namesake John Kitto and Silas Kitto, Anne also travelled widely in the Mediterranean. In terms of other Cornish influences, Anne admits to devouring the fiction of Arthur Quiller Couch and Daphne du Maurier, as well as the work of Charles Vyvyan and Mark Guy Pearse. Interestingly of course, it was her father Joseph, who had steered the Cornish historical novel away from religious tract and into historical romance, then most popularly shaped by du Maurier.

During 1953, W. H. Allen and Company were about to publish *Death Among the Tulips*[32] – a detective adventure set in the Netherlands. Two months earlier they had released *The Evil that Men Do* to acclaimed reviews.[33] Such a title is almost typically Hocking-like. In her later years, she continued to write from her retirement home in Wokingham, Berkshire, where she lived until her death on 20th March, 1966, at the age of seventy-four.[34] One of the most successful books of her career was titled *The Death in the Cup,* which is alluded to in Dr. F.D.M. Hocking's memoirs, *Bodies and Crimes* (1992),[35] where he explains the process of lacing a glass of spirits with tasteless barbiturates. F.D.M. Hocking was, for many years, the Cornwall County Pathologist, and was a relative of the Hockings referred to here.

Like her father and uncle, the literature of Anne Hocking has never been fully recognised. She managed the no mean feat of steering her vision of the crime novel from the 1930s to the 1960s – a period of considerable social and economic change. In evaluating her fiction, it is noticeable that her masterstroke as a crime novelist was to set the majority of her novels in the most normal and conventional settings, thus making the 'pulp' murder all the more shocking. Typical of all her work is *Ill Deeds Done,* which opens in Nottingham, at The Hollies Nursing Home. The heroine, Mildred Edwards, is almost a throwback to her father's novels, as stock a Hocking character as they come, who started 'parentless, penniless and plain', realising that 'marriage was unlikely for her'.[36] She does, however, think much of Peter Vernand, who has dreams of running his own garage, but the reader soon learns that Vernand needs money for the project, Edwards becoming the potential murderess. It is only later that we find the local police receiving an anonymous letter requesting them to investigate the circumstances concerning the death of Miss Weldon, a patient Mildred has cared for in her final illness. Suspicion falls on another suitor of Peter's, Roberta Gilbert, while Edward confesses her guilt. Reviewing the work from the twenty-first century, there is seemingly little difference between this vision of overambition and greed, and much of Joseph's work:

> *I killed them. You see, I had to. I've explained all that to you. You wanted the money and they had it, so I arranged that I would keep them for nothing while they lived if they left the money to me when they died. I was quite honest about it Peter. I refused to take more than £6,000.*[37]

This is sample enough of Anne Hocking's work. At the time of writing no other biographical material has come to light. This seems a great pity, since she was, during the middle years of the twentieth century, a famous author, though for the moment a revival of interest in her work, seems less likely than that of her more famous father and brother. *The Cornishman* newspaper of 10th March 1937 alludes to Joseph's other daughters. One wrote under the pseudonym of William Penmare from Geneva, where her husband was an an authority on jurisprudence; her books dealing with international intrigues. The youngest daughter, Mrs

Joan Shill, married a Government official and spent several years in Africa.[38]

Silas Kitto's books, meanwhile, continued to decline in sales in the second half of the twentieth century; new readers were easily catered for in the second-hand market. The only exceptions were reprints of *Her Benny: A Tale of Victorian Liverpool,* and *Chips: A Tale of Victorian Manchester,* by the Gallery Press of Liverpool in 1992.[39] Both editions promote the heritage of these two northern English cities. Several editions of Joseph's later novels continued to be reprinted in Britain until the onset of the 1970s, published by the Lythway Press of Bath. Titles like *The Secret of Trescobell* and *Davey's Ambition* were given new cover designs in the then late 1960s' style of gaudy, bold, modernist colours, with the heroes and heroines wearing contemporary fashions.[40] Given that *Davey's Ambition* was published over forty years earlier, this now seems proof of their long-lasting appeal to the reading public.

This mid-twentieth-century Hocking activity brings me back full circle to where, in my preface, I began this book – a performance of the musical *Her Benny* – in the city of Liverpool. Some history of the project is helpful in understanding this revival. The composer Anne Dalton, first began writing musicals in 1988. The musical *Her Benny* was written in 1990, after she discovered the Silas K. Hocking novel, and was initially developed and staged by the Andante Theatre Company. It was later submitted to the International Quest for New Musicals, initiated by the British television personality Richard Stilgoe. From an entry of 491 musicals, it was announced the winner. The production first played to sell-out audiences and standing ovations in Liverpool in 1993, with Dalton winning the *Scousology* award for Top Theatre personality.[41] *The Guardian* newspaper describes the show 'like an effective co-production between that upstart Lionel Bart, and the silver-tongued Andrew Lloyd Webber'.[42]

Admirably directed by Christopher G. Sanford and designed by David Shields, the show encapsulates the feel of Silas's original novel and his time at the Russell Street Church. Darkly lit and with a backdrop of the foggy Liverpool docklands, Dalton allows the characters of Joe and Sally Wragg, Benny and Mr. Lawrence to come alive. Like all musicals, there is a clever balancing act to be played between progressing the plot, and offering a range of music; some set dance routines involving the street children and the people of Liverpool, as well as some more evocative solo pieces. As composer, Dalton has given the story a contemporary pace, which greatly revived interest in Silas K. Hocking's connections to the city, and in the status of *Her Benny* – effectively Liverpool's very own *Oliver Twist*. Some of the most memorable sections of the drama remain Benny and Nelly's escape from their parents in the middle of the night, Nelly's death, Benny's arrival at Mr. Lawrence's, as well as a spectacular Christmas scene. Dalton was also careful to keep the diction and dialect of Silas's original text. Thanks to Dalton, the legacy of *Her Benny* in Liverpool is unlikely to be forgotten. It would perhaps be fitting if one day, the musical could be performed in Cornwall. If *Her Benny* can be revived, then perhaps, some other Hocking texts and their literary legacy is worth reconsidering.

Our story is almost complete, considering as we have, the legacy of Silas, Joseph and Salome's work, and their interaction with Jack and Eveline Clemo, Anne Hocking and the work of Anne Dalton. I now turn to the future of the 'old 'Ockings' in the literary and religious culture of contemporary Cornwall and Britain.

Notes

1. Jack Clemo (1988) *Selected Poems*. Newcastle upon Tyne: Bloodaxe Books, pp.116-7. The poem was originally published in Jack Clemo (1975) *Broad Autumn*, London: Methuen.
2. For a useful overview of Clemo's life, see Sally Magnusson (1986) *Clemo: A Love Story*, Tring: Lion.
3. Jack Clemo (1949) *Confession of a Rebel*, London: Chatto and Windus, pp.1-15. This would therefore make Jack first cousin, twice removed.
4. Ibid., p.1.
5. Ibid., p.8.
6. Ibid., p.36. Two writers Clemo pronounces an interest in were D.H. Lawrence and A.L. Rowse. For a useful biographies, see Brenda Maddox (1994) *The Married Man: A Life of D. H. Lawrence*, London: Sinclair Stevenson and Richard Ollard (1999) *A Man of Contradictions: A Life of A.L. Rowse*, London: Allen Lane.
7. Ibid., p.37-38.
8. Ibid., p.38.
9. Ibid.
10. Trethosa Chapel lies one mile from St Stephen-in-Brannel, and forms the focus of much of Clemo's life. He was married there. It is perhaps worth noting that rural and urban Methodism would have differed partly because of the size of congregations.
11. See John C.C. Probert, 'Dowran Chapel', in *Journal of the Cornish Methodist Historical Association*, No.5 (1995), pp.115-20.
12. Clemo (1949) op.cit., p.38.
13. Eveline Clemo, (c.1976) *I Proved Thee at the Waters: The Testimony of a Blind Writer's Mother*, Ilkeston, Derbyshire: Moorley's Bible and Bookshop.
14. Silas K. Hocking (1923) *My Book of Memory: A String of Reminiscences and Reflections*, London: Cassell and Company, pp.165-8.
15. Clemo (c.1976) op.cit., p.5. According to Cornish literary scholar Andrew C. Symons, Jack, unlike Eveline, was influenced by Reformed theology, but the experiential ethos remains in him. Information from correspondence with Andrew C. Symons, 1st September (2001)
16. Clemo (1949) op.cit., p.69.
17. Ibid., p.70.
18. Clemo (1988) op.cit., p.116-7. Symons argues convincingly that Clemo felt the Hockings had adopted the old British heresy of Pelagianism: that man is basically good and can win salvation through moral effort. Clemo felt the same way about Arthur Quiller Couch. Pelagianism was the position of Charlotte and Anne Brontë. Symons (2001) op.cit. For Clemo's observations on this, see Clemo (1949) op.cit., p.100 and p.107.
19. Ibid., p.117. This complex allusion brings in two themes: John Knox (1505-72) was the founder of Scottish Presbyterianism. He married the young Margaret Steward when aged fifty-nine. His enemies at the time thought he had cavorted with the devil to enable this. The second refers to the Scottish poet Robert Burns (1759-96) and his entanglement with Mary Campbell, best seen in the poem 'To Mary in Heaven'.
20. Jack Clemo 'The Hocking Brothers', in *Cornish Review*, Spring (1969), p.36.
21. Ibid., p.37.
22. See Clemo (1949) op.cit., p.88 and p.121. See Alan M. Kent (2000) *The Literature of Cornwall: Continuity, Identity, Difference 1000-2000*, Bristol: Redcliffe, pp.211-4.
23. Clemo (1969) op.cit., p.39.
24. George A. Greenwood, 'Daughter of famous Cornish novelist writers her 40th book: Anne Hocking's West Reminiscences', in *Western Morning News*, 2nd December (1953).
25. Ibid.
26. Ibid.
27. Ibid.
28. Ibid.
29. Ibid. Hocking also wrote under the name Mona Messer. H.R. Messer was not killed in action.

30. Ibid. Two other novels were Anne Hocking (1951) *Mediterranean Murder,* London: Evan Brothers, (1962) *He had to Die,* London: John Lang.
31. Ibid.
32. Anne Hocking (1953) *Death Among the Tulips,* London: W. H. Allen and Company.
33. Anne Hocking (1953) *The Evil that Men Do,* London: W. H. Allen and Company.
34. Attested in Harman MS.
35. F.D. M. Hocking (1992) *Bodies and Crimes,* London: The Book Guild.
36. Anne Hocking (n.d.) *Ill Deeds Done,* London: W. H. Allen and Company, p.12.
37. Ibid., p.190.
38. *Cornishman,* 10th March (1937), p.7. Penmare was the name of Joseph's residence in Hayle.
39. Silas Kitto Hocking (1992 [1879]) *Her Benny: A Tale of Victorian Liverpool,* Liverpool: Gallery Press; (1992 [1881]) *Chips: A Tale of Victorian Manchester,* Liverpool: Gallery Press.
40. Joseph Hocking (1969 [1931]) *The Secret of Trescobell.* Bath: Lythway Press; (1970 [1936]) *Davey's Ambition.* Bath: Lythway Press, 1970 [1936]. The novels continued to be reprinted until 1973.
41. Liverpool Empire Theatre (1994) *Her Benny: Programme,* Liverpool: Liverpool Empire Theatre Publications, p.20.
42. Cited on Liverpool Empire Theatre (1994) *Her Benny: Flyer,* Liverpool: Liverpool Empire Theatre Publications.

Conclusion

Pulp Methodism, Lost or Found?: Old 'Ockings; New Readings 1937-2001

> *I remember as a young girl being much perturbed by hearing a young preacher holding up the reading of fiction as a special sin to be shunned. He spoke so eloquently, and quoted with such thrilling effect that verse commencing: 'No room for mirth or trifling here, Or worldly hope or wordly fear, In life so soon, be gone', that I forswore novels for some weeks.*
>
> Salome Hocking, *Some Old Cornish Folk*, 1903[5]

This book has been an introductory biography to the lives of the Hockings and an initial survey of their writing and impact both on British and Cornish history. Within it, I hope to have told the story of the three novelists and along the way 'kicked into touch' several misnomers surrounding their work. As this book has shown, though emerging from the United Methodist Free Churches, much of their fiction illuminates the various strands of the Methodist tradition in Cornwall and elsewhere. Many of their books are a response to the crisis of industrialisation and modernism, the social progression of Methodists and the perceived threat of Anglo-Catholicism. The novels document the ideas and ideals of Methodism, visions of Cornwall and England and they tell us much about responses to War and national identity. From a cultural materialist position, the Hockings' set of novels are a case study example, where the transcendent significance of literary texts is revoked and where the evaluation and judgement of them is shown to be unproductive. In so doing we have come to better understand the implication of the Hockings' texts in recent Cornish and British history.

The novels also provide a continuum back to much earlier writing found in the territory. In just about the earliest Anglo-Cornish prose story set in Cornwall, *The Black Letter Pamphlet: News from Pe[n]rin in Cornwall*, we see a striking parallel to the works of the Hockings.[2] In effect, the chapbook narrative, published in 1618 is a moral fiction - a tale with a purpose, educating the reader and putting them on the straight and narrow. The themes of this early seventeenth-century text - a wicked stepmother, over-ambition, greed, love and faith conquering all - could be straight out of an 'old Joseph Hocking'. If a text from this period can survive down the ages and still have something to say to us now, then maybe the Hockings' work is more timeless and more lasting than we think. Literature is as affected by fashions, changes and rediscoveries as popular music, clothes, computer games and 'pop culture' in general. It all, it seems, eventually comes round again.

Having understood that, throughout this book, I have tended to steer away from comparing the Hockings with other Anglo-Cornish writers and fiction, but I intend to break that habit here. There have been many texts which have dealt with the themes of Methodism and its social effect - often comic and satirical - but nonetheless important components of the Anglo-Cornish literary continuum. One instantly thinks of the diary of the 'free trader' and 'precision Methodist' Harry Carter, the poetry of John Harris, R.M. Ballantyne's *Deep Down: A Tale of the Cornish Mines*, James F. Cobb's *The Watchers on the Longships,* F. Frankfurt Moore's *Tre, Pol and Pen*,[3] then later the work of Charles Lee, D.M. Thomas and K.C. Phillipps.[4]

Arthur Quiller Couch also wrote many interesting novels on Methodist themes, among them *Hetty Wesley* and *Sir John Constantine.*[5] Indeed, with regard to Quiller Couch's *Nicky Nan: Reservist,*[6] a novel set in a Cornish fishing village during the First World War, Appleby notes that 'ironically, there is more about Methodism in this novel than there is in any of the novels of the Methodist Joseph Hocking set in the same period'.[7] Joseph was not interested in writing *about* Methodism in this way during this phase. Methodism was a given theme already, and Joseph's written theology remained progressive, trying to deal with the complexities of the conflict. He wrote beyond Quiller Couch's more narrow Methodism. The projection in *Nicky Nan: Reservist* may meet a degree of approval but the novel is 'mythic'. Quiller Couch himself was later to comment how poorly he rated his own book.[8] Joseph's modernising vision made compromises in its literariness, but told it like it was for the population - who were then more interested in the Western Front. In essence, though Quiller Couch could be both sympathetic observer and critic of Methodism, Hocking was a believer. Therein, lies the difference, and also the problem.

The irony about all the Hocking books is that though they were intended to be a modernising influence, their language and debate was dated. We therefore have a problem in their novels: the maintenance of orthodoxy alongside modernity - but it is clear that the Hockings never really had the philosophising mentality to allow this debate to be resolved in their fiction. This may be related back to their childhood and education: Salome's education was limited; Silas studied, but did not go to College, and while Joseph did go to College, Methodist training during this phase was very narrow. Paradoxically, though Methodism had arisen as part of a wider pan-European radical response to the Enlightenment, the Hockings' own literary radicalism was too 'larded' with Methodism for its own good. Here we may ask two crucial and possibly unanswerable questions: Did the Hockings' novels merely confirm the views of the pew, saying what people wanted them to say, or did they actually bring more people into chapels throughout Britain?[9] Did their didacticism work or was their unctuousness (as viewed eventually by Eveline Clemo and the parish of St Stephen-in-Brannel) distasteful?

Another related comparison may be helpful in at least beginning to answer these questions: if William Carvasso's early nineteenth-century Methodism was all about spirituality and introspection,[10] then the Hocking's late-nineteenth and early twentieth-century Methodism was about social change, about being worldly-wise and perceptive. Perhaps their work would have been more canonized had it embraced a greater spirituality, like Carvasso or even Jack Clemo. That said, the 'great' novelists of the nineteenth century who depicted Cornwall, were actually visitors. Like Quiller Couch, but to a far greater extent, they wrote a mythic Methodism that never existed.[11] If we seek a more 'honest' Cornish Methodism in fiction, then as I hope, as this book has shown, we need only to look to the Hockings. In so doing, we look more honestly at ourselves and our own religious, cultural and literary past.

There might also be some benefit from moving our debate outside Cornwall, in comparing say Arnold Bennett's *Five Towns* sequence of Pottery novels[12] - generally regarded as some of the finest depictions of Methodist life in fiction - to the Hockings, but really this is unnecessary. We are back to judgement and the canon, and away from the people and the popular. Despite their novels sometimes reading as if they (in all seriousness) were the religious wing of the Liberal Party, their popularity, in the face of all the writers mentioned above, can never be denied. Joseph alone, sold four million copies of his novels.[13] A friend has joked with me that a useful comparison to the Hockings may be made with the best-selling romantic novelist, Barbara Cartland. In her fiction, female characters 'dream of the husbands they never got': in the Hocking novels, Methodists 'dream of the conversions they never got'. This may seem flippant, but there is much truth in it. It was the fictionalisation of the Methodist dream that leads us closest to understanding the Hockings' work and to answering the questions above.

Alongside this, an auxiliary outcome of this study is that the Hockings have facilitated a discussion of Methodism in Cornwall from a historical perspective, and in so doing has allowed us to examine the contribution of religion to a sense of 'national' identity in Cornwall, running from the Enlightenment to the Present. The Hockings, above any other Anglo-Cornish writers I am aware of, show that the history of a territory can only be truly understood when the religious dimension of issues of identity in writing are discussed at length. This fact has been ignored by too many literary observers and Methodist scholars, as well as those who write the history of Cornwall.

However, having studied their lives for some years, at the end of their story, I am reminded most of all here of Salome's slow realisation of modernity: how her 'hitherto unquestioned beliefs were subjected and exposed to the burning light of rational criticism, until one after another they shrivelled and died, dropping by the way like autumn leaves'.[14] It is both a sad and controversial note to finish on, but I am convinced that despite a lifetime's faith in Methodism, both Salome and Silas Kitto Hocking reached this point. Their journey to this realisation began in childhood, when they recognised the unfairness of the three-life system, and later the incapacity of the Anglican church to provide their spiritual needs, but due to the 'crisis' of industry, politics and war, at the end of the day, even nonconformist Methodism had, eventually, to be rethought. It was a sad day for both Salome and Silas Kitto when they realised this. Silas, in particular, was 'punch drunk' from modernity's blows.

The decline in interest in the Hockings also patterns this wider decline in Methodism in general. In a discussion paper written in 1979, Probert identified the core questions which Methodism needs to confront for its survival. The question he puts are as relevant now as they were then; they are also profoundly relevant to the eventual crisis of faith of Salome and Silas Kitto Hocking:

1. How much should a church partake of the spirit of the age and how much should it be a revolt against it?

2. How typical is Cornish Methodism? Is it the odd man out? Jabez Bunting called the Cornish 'the mob of Methodism'. Since Methodist Union it seems to have lost the Wesleyan tradition of worship to a much greater extent than elsewhere.

3. Does Methodism need to rediscover something of the order, and decorum of worship, and the taste of the classical age?[15]

Salome would have understood these questions. She had felt 'the burning light of rational criticism' as a woman and a feminist, and was someone, who, at the dawn of the twentieth century realised that the secular world of what eventually would become 'Green' politics, was the way forward. Silas Kitto had learnt that religion sometimes brought about conflict, and rationally, at the end of his life, he was more committed to peace and justice, than to Methodism. He had witnessed his own ministry fail him, realising its own outmodedness in communicating with the people - his reason for initially writing his vision of pulp Methodism. The writing on the wall told Silas that while his moral fiction had shaped British society in the past, it would no longer continue to do so.

Joseph is the anomaly. He is a different case. Younger, vitriolic and more confident than both his older brother and sister in the irrefutable destiny of Protestantism, he was not to undergo the same crisis of faith. Essentially Joseph was the last of his breed of Cornishmen - a man fighting a rearguard action, a battle having its roots in the Reformation and in Wesley's journeying to Cornwall two centuries earlier. Up until his death, I suspect Joseph Hocking blindly thought pulp Methodism the world's solution and that a new period of nonconformist evangelism would soon arrive.

Despite these shifts and differences, it is hard to imagine what all three of the Hockings would have made of contemporary Cornwall with industries so familiar to them - like fishing and tin mining in decline and stasis, its growing dependence on tourism - an anathema to all three siblings, and its further secularisation. John Angarrack has drawn attention to what he terms 'propaganda, censorship, deception and the manipulation of public opinion in Cornwall' in his controversial book *Breaking the Chains*,[16] exposing centralisation, repression and neo-colonialism. As our book here has shown, the Hockings would actually have had much to agree with Angarrack's position. One of his key targets in this repression in Cornwall is the Anglican Church, who had, and continue to have, many of the instruments of colonial control.[17] In the light of this, and a conference on the use and decline of Methodist chapels,[18] Angarrack has questioned in the *Western Morning News*: 'Is Cornwall ready for a religious merger?' between the Anglican and Methodist churches.[19]

Not only are religious issues of key consequence to Angarrack, but also land ownership, landlords and control, form a central pillar of the 'English' empire 'writing back' against the centre. Angarrack argues that generations of Cornish people have been exploited and ruined by the landed gentry (Anglican in beliefs), many of whom were part of the English mechanisms of control. Any merger between the Anglican church and Methodism would surely see the Hockings turn in their graves. When we read the Hocking novels in this light, we see that far from being cosy 'ethical fictions' or 'novels of purpose' their narratives had radical implications both against the methods of control of the Cornish and for promoting nonconformity. In line with Angarrack, the Hockings devoted much time in their work to celebrating their Cornishness and Celticity. For them, their identity would have been hard to frame in a 'nationalist' context (nationalism of this kind, was only just beginning to emerge as a pan-European philosophical system), yet from a social justice position, all three writers would have empathised with Angarrack's essential arguments.

There has been much to consider in this book about the place of Methodism within Cornwall. This is important since it seems to this observer at least that so much cultural activity in Cornwall (especially from the Anglican position) has keenly attempted to deny the occurrence of the Methodist Revival and the Industrial Revolution.[20] The one time Canon of Truro, H. Miles Brown, writing in 1976, is one of the few going against this trend, describing in a narrative way the prevalence of

Methodism in Cornwall, as well as its relationship to Anglicanism.[21] The argument however, of the linkage, not to mention lineage of Methodism in Cornwall's Christian history was put much more forcibly by the former Vicar of St Just-in-Penwith, Thomas Taylor, some sixty years earlier. Though still somewhat critical, Taylor, like the Hockings, did at least identify Methodism as part of his overall argument – part of the destiny of the religion in the territory:

During the last quarter of a century a remarkable change has passed over the face of Cornish nonconformity. Revivals have almost become a thing of the past. Conversion, theoretically the starting point of Methodist religion, is no longer required to be sudden. The class meeting has lost much of its effectiveness. There is less reverence for the Holy Scriptures. Many of the old doctrines are being recast. Methodism is in a state of transition. The drift is towards rationalism, but the end is not in sight. Under these circumstances it is not easy to form a right judgment or to forecast the future of Cornish Methodism, but to one who has spent twenty-five years in its midst and who knows how deeply and instinctively religious is the character of the people it would seem that at a no distant date there with be a volte-face, in other words, that the essentially religious instinct will reassert itself.[22]

However, Taylor continues by drawing attention to the future. In very many ways, his words are as relevant now to spiritual needs in Cornwall, as they were at the start of the twentieth century:

Two attitudes may supervene. There may be a return to the Catholic faith, Anglican or Roman, of which there are already signs or there may be a recourse to Christian Science, Spiritualism or some occult system, which attracts by its novelty and promises to satisfy religious craving. Rationalism, which may suit the Teutonic race and be a substitute for religion, is impossible to the emotional God-fearing Celt.[23]

Taylor might have been surprised that not only nonconformity, but also Catholicism and Anglicism, have not 'returned' in the way he felt was the natural course for the Celts of Cornwall. He would have been even more shocked to find Cornwall as a central space and place in much neo-pagan thought and theory.[24] Given this, it seems that the process 'worked-through' in the lifetime of Silas Kitto Hocking was actually eventually less spiritual and more rationalist, especially after events of the First World War. In any reading of Silas's texts, this process of change, in a way patterning the wider picture of religion and nonconformity in Cornwall, needs to be held in mind. This may also be said of Salome Hocking Fifield, who already had interests in alternative spirituality and lifestyle, which took her away from Taylor's 'religious craving'. The same, however, cannot be said for Joseph Hocking, who began as a hard-line Protestant and never faltered throughout his career. In the end, a more ecumenical world would show the effects of religious change and perhaps inevitably, down the road, merger.

Perceptively, Taylor also identifies rationalism, that one element, so lacking in the Hockings' fiction, but so much a part of Silas and Salome towards the ends of their life, as another possible future. Joseph may not have wanted to know it, but he knew it lurked beneath all that he said and wrote. As readers and thinkers, we know that, like many other peoples across the globe, 'the emotional God-fearing Celt' has embraced 'the burning light of rational criticism' too.[25] This is not, I suspect, a view or a conclusion that all will agree with, nor necessarily want to hear. It is, however, correct. Pulp Methodism is, in the end, as fleeting as those chapels which punctuate the childhood landscape of the Hockings, Clemo and myself. It would, however, be fitting to see the Hockings recognised by historians of Methodism, and for their home and origins to be incorporated into the wider Methodist heritage trail of Cornwall.[26]

Walking, as I often do, around a route which takes me past the Hockings' cottage at Terras, through Hallivick, Trelion, South Terras, it is hard now to see any remains of the tin industry there. Every time I pass through, I think of James Hocking's discovery of tin in the old Bible Christian chapel walls; Salome working on the fields of Broadmoor, Silas and friends telling stories in the old smith's shop, Joseph minded of wizards, wreckers and ghosts. The Hockings are still very much part of this landscape – a pulp Methodism found reverberating around the banks of the Fal Valley and far beyond. These were the old 'Ockings. I pause and test for echo. I know I shall hear new readings.

Notes

1. Salome Hocking (1903) *Some Old Cornish Folk,* London: Charles H. Kelly, pp.175-6.
2. *The Black Letter Pamphlet: News from Pe[n]rin in Cornwall of a most Bloody and un-exampled Murder.* Quarto, Bodley, 4 M G29(2), Oxford.
3. See John B. Cornish (ed.) (1971 [1894]) *The Autobiography of a Cornish Smuggler (Captain Harry Carter, of Prussia Cove) 1749-1809,* Truro: D. Bradford Barton; for John Harris, see Alan M. Kent (ed.) (2000) *Voices from West Barbary: An Anthology of Anglo-Cornish Poetry 1549-1928,* London: Francis Boutle, pp.125-44; R.M. Ballantyne (1868) *Deep Down: A Tale of the Cornish Mines,* London: Blackie and Son; Francis F. Cobb (1948 [1876]) *The Watchers on the Longships,* Redhill: Wells Gardner; F. Frankfurt Moore (1887) *Tre, Pol and Pen.* London: SPCK;
4. Arthur Quiller Couch (ed.) (1941) *Cornish Tales by Charles Lee,* London: J.M.Dent; D.M. Thomas (1983) *Selected Poems,* Harmondsworth: Penguin; K.C. Phillipps (1994) *Catching Cornwall in Flight.* St Austell: Cornish Hillside Publications.
5. Arthur Quiller Couch (1903) *Hetty Wesley.* London: Harper and Brothers; (1906) *Sir John Constantine,* London: Smith and Elder.
6. Arthur Quiller Couch (1915) *Nicky Nan: Reservist.* London: William Blackwood and Sons.
7. See Cedric J. Appleby, 'Sir Arthur Quiller Couch and Methodism in Polperro' in *Journal of the Cornish Methodist Historical Association,* No. 2 (1998), p.42-9. Quiller Couch's grandfather, the naturalist, Jonathan Couch, was a member of the Wesleyan Methodist Association. Generally there are two schools of thought on Quiller Couch's views on Methodism. The first suggests that he was both satirical and critical. The second is that he was sympathetic. This author's view is that he could be both, as indeed he was with Anglicanism.
8. Ibid., p.44. However, Quiller Couch's biographer, F. Brittain, disagreed with Q's own assessment.
9. As far as I can find, there is no evidence suggesting that a Hocking novel by itself converted anyone.
10. William Carvosso (1835) *The Efficacy of Faith in the Atonement of Christ: A Memoir,* London: Wesleyan Conference Office.
11. See observation in Alan M. Kent (2000) *The Literature of Cornwall: Continuity, Identity, Difference 1000-2000,* Bristol: Redcliffe, p.130-41.
12. See Arnold Bennett (2001 [1902]) *Anna of the Five Towns,* Harmondsworth: Penguin.
13. *Cornishman,* 10th March (1937), p.7. The same article commends Joseph for his fiction 'tinged with a religious spirit exceeded by low writers' and how 'more than any other writer he conveyed the atmosphere of nonconformity in Cornwall' yet ironically criticises him for his 'adherence to a mechanical plot'.
14. Salome Hocking (1905) *Belinda the Backward: A Romance of Modern Idealism,* London: Arthur C. Fifield, p.12.
15. John C.C. Probert, 'The Decline of Methodism: A Discussion Paper' in *Journal of the Cornish Methodist Historical Association,* No.3 (1979), pp.117-20. Bunting's comment may be attributed to Samuel Drew.
16. John Angarrack (1999) *Breaking the Chains: Propaganda, Censorship, Deception and the Manipulation of Public Opinion in Cornwall,* Camborne: Cornish Stannary Publications.
17. Ibid., pp.78-98.
18. English Heritage (2001) 'Historic Methodist Chapels in Cornwall: Bane or Blessing?' Conference, held at Truro School, 16th-18th July.
19. John Angarrack, 'Is Cornwall ready for a religious merger?' in *Western Morning News,* 7th August (2001), pp. 20-1. For background to this, see Cedric J. Appleby, 'When Cornish Methodist Ministers went to Prison' in *Journal of the Cornish Methodist Historical Association,* No.2 (1999), pp.32-38.
20. A position still perpetuated by the Cornish Gorseth, and perhaps symbolised by the fact that the Grand Bard's chair is held in the Anglican Truro Cathedral.

21. H. Miles Brown (1976) *A Century for Cornwall: The Diocese of Truro,* 1877-1977, Truro: Oscar Blackford, p.6 and p.13.
22. Thomas Taylor (1916) *The Celtic Christianity of Cornwall,* London: Longmans, Green and Company, pp.102-3. Interestingly, the myth of Cornish religiosity is challenged by the 1851 Census, which suggests that church attendance in Cornwall is worse than in Devon.
23. Ibid. For a useful perspective on this, see Thomas Shaw (1962) *Saint Petroc and John Wesley, Apostles in Cornwall: An Examination of the Celtic Background of Cornish Methodism,* Cornwall: Cornish Methodist Historical Association.
24. Core studies here include Hamish Miller and Paul Broadhurst (1989) *The Sun and the Serpent: An Investigation into Earth Energies.* Launceston: Pendragon Press; John Michell (1995) *The New View over Atlantis,* London: Thames and Hudson; Cheryl Straffon (1993) *Pagan Cornwall: Land of the Goddess,* St Just-in-Penwith: Meyn Mamvro Publications. See also *Meyn Mamvro* magazine.
25. See Peggy Pollard (1941) *Beunans Alysaryn,* St Ives: Lanham. For observations on agnosticism in this work, see Alan M. Kent (1998) *Wives, Mothers and Sisters: Feminism, Literature and Women Writers of Cornwall,* Penzance: The Jamieson Library, pp.33-5. See the depiction of this new Cornish spiritual order in the fiction and poetry of D.M. Thomas (1980) *Birthstone,* London: Victor Gollancz; Alan M. Kent (1995) *Out of the Ordinalia,* St. Austell: Lyonesse Press; N.R. Phillipps (1996) *The Horn of Strangers,* Tiverton: Halsgrove.
26. Cornish Methodist Heritage (n.d.) *A Guide to Trewint, Gwennap Pit, Carharrack, Kerley Downs, Innis, Gwithian and Other Places,* Pamphlet, Cornwall: Publisher unknown. St Stephen-in-Brannel does not feature.

Bibliography

Within the Primary Sources section, I offer what I believe is a full bibliography of all Hocking family titles, except for the work of Anne Hocking. For clarification, these are the earliest dates of publication I can trace with four entries of the most recent editions. Sometimes there were numerous editions published, often undated. Occasionally, as is the case with Joseph Hocking's *And Shall Trelawney Die?* and *The Mist on the Moor: A Romance of the Parish of Alternun*, the two stories were later placed in one volume. There were sometimes slight variations in titles and sub-titles, but I have taken the commonest in each case. The finest collection of Hocking titles currently held in Cornwall is to be found in the Cornish Studies Library, Cornwall Centre, Redruth.

Primary Sources

Hocking, Anne,

Ill Deeds Done. London: W. H. Allen and Company, n.d.

Mediterranean Murder. London: Evan Brothers, 1951

The Evil that Men Do. London: W. H. Allen and Company, 1953

Death Among the Tulips. London: W. H. Allen and Company, 1953

He had to Die. London: John Lang, 1962

Hocking [Fifield], Salome,

Granny's Hero: A Tale of Country Life. London: Publisher unknown, n.d.

The Fortunes of Riverside or Waiting and Winning. London: Partridge, 1885

Norah Lang: The Mine Girl. London: Andrew Crombie, 1886

Jacky: A Story of Everyday Life. London: Andrew Crombie, 1887

Chronicles of a Quiet Family: A Temperance Story. London: Andrew Crombie, 1888

Beginnings. London: Andrew Crombie, n.d.

A Conquered Self. London: Publisher unknown, n.d. (Written under the pseudonym of S. Moore Carew)

'Chats with Girls'. In: *Methodist Monthly,* I, 1894

Some Old Cornish Folk. London: Charles H. Kelly, 1903

Belinda the Backward: A Romance of Modern Idealism. London: Arthur C. Fifield, 1905

Hocking, Joseph,

Harry Penhale: The Trial of His Faith. London: Andrew Crombie, 1887

Gideon Strong: Plebeian. London: Andrew Crombie, 1888

From London to Damascus. London: Ward, Lock and Company, 1889

Elrad the Hic: A Romance of the Sea of Galilee. London: Ward, Lock and Company, 1890

Jabez Easterbrook: A Religious Novel. London: Ward, Lock and Company, 1890

The Weapons of Mystery. London: Ward, Lock and Company, 1890

Zillah: A Romance. London: Ward, Lock and Company, 1892

Ishmael Pengelly: An Outcast. London: Ward, Lock and Company, 1893

The Story of Andrew Fairfax. London: Ward, Lock and Company, 1893

The Monk of Mar-Saba. London: Ward, Lock and Company, 1894

'Novels and Novel Writers'. In: *Methodist Monthly,* IV, 1894

All Men are Liars. London: Ward, Lock and Company, 1895

The Mist on the Moors: A Romance of the Parish of Alternun. London: Ward, Lock and Company, 1895

Fields of Fair Renown. London: Ward, Lock and Company, 1896

And Shall Trelawney Die? London: Ward, Lock and Company, 1897

The Birthright: Being the Adventurous History of Jaspar Pennington of Pennington in the County of Cornwall. London: Ward, Lock and Company, 1897

Mistress Nancy Molesworth. London: Ward, Lock and Company, 1898

The Scarlet Woman. London: Ward, Lock and Company, 1899

The Romance of Michael Trevail. London: Cassell and Company, 1900

The Purple Robe. London: Ward, Lock and Company, 1900

The Madness of David Baring. London: Hodder and Stoughton, 1900

O'er Moor and Fen: A Tale of Methodist Life in Lancashire. London: Hodder and Stoughton, 1901

Lest We Forget. London: Ward, Lock and Company, 1901

Greater Love: A Cornish Romance. London: Ward, Lock and Company, 1902

A Flame of Fire: Being the History of the Adventures of Three Englishmen at the Time of the Great Armada. London: Cassell and Company, 1903

Follow the Gleam: A Tale of the Time of Oliver Cromwell. London: Hodder and Stoughton, 1903

Esau and *St Issey.* London: Ward, Lock and Company, 1904

The Coming of the King. London: Ward, Lock and Company, 1904

Roger Trewinion. London: Ward, Lock and Company, 1905

The Chariots of the Lord. London: The Religious Tract Society 1905

The Man Who Rose Again. London: Hodder and Stoughton, 1906

The Woman of Babylon. London: Cassell and Company, 1906

A Strong Man's Vow. London: Cassell and Company, 1907

The Trampled Cross. London: Hodder and Stoughton, 1907

The Soul of Dominic Wildthorne. London: Hodder and Stoughton, 1908

The Sword of the Lord: A Romance of the Time of Martin Luther. London: Cassell and Company, 1909

The Prince of this World. London: Ward, Lock and Company, 1910

The Wilderness. London: Hodder and Stoughton, 1911

The Bells of St Ia. London: Hodder and Stoughton, 1911

The Jesuit. London: Cassell and Company, 1911

God and Mammon. London: Ward, Lock and Company, 1912

Rosaleen O'Hara: A Romance of Ireland. London: Hodder and Stoughton, 1912

Is Home Rule Rome Rule? London: Publisher unknown, 1912

The Reformation: The Anglo-Catholic Peril. London: Publisher unknown. c.1912

The Spirit of the West. London: Cassell and Company, 1913

Facing Fearful Odds. London: Hodder and Stoughton, 1914

An Enemy Hath Done This. London: Ward, Lock and Company, 1914

Dearer than Life: A Romance of the Great War. London: Hodder and Stoughton, 1915

All for a Scrap of Paper: A Romance of the Present War. London: Hodder and   Stoughton, 1915

The Dust of Life. London: Cassell and Company, 1915

The Day of Judgement. London: Cassell and Company, 1915

Tommy: A War Story. London: Hodder and Stoughton, 1916
The Passion for Life. London: The Religious Tract Society, 1916
The Curtain of Fire. London: Hodder and Stoughton, 1916
The Path of Glory. London: Hodder and Stoughton, 1917
Tommy and the Maid of Athens. London: Hodder and Stoughton, 1917
The Pomp of Yesterday. London: Hodder and Stoughton, 1918
The Price of a Throne. London: Hodder and Stoughton, 1918
The Kaiser's Investments. London: Ward, Lock and Company, 1920
In the Sweat of Thy Brow. London: Hodder and Stoughton, 1920
The Everlasting Arms. London: Hodder and Stoughton, 1920
Out of this Wreck. London: Hodder and Stoughton, 1920*
The Ring of Destiny. London: Hodder and Stoughton, 1921
The Man who Almost Lost. London: Hodder and Stoughton, 1922
The Girl who Defied the World. London: Hodder and Stoughton, 1922
Prodigal Daughters. London: Cassell and Company, 1922
The Game and the Candle. London: Hodder and Stoughton, 1923
The Case of Miss Dunstable. London: Hodder and Stoughton, 1923
Prodigal Parents. London: Hodder and Stoughton, 1923
What Shall it Profit a Man? London: Hodder and Stoughton, 1924
Rosemary Carew: Just a Love Story. London: Hodder and Stoughton, 1925
The All Conquering Power. London: Hodder and Stoughton, 1925
The Wagon and the Star. London: Hodder and Stoughton, 1925
Heartsease: The Story of a Feud. London: Ward, Lock and Company, 1926
Andrew Boconnoc's Will: The Story of a Crisis. London: Cassell and Company, 1926
Bevil Granville's Handicap. London: Hodder and Stoughton, 1926
The Tenant of Cromlech Cottage. London: Ward, Lock and Company, 1927
The Eternal Challenge. London: Hodder and Stoughton, 1928
Felicity Treverbyn: A Love Story. London: Hodder and Stoughton, 1928
Nancy Trevanion's Legacy. London: Ward, Lock and Company, 1928
Sham. New York: Publisher unknown, 1929
The Constant Enemy. London: Hodder and Stoughton, 1929
The Sign of the Triangle. London: Ward, Lock and Company, 1929
The God that Answers by Fire. London: Cassell and Company, 1930
Out of the Depths. London: Ward, Lock and Company, 1930
The Secret of Trescobell. London: Ward, Lock and Company, 1931
The Man Who was Sure. London: Hodder and Stoughton, 1931
The Eternal Choice. London: Hodder and Stoughton, 1932
Caleb's Conquest. London: Ward, Lock and Company, 1932
The Man Who Found Out. London: Ward, Lock and Company, 1933
Not One in Ten. London: Hodder and Stoughton, 1933
And Grant a Leader Bold. London: Hodder and Stoughton, 1934
No Other Name. London: Ward, Lock and Company, 1934
The Squire of Zabuloe. London: Hodder and Stoughton, 1935

Deep Calleth Unto Deep. London: Hodder and Stoughton, 1936

Davey's Ambition. London, Ward, Lock and Company, 1936

The Secret of Trescobell. Bath: Lythway Press, 1969 [1931]

Davey's Ambition. Bath: Lythway Press, 1970 [1936]

Hocking, Joseph and Horton, R.F.,

Shall Rome Reconquer England? London: National Council of Evangelical Free Churches, 1910

Hocking, Silas Kitto,

Alec Green: A Tale of Sea Life. London: Frederick Warne and Company, 1878

Her Benny: A Story of Street Life. London: Frederick Warne and Company, 1879

His Father or A Mother's Legacy. London: Frederick Warne and Company, 1880

Reedyford or Creed and Character. London: Frederick Warne and Company, 1880

Chips: A Story of Manchester Life. London: Frederick Warne and Company, 1881

Ivy: A Tale of Cottage Life. London: Frederick Warne and Company, 1881

Poor Mike: The Story of a Waif. London: Frederick Warne and Company, 1882

Sea Waif: A Tale of the Cornish Cliffs. London: Frederick Warne and Company, 1882

Dick's Fairy: A Tale of the Streets. London: Frederick Warne and Company, 1883

Caleb Carthew: A Life Story. London: Frederick Warne and Company, 1884

Our Joe. London: Frederick Warne and Company, 1885

Cricket: A Tale of Humble Life. London: Frederick Warne and Company, 1886

Up the Rhine and Over the Alps. London: Andrew Crombie and the Denominational Press of UMFC, 1886

For Such is Life. London: Frederick Warne and Company, 1887

Real Grit. London: London: Frederick Warne and Company, 1887

Crookleigh: A Village Story. London: Frederick Warne and Company, 1888

For Abigail: A West Country Story. London: Frederick Warne and Company, 1888

Social Models: A Series of Addresses on Social Themes. London: Frederick Warne and Company, 1889

Rex Raynor, Artist: A Story of Sowing and Reaping. London: Frederick Warne and Company, 1890

Tregeagle's Head: A Romance of the Cornish Cliffs. London: Frederick Warne and Company, 1890

'Chips', Joe and Mike. London: Frederick Warne and Company, 1890

For Light and Liberty. London: Frederick Warne and Company, 1892

Where Duty Lies. London: Frederick Warne and Company, 1892

One in Charity. London: Frederick Warne and Company, 1893

Sweethearts Yet: Chapters on Love and Home. London: Frederick Warne and Company, 1894

A Son of Reuban. London: Frederick Warne and Company, 1894

The Blindness of Madge Tyndall. London: Frederick Warne and Company, 1894

Doctor Dick and Other Tales. London: Frederick Warne and Company, 1895

The Heart of Man. London: Frederick Warne and Company, 1895

In Spite of Fate. London: Frederick Warne and Company, 1897

For Such is Life. London: Frederick Warne and Company, 1897

God's Outcast. London: Frederick Warne and Company, 1898

Tales of a Tin Mine. London: Horace Marshall and Son, 1898

The Culture of Manhood. London: Publisher unknown, 1898
The Day of Recompense. London: Frederick Warne and Company, 1899
The Strange Adventures of Israel Pendray. London: Frederick Warne and Company, 1899
To Pay the Price. London: Frederick Warne and Company, 1900
When Life is Young. London: Frederick Warne and Company, 1900
The Fate of Endilloe. London: Frederick Warne and Company, 1901
The Awakening of Anthony Weir. London: The Religious Tract Society, 1901
Gripped. London: Frederick Warne and Company, 1902
The Wizard's Light. London: Frederick Warne and Company, 1902
A Bonnie Saxon. London: Frederick Warne and Company, 1903
The Tempter's Power. London: Frederick Warne and Company, 1903
The Adventure of Latimer Field, Curate. London: Frederick Warne and Company, 1903
Smoking Flax. London: S.W. Partridge and Company, 1904
Chapters in Democratic Christianity. London: Publisher unknown, 1904
Meadowsweet and Rue. London: T. Fisher Unwin, 1904
The Scarlet Clue. London: Frederick Warne and Company, 1904
Pioneers. London: Frederick Warne and Company, 1905
The Flaming Sword. London: Frederick Warne and Company, 1905
The Earnest Life. London: S.W. Partridge, 1905
The Conquering Will. London: Frederick Warne and Company, 1905
A Gamble with Life. London: James Clarke and Company, 1906
A Human Face. London: Cassell and Company, 1906
The Squire's Daughter. London: Frederick Warne and Company, 1906
St. Gwynifer. London: Hodder and Stoughton, 1907
A Modern Pharisee. London: Frederick Warne and Company, 1907
The Silent Man. London: Frederick Warne and Company, 1907
The Shadow Between. London: Frederick Warne and Company, 1908
Yours and Mine. London: Frederick Warne and Company, 1908
A Desperate Hope. London: Frederick Warne and Company, 1909
Who Shall Judge? London: Frederick Warne and Company, 1910
The Quenchless Fire. London: Frederick Warne and Company, 1911
The Third Man. London: Cassell and Company, 1911
The Wrath of Man. London: Frederick Warne and Company, 1912
Smuggler's Keep. London: Frederick Warne and Company, 1913
A Woman's Love. London: Cassell and Company, 1913
Sword and Cross. London: Stanley Paul, 1914
Uncle Peter's Will. London: Ward, Lock and Company, 1914
In Self Defence. London: Publisher unknown, 1914
The Angel of the Desert. London: Ward, Lock and Company, 1915
The Great Hazard. London: Publisher unknown, 1915
The Beautiful Alien. London: Sampson Low, Marston and Company, 1916
A Man's Work. London: Publisher unknown, 1916
When He Came to Himself. London: Publisher unknown, 1916

His Own Accuser. London: Sampson Low, Marston and Company, 1917

Camouflage. London: Sampson Low, Marston and Company, 1918

Nancy. London: Sampson Low, Marston and Company, 1919

Without the Gate. London: Publisher unknown, 1919

Watchers in the Dawn. London: Sampson Low, Marston and Company, 1920

An Interrupted Romance. London: Sampson Low, Marston and Company, 1921

The Greater Good. London: Sampson Low, Marston and Company, 1922

Where the Roads Cross. London: Sampson Low, Marston and Company, 1922

My Book of Memory: A String of Reminiscences and Reflections. London: Cassell and Company, 1923

The Lost Lode. London: Sampson Low, Marston and Company, 1923

The Guarded Way. London: Sampson Low, Marston and Company, 1924

Lonehead Farm. London: Sampson Low, Marston and Company, 1925

The Crooked Trail. London: Sampson Low, Marston and Company, 1925

The Conquering Will. London: Publisher unknown, 1925

The Sinister Shadow. London: Sampson Low, Marston and Company, 1926

Miss Ann's Lodger. London: Sampson Low, Marston and Company, 1927

The Broken Fence. London: Sampson Low, Marston and Company, 1928

The Winds of Chance. London: Sampson Low, Marston and Company, 1928

The Exile's Return. London: Sampson Low, Marston and Company, 1929

The Mystery Man. London: Sampson Low, Marston and Company, 1930

The Perplexities of Peter. London: Publisher unknown, 1933

Gerry Storm: A Novel. London: Sampson Low, Marston and Company, 1934

Looking Back. London: Cassell and Company, 1936

Her Benny: A Tale of Victorian Liverpool. Liverpool: Gallery Press, 1992 [1879]

Chips: A Tale of Victorian Manchester. Liverpool: Gallery Press, 1992 [1881]

Secondary Sources
Manuscripts & Papers

The Black Letter Pamphlet: News from Pe[n]rin in Cornwall of a most Bloody and un-exampled Murder. Quarto, Bodley, 4 M G29(2), Oxford.

Borlase, William C. (1871) *Ancient Cornwall, a collection of drawings etc, Original and copied, illustrative of the Antiquities of that County,* MS., Courtney Library, Royal Institution of Cornwall.

Census 1851, Cornwall Records Office, Truro.

Census 1861, Cornwall Records Office, Truro.

Census 1871, Cornwall Records Office, Truro.

Charles Henderson Collection, Courtney Library, Royal Institution of Cornwall, Truro.

Ground Rent Receipts collection, Courtney Library, Royal Institution of Cornwall, Truro.

Last Will and Testament of Arthur C. Fifield, Probate Registry, Purley.

Last Will and Testament of Joseph Hocking, Probate Registry, Bodmin.

Last Will and Testament of Salome Hocking Fifield, Probate Registry, Purley.

Last Will and Testament of Silas Kitto Hocking, Probate Registry, Bodmin.

Leonard W. Harman MS. In possession of the author.

Parish Index, Cornwall Records Office, Truro.

Shaw Cornish Methodism Collection, Courtney Library, Royal Institution of Cornwall, Truro.
Treffry Deeds, Cornwall Records Office, Truro.

Newspapers, Magazines & Periodicals

An Baner Kernewek / The Cornish Banner
Bible Christian Magazine
Bioscope
British Weekly
Cornish Guardian
Cornish Magazine
Cornishman
Cornish Methodism
Cornish Review
Cornish Scene: New Series
Cornubian
Daily Mail
Diegesis: Journal of the Association of Research in Popular Fictions
Family Circle
Horner's Penny Stories
John Harris Society Newsletter
Journal of the Cornish Methodist Historical Association
Journal of the Royal Institution of Cornwall
Kinematograph
Leisure Hour
Liverpool Mercury
Methodist Monthly
Meyn Mamvro
Mining Journal
Mining World
Old Cornwall
Plymouth Evening Herald
Sunday Guardian
Temple Magazine: Silas K. Hocking's Illustrated Monthly
Vanity Fair
West Briton and Cornish Adverstiser
Western Morning News

Books, Articles & Pamplets

Ackroyd, Peter, *Dickens*. London: Minerva, 1991 [1990]
    London: The Biography. London: Chatto and Windus, 2000

Adamson, Ian, *Cruthin: The Ancient Kindred*. Belfast: Pretani Press, 1974

Alvarez, A. and Skilton, David (eds.), *Thomas Hardy: Tess of the D'Urbervilles*. Harmondsworth: Penguin, 1978 [1871]

Angarrack, John, *Breaking the Chains: Propaganda, Censorship, Deception and the Manipulation of Public Opinion in Cornwall*. Camborne: Cornish Stannary Publications, 1999
    'Is Cornwall ready for a religious merger? In: *Western Morning News*, 7th August, 2001

Appleby, Cedric J., "Marching as to War': Cornish Methodists and the "Great War"'. In: *Journal of the Cornish Methodist Historical Association*, No.4, 1994
    'Sir Arthur Quiller Couch and Methodism in Polperro'. In: *Journal of the Cornish Methodist Historical Association*, No. 2, 1998
    'When Cornish Methodist Ministers went to Prison'. In: *Journal of the Cornish Methodist Historical Association*, No.2, 1999

Ashcroft, Bill, Griffiths, Gareth and Tiffin, Helen, *The Empire Writes Back: Theory and Practice in Post-Colonial Literatures*. London and New York: Routledge 1989

Atkins, G. Douglas and Morrow, Laura (eds.), *Contemporary Literary Theory*. London and Boston: Macmillan, 1989

Ballantyne, R.M., *Deep Down: A Tale of the Cornish Mines*. London: Blackie and Son, 1868

Barton, R. M., *A History of the Cornish China Clay Industry*. Truro: Bradford Barton, 1966

Bibliography

Beckerlegge, Oliver A., *The United Methodist Free Churches: A Study in Freedom*. London: Epworth Press, 1957

United Methodist Ministers and their Circuits 1797-1932. London: Epworth Press, 1968

Behenna, P. and Caddy, Kathleen, 'Our Village – St Stephen-in-Brannel'. In: Bishop, Peter *et al* (eds.), 1994

Bennett, Arnold, *Anna of the Five Towns*. Harmondsworth: Penguin, 2001 [1902]

Bennett, Tony (ed.), *Popular Fiction: Technology, Ideology, Production, Reading*. London and New York, Routledge, 1990

Bell, Ian A. (ed.), *Peripheral Visions: Images of Nationhood in Contemporary British Fiction*. Cardiff: University of Wales Press, 1995

Bishop, Peter, Morcom, Susan, Bennett, Babs, Toms, Liz (eds.), *A Century of Change: One Hundred Years of St Stephen-in-Brannel Parish Council 1894-1994*. St Stephen-in-Brannel: St Stephen-in-Brannel Parish Council, 1994

Boconnoc, *A History of Boconnoc*. Boconnoc: Boconnoc Church, n.d.

Bott, George (ed.), *George Orwell: Selected Essays*. London: Heinemann, 1958

Bowen, Desmond, *The Protestant Crusade in Ireland*. Dublin: Gill and Macmillan, 1990

Brack, Alan, *All they need is love: The Story of the Liverpool Society for the Prevention of Cruelty to Children*. Liverpool: The Liverpool Society for the Prevention of Cruelty to Children, 1983

Bradley, Katherine, *Friends and Visitors: A History of the Woman's Suffrage Movement in Cornwall 1870-1914*. Penzance: The Jamieson Library, 2000

Bradshaw, Brendan and Morrill, John (eds.), *The British Problem c.1534-1707: State Formation in the Atlantic Archipelago*. Basingstoke: Macmillan, 1996

Brooke, Peter, *Ulster Presbyterianism*. Belfast: Athol Books, 1994

Brown, Callum G., *The Death of Christian Britain: Understanding Secularisation 1800-2000*. London and New York; Routledge, 2001

Brown, H. Miles, *A Century for Cornwall: The Diocese of Truro, 1877-1977*. Truro: Oscar Blackford, 1976

Browne, Douglas G., *Too Many Cousins*. London: MacDonald, 1948

Brunswick Chapel, *Brunswick Chapel 1869-1959 and the original Mount "Pleasant"*. Burnley: Brunswick Chapel, 1959

Busby, Graham and Hambly, Zoë, 'Literary Tourism and the Daphne du Maurier Festival'. In: Payton, Philip (ed.), 2000

Carey, John, *The Intellectuals and the Masses: Pride and Prejudice among the Literary Intelligentsia, 1880-1939*. London: Faber and Faber, 1992

Carvosso, William, *The Efficacy of Faith in the Atonement of Christ: A Memoir*. London: Wesleyan Conference Office, 1835

Chapman, Malcolm, *The Celts: The Construction of a Myth*. Basingstoke: Macmillan, 1992

Clemo, Eveline, *I Proved Thee at the Waters: The Testimony of a Blind Writer's Mother*. Ilkeston, Derbyshire: Moorley's Bible and Bookshop Ltd, c.1976

Clemo, Jack, *Wilding Graft*. London: Chatto and Windus, 1948

Confession of a Rebel. London: Chatto and Windus, 1949

The Invading Gospel: A Return to Faith. Basingstoke: Marshall Pickering, 1986 [1958]

'The Hocking Brothers'. In: *Cornish Review,* Spring, 1969

The Shadowed Bed. Tring: Lion, 1986

Selected Poems. Newcastle upon Tyne: Bloodaxe Books, 1988

The Clay Kiln. St Austell: Cornish Hillside Publications, 2000

Cobb, Francis F., *The Watchers on the Longships*. Redhill: Wells Gardner, 1948 [1876]

Collins, Wilkie, *Rambles Beyond Railways.* London: Westaway Books, 1948 [1951]

Combellack-Harris, Myrna (ed.), *Cornish Studies for Cornish Schools,* Redruth: Institute of Cornish Studies, 1989

Combined Universities in Cornwall, *Pathways to Success: Higher Education Opportunities in Cornwall.* Penryn: Combined Universities in Cornwall, 2001

Connolly, S.J. (ed.), *Kingdoms United? Great Britain and Ireland Since 1500: Integration and Diversity.* Dublin: Four Courts Press, 1999

Cornish Gorsedd at Boscawen Ün Stone Circle, near St Buryan, September 21st. In: *Cornishman,* Penzance, 1928

Cornish, John B. (ed.), *The Autobiography of a Cornish Smuggler (Captain Harry Carter, of Prussia Cove) 1749-1809.* Truro: D. Bradford Barton, 1971 [1894]

Cornish Methodist Heritage (n.d.) *A Guide to Trewint, Gwennap Pit, Carharrack, Kerley Downs, Innis, Gwithian and Other Places.* Pamphlet, Cornwall: Publisher unknown,

Courtney, Margaret, *Folklore and Legends of Cornwall [Cornish Feasts and Folklore].* Exeter: Cornwall Books, 1989 [1890]

Crago, Treve, "Play the Games as Men Play It': Women in Politics during the Era of the 'Cornish Proto-Alignment' 1918-1922'. In: Payton, Philip (ed.), 2000

Crystal, David, *The Cambridge Encyclopedia of the English Language.* Cambridge: Cambridge University Press, 1995

Cubitt, Geoffrey (ed.), *Imagining Nations.* Manchester: Manchester University Press, 1998

Daiches, David (ed.), *Emily Brontë: Wuthering Heights.* Harmondsworth: Penguin, 1965 [1847]

Darke, Nick, *Plays: 1.* London: Methuen, 1999

Davies, Rupert E., *Methodism.* Peterborough: Epworth Press, 1985 [1963]

Dawe, Richard D., *Cornish Pioneers in South Africa: Gold and Diamonds, Copper and Blood.* St Austell: Cornish Hillside Publications, 1998

Deacon, Bernard, 'Proto-Industrialization and Potatoes: A Revised Narrative for Nineteenth-Century Cornwall'. In: Payton, Philip (ed.), 1997

Deacon, Bernard and Payton, Philip, 'Re-inventing Cornwall: Cultural Change on the European Periphery'. In: Payton, Philip (ed.), 1993

Deane, Tony and Shaw Tony, *The Folklore of Cornwall.* Totowa, New Jersey: Rowman and Littlefield, 1975

Dixon, John, *A Schooling in 'English': Critical Episodes to Shape Literary and Cultural Studies.* Buckingham: Open University Press, 1991

Dorey, Michael, 'Joseph Hocking'. In: *Cornish Scene,* No.15, 1992

Doyle, Arthur Conan, *The Hound of the Baskervilles,* Harmondsworth: Penguin, 2000 [1902]

'The War in South Africa', Pamphlet, 1902

The British Campaign in France and Flanders 1915. London: Hodder and Stoughton, 1917

Dunnerdale, John, 'Joseph Hocking: The Man and His Books'. In: Lyall, David (ed.) (1903)

During, Simon (ed.), *The Cultural Studies Reader.* London and New York: Routledge, 1993

Ebbatson, Roger (ed.), *Thomas Hardy: A Pair of Blue Eyes.* Harmondsworth: Penguin, 1986 [1873]

Edmunds, Rosemary (ed. and tr.), *Leo Tolstoy: War and Peace,* 2 vols. Harmondsworth: Penguin, 1957 [1863-9]

(ed. and tr.), *Leo Tolstoy: Anna Karenina.* Harmondsworth: Penguin, 1973 [1873-7]

Ellis, Peter Berresford, *The Celtic Dawn: A History of Pan Celticism.* London: Constable, 1993

English Heritage, 'Historic Methodist Chapels in Cornwall: Bane or Blessing?' Conference, held at Truro School, Conference Programme, 16th-18th July, 2001

Evans, C.A., 'A Tudor Mansion in the Clay Country: The Story of Meledor at St. Stephen'. In: *Cornish Guardian,* n.d.

Fifield, Arthur C., *Salome Hocking Fifield: In Memoriam.* Coulsdon: Arthur C. Fifield, 1927

Fisher, Trevor, *Prostitution and the Victorian.* Stroud: Sutton, 2001

Foot, Sarah (ed.), *Methodist Celebration: A Cornish Contribution.* Redruth: Dyllansow Truran, 1988

Fuller, Simon (ed.), *The Poetry of War 1914-1989.* Harlow: Longman, 1990

Galley, R.L., *The History of Woodford Union Church.* London: Woodford Union Church, n.d.

Gazamian, Louis, *The Social Novel in England.* London and Boston: Routledge and Kegan Paul, 1973 [1903]

Giles, Judy and Middleton, Tim (eds.), *Writing Englishness 1900-1950: An Introductory Sourcebook on National Identity.* London and New York, 1995

Gillespie, Jack (ed.), *Our Cornwall: The Stories of Cornish Men and Women.* Padstow: Tabb House, 1988

Graham, Winston, *Ross Poldark 1783-87.* London: Werner Laurie, 1945

Greenwood, George A., 'Daughter of famous Cornish novelist writes her 40th book: Anne Hocking's West Reminiscences'. In: *Western Morning News,* 2nd December, 1953

Hale, Amy, 'Rethinking Celtic Cornwall: An Ethnographic Approach'. In: Payton, Philip (ed.), 1997 'Genesis of the Celto-Cornish Revival? L.C. Duncombe-Jewell and the Cowethas Kelto-Kernuack'. In: Payton, Philip (ed.), 1997

Hale, Amy and Payton, Philip (eds.), *New Directions in Celtic Studies.* Exeter: University of Exeter Press, 2000

Hale, Amy, Kent, Alan M. and Saunders, Tim (eds.), *Inside Merlin's Cave: A Cornish Arthurian Reader 1000-2000.* London: Francis Boutle, 2000

Halliday, F.E., *A History of Cornwall.* London: Duckworth, 1959

Hampton, Christopher (ed.) *A Radical Reader: The Struggle for Change in England 1381-1914.* Harmondsworth: Penguin, 1984.

The Ideology of the Text. Milton Keynes: Open University Press, 1990

Hardy, Dennis, *Utopian England: Community Experiments 1900-1945,* London: E & F. N. Spon, 2000

Harrison, George, *A Report on the Laws and Jurisdiction of the Stannaries in Cornwall.* London: Longman, Rees, Orme, Brown, Green, and Longman, 1835

Hechter, Michael, *Internal Colonialism: The Celtic Fringe in British National Development, 1536-1966.* London: Routledge and Kegan Paul, 1975

Hempton, David, *Methodism and Politics in British Society 1750-1850.* London: Hutchinson, 1984

Herring, Peter and Smith, John R., *The Archaeology of the St Austell China Clay Area.* Truro: Cornwall Archaeological Unit, 1991

Hill, Kerrow, *The Brontë Sisters and Sir Humphry Davy: A Sharing of Visions.* Penzance: The Jamieson Library, 1994

Hirst, Derek, 'The English Republic and the Meaning of Britain'. In: Bradshaw, Brendan and Morrill, John (eds.), 1996

Hoare, George and Stanhope, Alan, *Towards a University in Cornwall: Developments in Higher Education – an update.* Camborne: Cornwall College, 1999

Hocking, F.D.M., *Bodies and Crimes.* London: The Book Guild, 1992

Horton, Robert Forman: *An Autobiography.* London: George Allen and Unwin Ltd, 1917

Hudson, W.H., *The Land's End: A Naturalist's Impressions in West Cornwall.* London: Wildwood House, 1981 [1908]

Hunt, Robert (ed.), *The Drolls, Traditions, and Superstitions of Old Cornwall: Popular Romances of the West of England (First Series).* London: John Camden Hotton, 1865

Hurst, John, 'Literature in Cornwall'. In: Payton, Philip (ed.), 1993 'Voice From a White Silence: The Manuscripts of Jack Clemo'. In: Payton, Philip (ed.), 1995 'Mine, Moor and Chapel: The Poetry of John Harris'. In: Westland, Ella (ed.), 1997

Ingham, Patricia (ed.), *Thomas Hardy: The Woodlanders*. Harmondsworth: Penguin, 1998 [1887]

Isaac, Peter, *A History of Evangelical Christianity in Cornwall*. Cornwall: Peter Isaac, 2000

Ivey, Allen E., and Payton, Philip, 'Towards a Cornish Identity Theory'. In: Payton, Philip (ed.), 1994

James-Korany, Margaret, ''Blue Books' as Sources for Cornish Emigration History'. In: Payton, Philip (ed.), 1993

James, Louis, *Fiction for the Working Man 1830-50*. Oxford: Oxford University Press, 1963

Jenner, Henry, *A Handbook of the Cornish Language*. London: David Nutt, 1904

Johnston, Dafydd, *The Literature of Wales*. Cardiff: University of Wales Press, 1994

Jones, R. Ben, *A Political, Social and Economic History of Britain 1760-1914: The Challenge of Greatness*. London: Hodder and Stoughton, 1987

Jones, R. Brinley, *William Salesbury*. Cardiff: University of Wales Press, 1994

Julian, Herbert, 'Music in Cornish Methodism: The First 250 Years'. In: Foot, Sarah (ed.), 1988

Jump, John D. (ed.), *Tennyson: In Memoriam, Maud and Other Poems*. London: J.M. Dent, 1974

Keast, Horace, *The Catholic Revival in Cornwall*. Cornwall: Catholic Advisory Council for Cornwall, 1983

Keating, J., *A Brace of Bigots: Dr Horton and Mr Hocking*. London: Catholic Truth Society, 1909

Keen, J.O.,'*Midst Mine and Moor and Cornish Folk, or Idylls of Cornwall*, London: Bible Christian Reading Room, n.d.

Kent, Alan M., *Out of the Ordinalia*. St Austell: Lyonesse Press, 1995

'The Cornish Alps: Resisting Romance in the Clay Country'. In: Westland, Ella (ed.), 1997

Wives, Mothers and Sisters: Feminism, Literature and Women Writers of Cornwall. Penzance: The Jamieson Library, 1998

(ed.), *Voices from West Barbary: An Anthology of Anglo-Cornish Poetry 1549-1928*. London: Francis Boutle, 2000

The Literature of Cornwall: Continuity, Identity, Difference 1000-2000. Bristol: Redcliffe, 2000

Kent, Alan M. and Saunders, Tim (eds. and trs.), *Looking at the Mermaid: A Reader in Cornish Literature 900-1900*. London: Francis Boutle, 2000

Kentish, Jane (ed. and tr.), *Leo Tolstoy: A Confession and Other Religious Writings*. Harmondsworth: Penguin, 1987

Kitto, John, *The Pictorial Bible,* 3 vols. London: Charles Knight and Co., 1835-8

The Pictorial History of Palestine and the Holy Land, including a complete History of the Jews, 2 vols. London: Charles Knight and Co., 1840

The Lost Senses. London: Charles Knight and Co., 1845

Lake, Jeremy, Cox, Jo and Berry, Eric, *Diversity and Vitality: The Methodist and Nonconformist Chapels of Cornwall*. Truro: Cornwall Archaeological Unit, 2001

Langford, Thomas A., *Methodist Theology,* Peterborough: Epworth Press, 1998

Laurence, Dan H. (ed.), *Bernard Shaw: Plays Pleasant*. Harmondsworth: Penguin, 1946

Lawrence, D.H., *Lady Chatterley's Lover*. Harmondsworth: Penguin,1960 [1928]

Kangaroo. Harmondsworth: Penguin, 1975 [1923]

Lee, A. Robert (ed.), *Other Britain, Other British: Contemporary Multicultural Fiction*. London: Pluto Press, 1995

Light, Alison, *Forever England: Feminity, Literature and Conservatism between the Wars*. London: Routledge, 1991

Liverpool Empire Theatre, *Her Benny: Programme*. Liverpool: Liverpool Empire Theatre Publications, 1994

Her Benny: Flyer. Liverpool: Liverpool Empire Theatre Publications, 1994

Lyall, David (ed.), *The Secrets of Upland Farm*. London: United Methodist Free Church, 1903

MacDonald, George, *Alec Forbes of Howglen*. London: Hurst and Blackett, 1895

    The Princess and Curdie. London: Chatto and Windus, 1883

    At the Back of the North Wind. London: Blackie and Son, 1886

Maddox, Brenda, *The Married Man: A Life of D. H. Lawrence*. London: Sinclair Stevenson, 1994

Magnusson, Sally, *Clemo: A Love Story*. Tring: Lion, 1986

Maker, Lawrence, *Cob and Moorstone: The Curious History of some Cornish Methodist Churches*. London: Epworth Press, 1935

Mason, Daniel, *Cousin Jack*. Fowey: Alexander Associates, 1996

Massie, Allan, *The Novel Today*. Harlow: Longman, 1990

Matthews, John, *Amos: Amos B. Matthews, Victorian Methodist Traveller*. London: Bryant, 1992

McCann, P., *Popular Education and Serialization in the Nineteenth Century*. London: Methuen, 1977

McCord, Norman, *British History 1815-1906*. Oxford: Oxford University Press, 1991

McKinney, Gage, *A High and Holy Place: A Mining Camp Church at New Almaden*. New Almaden, California: Pine Press, 1997

Mee, Arthur, *The King's England: Cornwall*. London: Hodder and Stoughton, 1967 [1930]

Michell, John, *The New View over Atlantis*. London: Thames and Hudson, 1995

Miller, Hamish and Broadhurst, Paul, *The Sun and the Serpent: An Investigation into Earth Energies*. Launceston: Pendragon Press, 1989

Moody, Nickianne, 'Poldark Country and National Culture'. In: Westland, Ella (ed.), 1997

Moore, F. Frankfurt, *Tre, Pol and Pen*. London: SPCK, 1887

Munson, James, *The Nonconformists: In Search of a Lost Culture*. London: SPCK, 1991

Murdoch, Brian, *Cornish Literature*. Cambridge: D.S. Brewer, 1993

Newman, Paul, *The Meads of Love: The Life and Poetry of John Harris*. Redruth: Dyllansow Truran, 1994

Ollard, Richard, *A Man of Contradictions: A Life of A.L. Rowse*. London: Allen Lane, 1999

Olver, T.J., *An Account of the History of St Stephen-in-Brannel*. St Stephen-in-Brannel: St Stephen-in-Brannel Parish Church Publication, n.d.

Ordnance Survey of England, *Book of Reference to the Plan of the Parish of St Stephen-in-Brannel (Hundred of Powder)*. London: George M. Eyre and William Spottiswoode, 1880

Padel, O.J., *A Popular Dictionary of Cornish Place-Names*. Penzance: Alison Hodge, 1988

Parker, Simon, *A Star on the Mizzen*. Liskeard: Giss' On Books, 1997

Pawling, Christopher (ed.), *Popular Fiction and Social Change*. London: Macmillan, 1984

Payne, H. M. Creswell, 'Cornish Methodism in Fiction'. In: *Old Cornwall*, Vol. 5, 1958

    'Pages from the Book of Memory: A Cornish Novelist'. In: *Cornish Methodism*, 24th December, 1953

    'Pages from Book of Memory: Joseph Hocking'. In: *The Cornish Guardian*, 20 May, 1954

Payton, Philip, *The Making of Modern Cornwall: Historical Experience and the Persistence of 'Difference'*. Redruth: Dyllansow Truran, 1992

    (ed.), *Cornish Studies: One*. Exeter: University of Exeter Press, 1993

    (ed.), *Cornwall Since the War: The Contemporary History of a European Region*. Redruth: Dyllansow Truran and the Institute of Cornish Studies, 1993

    (ed.) *Cornish Studies: Two*. Exeter: University of Exeter Press, 1994

    (ed.), *Cornish Studies: Three*. Exeter: University of Exeter Press, 1995

    (ed.), *Cornish Studies: Five*. University of Exeter: University of Exeter Press, 1997

    The Cornish Overseas. Fowey: Alexander Associates, 1999

    (ed.), *Cornish Studies: Eight*. Exeter: University of Exeter Press, 2000

Pearce, John, *The Wesleys in Cornwall.* Truro: D. Bradford Barton, 1964

Pearce, Keith and Fry, Helen (eds.), *The Lost Jews of Cornwall.* Bristol: Redcliffe, 2000

Pearse, Mark Guy, *West Country Songs,* London: Horace Marshall and Co, 1902

Pellowe, Susan (ed.), *A Wesley Family Book of Days.* Aurora, Illinois, Renard Publications, 1994

Penhallurick, Roger, *Tin in Antiquity.* London: The Institute of Metals, 1986

Pennick, Nigel, *Celtic Sacred Landscape.* London: Thames and Hudson, 1996

Pevear, Richard (ed. and tr.), *Leo Tolstoy: What is Art?* Harmondsworth: Penguin, 1995

Phelps, Kenneth, *The Wormwood Cup – Thomas Hardy in Cornwall: A Study in Temperament, Topography and Timing.* Padstow: Lodenek Press, 1975

Phillipps, K.C., 'A Calling Sacrificed to Writing Novels'. In: *Western Morning News,* July, 1976

    Catching Cornwall in Flight. St Austell: Cornish Hillside Publications, 1994

Phillipps, N.R., *The Horn of Strangers.* Tiverton: Halsgrove, 1996

Pittock, Murray G.H., *Celtic Image and the British Image.* Manchester and New York: Manchester University Press, 1999

Pollard, Peggy, *Beunans Alysaryn.* St Ives: Lanham, 1941

Powys, John Cowper, *A Glastonbury Romance.* Harmondsworth: Penguin, 1999 [1932]

Prescott, Peter, *The Case of Cornish Methodism Considered; The Missing Lynch-Pin.* London: A. Osbourne, 1871

Probert, John C. C., *The Sociology of Cornish Methodism.* Truro: Cornwall Methodist Historical Association, 1971

    'The Decline of Methodism: A Discussion Paper'. In: *Journal of the Cornish Methodist Historical Association,* No.3, 1979

    'Dowran Chapel'. In: *Journal of the Cornish Methodist Historical Association,* No.5, 1995

    'Recruiting for the 1914-18 War and the 1851 Religious Census Etc'. In: *Journal of the Cornish Methodist Historical Association,* No.4, 2000

Quiller Couch, Arthur, *Hetty Wesley.* London: Harper and Brothers, 1903

    Sir John Constantine. London: Smith and Elder, 1906

    Nicky Nan: Reservist. London: William Blackwood and Sons, 1915.

    On the Art of Writing. Fowey: Fowey Rare Books, 1995 [1916]

    (ed.) *Cornish Tales by Charles Lee.* London: J.M.Dent, 1941

Rack, Henry D., *Reasonable Enthusiast: John Wesley and the Rise of Methodism.* London: Epworth Press, 1989

Raley, P. (ed.), *Samuel Butler: The Way of All Flesh.* London: Dent, 1993 [1903]

Rawe, Donald R., *A Prospect of Cornwall.* London: Robert Hale, 1986

Reis, Richard H., *George MacDonald.* New York: Twayne Publications, 1972

Rose, Jonathan, *The Intellectual Life of the British Working Classes.* New Haven and London: Yale University Press, 2001

Rowe, John, *Cornwall in the Age of the Industrial Revolution.* St Austell: Cornish Hillside Publications, 1993 [1953]

    The Hard Rock Men: Cornish Immigrants and the North American Mining Frontier. Liverpool: Liverpool University Press, 1974

    Changing Times and Fortunes: A Cornish Farmer's Life 1828-1904. St Austell: Cornish Hillside Publications, 1996

Rowse, A.L., *A Cornish Childhood.* Mount Hawke: Dyllansow Truran, 1998 [1942]

    The Cornish in America. Redruth: Dyllansow Truran, 1991 [1961]

St Stephen Methodist Church, *St. Stephen Methodist Church Centenary 1870-1970.* St Stephen-in-

Brannel: St Stephen-in-Brannel Methodist Church, 1970

Saunders, Tim (ed.), *The Wheel: An Anthology of Modern Poetry in Cornish 1850-1980*. London: Francis Boutle, 1999

Schwartz, Sharron P., 'No Place for a Woman: Gender at Work in Cornwall's Metalliferous Mining Industry'. In: Payton, Philip (ed.), 2000

Seaman, L.C.B., *Victorian England: Aspects of English and Imperial History 1837-1901*. London and New York: Routledge, 1973

Selleck, A. Douglas, *Cookworthy: A Man of No Common Clay*. Plymouth: Baron Jay Ltd, 1978

Semmel, Bernard, *The Methodist Revolution*. London: Heinemann, 1974

Sharrock, Roger (ed.), *John Bunyan: The Pilgrim's Progess*. Harmondsworth: Penguin, 1987

Shaw, Nellie, *A Colony on the Cotswolds*. London: C.W. Daniel, 1935

Shaw, Thomas, *Saint Petroc and John Wesley, Apostles in Cornwall: An Examination of the Celtic Background of Cornish Methodism*. Cornwall: Cornish Methodist Historical Association, 1962

The Bible Christians. London: Epworth Press, 1965

A History of Cornish Methodism. Truro: D. Bradford Barton, 1967

The Pastoral Crook: The State of Religion in the Diocese of Exeter in the Mid-Nineteenth Century. Cornwall: The Cornish Methodist Historical Association, 1970

Methodism at Fraddon 1819-1977. Fraddon: Fraddon Methodist Chapel, 1978

A Methodist Guide to Cornwall. London: Methodist Publishing House, 1991

Shirer, William L., *Love and Hatred: The Stormy Marriage of Leo and Sonya Tolstoy*. London: Aurum Press, 1994

Sinfield, Alan (ed.), *Society and Literature 1945-1970*. London: Methuen, 1983

Literature, Politics and Culture in Postwar Britain. Oxford: Blackwell, 1989

Smale, Courtney V., 'Cornwall's Premier Uranium and Radium Mine'. In: *Journal of the Royal Institution of Cornwall*, 1993

Straffon, Cheryl, *Pagan Cornwall: Land of the Goddess*. St Just-in-Penwith: Meyn Mamvro Publications, 1993

Symons, Andrew C., 'She, 'Er and 'Un: Study II in Language and History'. In: *An Baner Kernewek / The Cornish Banner*, No.94, 1998

'Jack Clemo's Italian Holiday'. In: *Journal of the Royal Institution of Cornwall*, 2000

Symons, Brenton, *Geology of Cornwall*. London: The Mining Journal, 1882

Taylor, Thomas, *The Celtic Christianity of Cornwall*. London: Longmans, Green and Company, 1916

Thacker, Joy, *Whiteway Colony: The Social History of a Tolstoyan Community*. Stroud: Joy Thacker, 1993

Thomas, Charles, *Methodism and Self-Improvement in Nineteenth-Century Cornwall*. Cornwall: Cornish Methodist Historical Association, 1965

'The Reflection of Methodism in Cornwall's Literature'. In: Foot, Sarah (ed.), 1988

"Let... us praise one another a bit': The Writing of Cornish Methodist History'. In: *Journal of the Cornish Methodist Historical Association*, No.5, 2001

Thomas, Charles and Mattingly, Joanna, *The History of Christianity in Cornwall AD 500 – 2000*. Truro: Royal Institution of Cornwall, 2000

Thomas, Chris 'See Your Own Country First: The Geography of a Railway'. In: Westland, Ella (ed.), 1997

Thomas D.M., *Birthstone*. London: Victor Gollancz, 1980

Selected Poems. Harmondsworth: Penguin, 1983

Thompson, E.V., *Chase the Wind*. London: Macmillan, 1977

Ben Retallick. London: Macmillan, 1977

Thorn, Caroline and Frank (eds.), *Domesday Book: Cornwall*. Chicester: Phillimore, 1979

Thorne, Roger F.S., *Hocking: Or the Tales of Two Brothers. A Catalogue of the Works of the Hockings (Joseph, Silas and Salome) in the collection of the late Michael E. Thorne*. Exeter: Heatherdene, 2000 [1978]

Thorpe, Lewis (ed. and tr.), *Geoffrey of Monmouth: The History of the Kings of Britain*. Harmondsworth: Penguin, 1966

Thurlow, Charles, *China Clay from Cornwall and Devon: The Modern China Clay Industry*. St Austell: Cornish Hillside Publications, 2001

Todd, A.C., *The Search for Silver: Cornish Miners in Mexico 1824-1947*, St Austell: Cornish Hillside Publications, 2000 [1977]

Tóibín, Colm, *The Irish Famine*. London: Profile Books, 1999

Tolstoy, Nikolai, *The Half-Mad Lord: Thomas Pitt, 2nd Baron, Camelford (1775 – 1804)*. London: Jonathan Cape, 1978

Tooby, Michael, *Tate St Ives: An Illustrated Companion*. London: Tate Gallery Publications, 1993

Toorians, Lauran (ed.), *The Middle Cornish Charter Endorsement: The Making of a Marriage in Medieval Cornwall*. Innsbruck: Institut für Sprachwissenschaft der Universität Innsbruck, 1991

Townsend, Michael, *Burnley*. Stroud: Tempus Publishing, 1999

Toy, H. Spencer, *The Methodist Church at Launceston*. Launceston: Wesley Methodist Church, 1964

Tregidga, Garry, *The Liberal Party in South-West Britain Since 1918: Political Decline, Dormancy and Rebirth*. Exeter: University of Exeter Press, 2000

Trelyon Consols, *Terras, Hallivick and Trelyon Mines*. Grampound Road: James and Company, n.d.

Trezise, Simon, *The West Country as a Literary Invention: Putting Fiction in its Place*. Exeter: University of Exeter Press, 2000

Van Reemen, Rybie (ed.), *Emily Hobhouse: Boer War Letters*. Capetown and Pretoria: Human and Rousseau, 1984

Vernon, James, 'Cornwall and the Engish Imagi(nation)'. In: Cubitt Geoffrey (ed.), 1998

Vickers, John A. (ed.), *A Dictionary of Methodism in Britain and Ireland*. London: Epworth Press, 2000

Vicinus,Martha, *The Industrial Muse: A Study of British Working Class Literature*. London: Croom Helm, 1974

Walke, Bernard, *Twenty Years at St Hilary*. London: Anthony Mott, 1982 [1935]

Walkowitz, Judith R., *Prostitution and Victorian Society*. Cambridge: Cambridge University Press, 1983

Warnes, Frank, 'The Christian Church in Cornwall'. In: Combellack-Harris, Myrna (ed.), 1989

Weatherhill, Craig, *Cornovia: Ancient Sites of Cornwall and Scilly*. Penzance: Alison Hodge, 1985
Cornish Place Names and Language. Wilmslow: Sigma, 1995

Westland, Ella, 'The Passionate Periphery: Cornwall and Romantic Fiction'. In: Bell, Ian A. (ed.), 1995

(ed.) *Cornwall: The Cultural Construction of Place*. Penzance: The Patten Press and the Institute of Cornish Studies, 1997

Whetter, James, *The Cornish Farmer*. Gorran: Lyfrow Trelyspen, 2001

Williams, Ian, *The Realist Novel in England: A Study in Development*. London and Basingstoke: Macmillan, 1974

Williams, Raymond, *The Long Revolution*. Harmondsworth: Penguin, 1961
The Country and the City. St. Albans: Paladin, 1975 [1973]

Wilson, A.N., *Tolstoy: A Biography*. New York: Norton, 1988

Wilson, Scott, *Cultural Materialism: Theory and Practice*. Oxford: Blackwell, 1995

Wright, David (ed.), *Thomas Hardy: Selected Poetry*. Harmondsworth: Penguin, 1978

Wright, W.H.K., *John Kitto, D.D., F.S.A.* Publisher unknown, n.d.

Unpublished Sources

Appleby, Cedric J., *The Hockings and the First World War*. Unpublished paper, 2001.

Luker, David, *Cornish Methodism, Revivalism, and Popular Belief, c.1780-1870*. Ph.D. Oxford: University of Oxford, 1987

Audio-Visual Sources

Film

Her Benny (5900) (U) 1920

British Film Institute Catalogue Number 06826

Diamond Super (Granger)

Producer: W.H. Baker

Director. A.V. Bramble

Source: (Novel) Silas K. Hocking

Screenplay: George Dewhurst

Sydney Wood ....Benny (child)
Babs Reynolds....................................Nellie Bates
Charles Buckmaster..........................Benny Bates
Peggy Patterson ....Eva Lawrence
C. Hargreave Mansell ....Joe Wragg
Lotie Blackford ....Mrs Wragg
Robert Vallis..Dick Bates
Anthony St John...Perks

Romance: Liverpool slum boy, blamed for theft, becomes farmer in Wales and saves life of childhood sweetheart.

Television

The Rebel Heiress: A Cornish adventure in six parts adapted by David Goddard from the book *Mistress Nancy Molesworth* by Joseph Hocking – Broadcast in 1958

Nancy Molesworth........................Mary Holland
Roger Trevanion.....................Patrick Troughton
Mr. Hendy ....John Kidd
Daniel..Richard Statman
Old Peter Trevisa. ....Derek Smee
Innkeeper ....David Oddie
Uncle Anthony ....Nigel Arkwright
Amelia Lanteglos ....Sheila Shand Gibbs
Benet Killigrew ....Colin Douglas
Clement Killigrew..............................Terry Baker
David Killigrew ....Alec Beegonzi
Colman Killigrew........................Lionel Marson
John Polperro................................Derek Waring
Sam Daddo ....John King

Other parts played by Claire Wyton, Denis Cleary, Michael Hutton, Anthony Wiles.

Fight director: Terry Baker

Film cameraman: John Turner

Film editor: Ton de Mattos

Designer: Fanny Taylor

Producer: David Goddard

Index

A

Advertiser, The 66
Ainsworth, Harrison 61
Alec Green: A Tale of Sea Life 66, 67, 68
Algiers 73
All for a Scrap of Paper: A Romance of the Great War 170, 171
All Men are Liars 107, 163
America, 41, 42, 48, 49, 66, 69, 72, 73, 76, 85, 118, 148, 155, 157, 158, 184, 196
Andrew Boconnoc's Will: The Story of a Crisis 172
Andrews, T.N. 59
And Shall Trelawney Die? 163
Angarrack, John 215
Anglican church 7, 17, 18, 20, 21, 27, 38, 62, 76, 102, 146, 147, 149, 154, 180, 199. 214, 215, 216
Anglo-Catholicism 7, 73, 111, 146, 168, 169, 211
Anglo-Cornish literature 11, 14, 23, 97, 127,143, 144, 181, 187, 203, 211, 212, 213
Anthony, Frederick 74
Anti-Catholicism 7, 12, 24, 82, 105, 106, 109, 120, 166, 167, 168, 169
Appleby, Cedric J. 144, 157, 170
Armenia 47
Arthuriana 16, 25
Arundell, Humphry 34
Asquith, Herbert 86
Atchinson, George 104
Atheism 21, 161
Austria 57

B

Ballantyne, R.M. 212
Band of Hope Union 60, 98
Baptists 62, 82
Beatles, The 9
Becquerel, Antoine Henri 44
Beginnings 135, 182
Belinda the Backward: A Romance of Modern Idealism 135, 186, 187
Bells of St Ia, The 188
Bennett, Arnold 213
Bennett, Tony 13, 73
Bernal 32, 33
Besant, Walter 76, 119
Better Treatment of Children Act 1889 65
Bevil Grenville's Handicap 172
Bevill, John 34
Bible Christians 18, 20, 39, 40, 46
  - Bible Christian Magazine 39, 40
  - Bryant, Catherine 21
  - Bryant, William 20
  - Chapel at Trelion 39, 40, 41, 60, 88, 217
  - Kinsman, William 39
  - Welsh, Henry 39
Bioscope 84
Birstall 100
Birthright, The 107, 163
Black Letter Pamphlet: News from Pe[n]rin in Cornwall, The 211
Blindness of Madge Tyndall, The 151
Boconnoc 33, 38, 192

Boer War 58, 74, 77, 78, 79, 80, 82, 196, 198
Bonnie Saxon, A 15, 77
Borlase, William C. 35
Bosanketh, Edward 70
Bottrell, William 69
Brace of Bigots, A 12
Brack, Alan 65
Bray, Billy 21, 40, 41, 60
Breton return 33, 51
British Weekly 101, 108
Brittany 24, 34
Broad Moor 38, 39, 44
Broken Fence, The 153
Brontë Emily 22, 57, 187
Broome, Douglas G. 57, 86
Brown [Hocking], Annie 73, 100, 102, 112, 119, 203
Brown, Ford Madox 132
Brown, H. Miles 215, 216
Brownies 49
Brown, Joseph 100, 203
Bunyan, John 22
Burnett, William 103
Burnley 66, 68, 69, 70, 71, 72, 82, 83, 88, 102, 160, 163
  - Brunswick Chapel 66, 67, 71, 102
  - St Mary's Church 103
Butler, Samuel 132

C

Caleb Carthew: A Life Story 151
California 41, 42, 154, 180, 181, 186
Calvinsim 32, 63
Camborne 69, 76, 79, 111
Campbell-Bannerman, Henry 86
Canada 49, 69, 72, 76, 83, 155
Canstatt 47
Carloggas 35, 153
Carter, Harry 212
Cartland, Barbara 213
Carvasso, William 21, 213
Catholicism 7, 8, 17, 20, 24, 32, 66, 105, 143, 166, 172, 216
Catholic Truth Society 12, 168
Celtic 23, 24, 34, 49, 62, 107, 171, 172, 173, 176, 185, 201, 202
  - Celticity 23, 49, 50, 88, 215, 216, 217
  - Celtic Revival 23, 49, 173, 201
  - church 34, 216, 217
Chariots of the Lord, The 167
Charter Endorsement 31, 32
Chips: A Story of Manchester Life 68, 206
Cholera 148
Christian anarchy 132, 133
Christian Perfection 17, 18
Christian rebellion 22, 104, 201
Christie, Agatha 203, 204
Christmas 87, 132, 206
Chronicles of a Quiet Family: A Temperance Story 129, 131, 182
City Temple 75, 82
Clemo, Eveline 198, 199, 203, 207, 213
Clemo, Jack 11, 21, 22, 23, 32, 51, 58, 63, 175, 180, 195, 196, 197, 198, 199, 200, 201, 202, 203, 207, 213
Clemo, Reginald 199

Cobb, James F. 212
Collins, Wilkie 61, 91
Columbia University 75
Combined University of Cornwall 25
Coming of the King, The 116
Confession of a Rebel 22, 195
Conquered Self, A 130, 183
Cookworthy, William 35
Cornish emigration 41, 42, 50, 77, 78, 155, 156
Cornish ethnicity and identity 20, 23, 109, 110, 139, 146, 149, 150, 154, 171, 176, 185, 186, 204, 213, 215
Cornish Gorseth 49, 111, 176, 218
Cornish industrialization 16, 37, 50, 58, 130, 143, 145, 156, 173, 215
Cornish language 24, 31, 34
Cornish literature 11, 31, 187
Cornish nationalism 24, 175, 176, 215
Cornish Revival 24, 49, 111, 154, 173, 201
Cornish Studies 25, 124
Cornu-English 16, 23, 24, 69, 109, 139, 149, 164, 183, 185
Coulsdon, Surrey 136, 137
Courtney, Elizabeth 33
Courtney, Leonard 78, 82
Crewe 76
Crooked Road, The 57
Croydon Brotherhood Church 134
Cullompton 33
Cultural Materialism 32
Cultural studies 13, 14
Curie, Marie Sklodowska, and Pierre 44
Curtain of Fire, The 170

D

Dalton, Anne 9, 206, 207
Davey's Ambition 112, 113, 206
Davies, Rupert E. 17
Dawe, Richard 77
Deacon, Bernard 24, 37
Death Among the Tulips 204
Death in the Cup, The 205
de Cornubia, Walter 33
Del Val, Cardinal Merry 169
Dent, Joseph Malaby 105
Desperate Hope, A 151, 152
de Valletort, Joan 33
Diamond Super Film Company 84
Dickens, Charles 14, 57, 119
Dictionary of National Biography 7, 48
Domesday Book 32
Dorey, Michael 99, 100, 114, 115
Dowran Chapel 26, 198
Doyle, Arthur Conan 73, 74, 115
Drew, Samuel 21
du Maurier, Daphne 11, 137, 187, 204
Dunnerdale, John 98, 99, 115, 116

E

Edgcumbe, Piers 33
Edward I 33
Edward III, 35
Eliot, George 57, 187
Elrad the Hic 101, 160
England 68, 69, 98, 100, 116, 130, 146, 149, 154, 166, 175, 176, 183, 186, 211

English studies 13, 69, 116, 187
Enlightenment, The 17, 21, 22, 111, 146, 212, 213
Eternal Challenge, The 102, 120, 169
Eternal Choice, The 112,
Ethical fiction 14, 90, 118, 215
Existentialism 18

F
Fal, River 32, 34, 35, 37, 41, 44, 128, 136, 217
Family Circle 75
Farming 37, 38, 44, 48, 50, 97, 100, 128, 130, 139, 151
Felicity Treverbyn: A Love Story 172
Ferrel's Van 48, 184, 185
Fifield, Arthur C. 12, 76, 128, 130, 131,132, 133, 134, 136, 137, 138, 139
First World War 8, 12, 21, 22, 57, 74, 80, 83, 84, 102, 109, 111, 134, 137, 157, 159, 166, 169, 170, 171, 172, 173, 198, 212, 216
Fisherman's Children, The 99
Flamank, William 21
Flame of Fire: Being the History of the Adventures of Three Englishmen at the Time of the Great Armada, A 166
Follow the Gleam: A Tale of the Time of Oliver Cromwell 107, 108, 164
Forfar, W. B. 16, 69
For Such is Life 151
Fortescue family 33, 38, 197
Fortunes of Riverside or Waiting and Winning, The 129, 182
Fowey 11, 109
Foxhole 38
France 57, 73
Frederick Warne and Company 67, 68
From London to Damascus 101, 160

G
Garstin, Crosbie 111
General Elections
 - 1900 78, 79
 - 1906 80
 - 1910 80
Gentleman's Magazine 14
George, David Lloyd 76, 78
Germany 47, 73, 85, 166, 170, 171, 172
Gideon Strong: Plebeian 101, 160
God and Mammon 169
Golding, William 11
Goonamarris 11, 195
Grampound 60,
Grampound Road 39, 45
Granny's Hero: A Tale of Country Life 129, 182
Great Britain 16, 32, 57, 58, 83
Greater Love: A Cornish Romance 163
Great Exhibition, The 58
Great Western Railway 45, 156
Grenville, Lady Ann 33
Gwennap 21, 37, 47, 48, 102
Gwindra 33, 35
Gypsies 46, 59

H
Hale, Amy 23
Hampton, 'Foolish Dick' 21
Hardy, Dennis 133
Hardy, Thomas 57, 115
Harman, Leonard W. 4, 12, 120

Harris, John 11, 212
Harry Penhale: The Trial of his Faith 101, 160
Harry Potter 57
Hawkins family 34
Heart of Man, The 75
Helston 76, 79, 82
Henry II, 35
Henry III 33, 35
Henry VII 34
Hensbarrow Downs 34, 61
Her Benny 7, 9, 57, 64, 68, 69, 72, 75, 89, 146, 163, 206
 - film 84, 85, 120
 - musical adaptation 9, 10, 206, 207
Hetty Wesley 212
His Father or A Mother's Legacy 68
His Own Accuser 157
Historical romance 97, 160
Hobhouse, Emily 78
Hoblyn family 52,
Hocking, Anne 12, 37, 46, 47, 102, 109, 202, 203, 204, 205
Hocking, Arthur Vivian 66, 83, 170
Hocking, Cuthbert 102, 103, 170
Hocking family cottage 36, 217
Hocking, F.D.M. 205
Hocking, Jabez 39, 41, 42, 49
Hocking, James 7, 31, 36, 37, 38, 39, 40, 41, 42, 46, 47, 60, 62, 63, 67, 88, 128, 138, 153, 195, 196, 197, 217
Hocking, Joseph 7, 9, 11, 12, 16, 19, 20, 21, 22, 23, 24, 25, 31, 36, 37, 38, 40, 42, 45, 66, 71, 80, 82, 83, 96, 97, 98, 99, 100, 101, 102, 103, 104, 105, 106, 107, 108, 109, 110, 111, 112, 113, 114, 115, 116, 117, 118, 119, 120, 136, 188, 196, 203, 207, 211, 216
 - birth 39, 97
 - children 83, 102, 103
 - death 112, 114, 119
 - education 71, 97, 98, 100
 - Hayle 111, 139, 199
 - humour 109
 - illness 111, 112
 - literature 160, 161, 162, 163, 164, 165, 166, 167, 168, 169, 170, 171, 172, 173, 174, 175, 176, 177, 178, 206
 - marriage 100
 - ministry 72, 100, 120
 - Perranporth 111, 112
 - resignation from the ministry 20, 90, 109
 - St Ives 111, 112
 - schoolfriends 97
 - surveying 99, 100
 - Thornton Heath 100, 130, 136, 203
 - travel 100, 109
 - views on novels 105, 116, 117
 - views on recruitment and war 12, 169, 170, 171, 172
 - Will 123
Hocking, Mahala Mary 39, 49, 50
Hocking [Fifield], Salome 7, 9, 11, 12, 19, 20, 21, 22, 23, 24, 25, 36, 37, 38, 40, 45, 48, 71, 76, 100, 120, 126, 127, 128, 129, 130, 131, 132, 133, 134, 135, 136, 137, 138, 139, 196, 203, 207, 211, 214, 217
 - birth 39, 127
 - death 137, 141
 - disability and illness 128, 136, 141

 - idealism 21, 127, 130, 135
 - literature 178, 179, 180, 181, 182, 183, 184, 185, 186, 187
 - marriage 126, 132
 - Will 137
Hocking, Samuel 196
Hocking, Silas Kitto 7, 9, 11, 12, 15, 16, 19, 20, 21, 22, 23, 24, 25, 31, 36, 38, 42, 45, 46, 50, 56, 57, 58, 59, 60, 61, 62, 63, 64, 65, 66, 67, 68, 69, 70, 71, 72, 73, 74, 75, 76, 77, 78, 79, 80, 81, 82, 83, 84, 85, 86, 87, 88, 89, 90, 100, 135, 136, 145, 195, 196, 203, 204, 206, 207, 214, 217
 - birth 39, 57
 - children 58, 66, 72, 83
 - crisis of faith 83, 214
 - death 87
 - doctrine 60, 62, 63, 83
 - education 59, 60, 61
 - Highgate, London 74, 79
 - literature 144, 145, 146, 147, 148, 149, 150, 151, 152, 153, 154, 156, 157, 158, 159, 206
 - marriage 66
 - ministry 57, 61, 62, 64, 65, 66, 71, 72, 76, 83, 120
 - pacifist career 57, 83, 157
 - political career 57, 77, 78
 - recreation 82, 87, 95, 197
 - resignation from the ministry 12, 20, 58, 72, 73, 74
 - travel 60
 - Will 87, 95
Hocking, Simeon 39, 41, 49
Hocking, Thirza 39, 50
Hocking, Thomas 36, 196
Holbeach 64
Holmes, Sherlock 73, 74
Horner's Penny Stories 14, 15
Horton, R.F. 12, 168, 169
Hound of the Baskervilles, The 74
Hungary 57
Hunt, Robert 69
Hurling 24

I
Ill Deeds Done 205
In Memoriam 128, 137
In Spite of Fate 74
In the Sweat of Thy Brow 11
Invading Gospel: A Return to Faith, The 22
I Proved Thee at the Waters: The Testimony of a Blind Writer's Mother 198, 199
Ireland 24, 167, 168, 176
Ishmael Pengelly: An Outcast 116, 163
Isles of Scilly 158
Italy 73, 85
Ivy: A Tale of Cottage Life 68, 70, 147, 148

J
Jabez Easterbrook 101, 102, 160, 163
Jacky: A Story of Everyday Life 129, 181, 182
Jacobite Rebellion 20, 165
Jacobs, W.W. 75, 105
Jameson, Leander Starr 78
Jenner, Henry 25, 31, 123
Jesuits 105, 168

Index

Jesuit, The 169
Judaism 20, 46, 66, 127

K

Kailyard School 63
Kaiser, The 83, 171
Kaiser's Investments, The 170
Kent, Alan M. 3, 7, 13, 16, 175
Kinematograph 85
Kingsley, Charles 75
Kitto, Benedict 44
Kitto [Hocking], Eliza 37, 38, 39, 40, 45, 46, 47, 48, 49, 50, 63, 128, 130, 138, 196, 204
 - charming 46, 48, 49
 - healing powers 46, 48, 49
 - Pole-Carew connection 46, 130, 183
 - Spanish and Gypsy connection 37, 46, 48
 - storytelling skills 49, 98
Kitto Jr., John 47, 73, 80
 - John Kitto School 48
Kitto Sr., John 47

L

Lancashire 69
Lancashire Idylls 69
Lawrence, D.H. 114, 115, 118
League of Nations, The 58, 85
Lee, Charles 212
Lest We Forget 107
Liberal Party, The 12, 24, 76, 78, 79, 86, 111, 114, 146, 167, 213
Liskeard 78, 82
Literacy 14, 16, 101
Liverpool 7, 9, 10, 23, 64, 65, 66, 71, 72, 82, 88, 146, 206, 207
 - Docks 9, 64, 66, 146, 147, 206
 - Empire Theatre 9, 10, 206
 - Grove Street Methodist Church 65, 66
 - slums 65
 - Russell Street Church 65, 206
 - Wellington Road Chapel 65
Lloyd, Esther Mary 66
Lloyd, Richard 65, 66
London 48, 58, 74, 76, 88, 100, 110, 112, 187, 203
Looking Back 58
Lost Lode, The 155
Lost Senses, The 47
Lubbock, Sir John 16
Luker, David 19
Luther, Martin 17, 166
Luxulyan 20
Lyall, David 83, 98
Lytton, Bulworth 61

M

MacDonald, George 62, 63
Madness of David Baring, The 164
Magazines: Christian, Monthly and Weekly 14, 15, 101, 106, 107, 108, 120, 127, 131, 136
Maker, Lawrence 18
Malta 47, 73
Manchester 23, 70, 71, 72, 82, 88, 100, 160
 - Owens College 100
 - United Methodist Free Churches College 71, 72, 100
Man Who Almost Lost, The 173

Man Who Found Out, The 108, 173
Man Who Rose Again, The 108, 173
Man Who was Sure, The 173, 174
Materialism 21, 151, 186
Mather, J. Marshall 69
Matthews, Amos B. 60, 88
Mattingly, Joanna 20
McGough, Roger 9
Meadowsweet and Rue 79, 80, 144
Mediterranean Murder 202
Meledor 33, 34, 36, 201
 - John Melledor 34
Methodism 7, 8, 12, 16, 17, 18, 19, 21, 22, 24, 27, 32, 35, 39, 40, 50, 62, 71, 72, 90, 98, 110, 111, 119, 127, 129, 138, 143, 146, 148, 149, 150, 158, 175, 176, 177, 180, 184, 211, 212, 213, 215, 216, 217
 - Archaeological Survey 19, 120
 - Chapels 16, 18, 21, 22, 35, 40, 50, 64, 120, 215, 217
 - Cornish Methodism 16, 18, 19, 143, 211, 212, 214
 - Cornish Methodist Historical Association 19
 - myth 20, 21, 161, 212, 213
 - Preachers 21, 40, 103
 - Primitive 175
 - Revolution 19, 143
 - United Methodist Free Churches 7, 12, 20, 39, 61, 62, 68, 69, 71, 72, 73, 76, 87, 103, 104, 112, 114, 130, 175, 211
 - Wesleyans 7, 40, 94, 103, 112, 175, 214
Methodist Magazines 66, 88, 116, 127, 132
Million copies 7, 57, 68, 90
Mining
 - Cap'ns 28, 37, 49, 60, 128, 178, 180, 181, 182, 183
 - china clay 9, 32, 35, 36, 153, 197, 201
 - iron 44
 - tin 31, 34, 35, 37, 41, 42, 43, 44, 49, 58, 128, 130, 177, 178, 180, 217
 - radium 44, 45
 - uranium 44, 45
Mining Journal 41, 42, 43
Mining World 44, 45
Mistress Nancy Molesworth 107, 164, 165
 - television adaptation 120
Modern Pharisee, A 75
Monk of Mar-Saba, The 116, 163
Moody and Sankey 66
Moore, F. Frankfurt 212
Moravian Pietis Community 17
Mortain, Robert of 33
My Book of Memory 7, 12, 58, 60, 62, 73, 76, 97, 201

N

Nancy 84
Nancy Trevanion's Legacy 172
Napoleonic Wars 16
National Council of Evangelical Free Churches 76
Newman, John Henry 8
Newport Circuit 62
Newquay 11, 156
Nicky Nan: Reservist 212

Nonconformity 18, 19, 20, 22, 23, 50, 62, 67, 73, 82, 90, 129, 131, 143, 146, 147, 152, 154, 159, 162, 166, 180, 184, 186, 200, 201, 213, 215, 216
No Other Name 112
Norah Lang: The Mine Girl 129, 130, 178, 179, 180, 181
Norman Conquest 33, 51
Northern Ireland 24, 29
Norway 73
Not One in Ten 112, 174, 175

O

Oberammergau 11
O'er Moor and Fen: A Tale of Methodist Life in Lancashire 163
Olver, T.J. 32, 35, 38
Ordinalia 11, 24
Owen, Daniel 51
Oxford Movement 8

P

Padel, Oliver 34
Paganism 20, 24, 46, 201, 216
Paraliterature 14
Parkin, Mary 36, 196
Paul, Stanley 80
Payne, H.M. Cresswell 13, 49, 105, 122, 143
Payton, Philip 23, 24, 154, 155
Pearce, John 18
Pearse, Mark Guy 21, 42, 69, 111, 129, 204
Pellowe, Susan 19
Pensweeta manuscript 137
Penvose Quay 37
Persia 47
Philanthropists 86
Phillipps, K.C. 4, 13, 97, 120, 165, 212
Pictorial Bible 47
Pictorial History of Palestine and the Holy Land 47
Pitt family 33, 38, 53
Pittock, Murray G.H. 23
Plantagenet, Elizabeth 33
Plymouth 35, 45, 47, 48, 60, 99, 114
Poldark 11, 175
Pomp of Yesterday, The 170
Pontypool 62, 80, 88
Poor Mike: The Story of a Waif 68
Popular literature 7, 8, 13, 14, 16, 17, 22, 97, 115, 146, 187
Poverty 64, 65, 68, 100, 146, 147, 154
Powys brothers 22
Prayer Book Rebellion 34
Prescott, Peter 18
Probert, John C.C. 3, 7, 8, 18, 19, 214
Prostitution 65, 71, 72
Protestantism 16, 17, 18, 24, 63, 66, 69, 89, 109, 115, 118, 120, 143, 160, 163, 164, 166, 167, 169, 176, 186, 187, 214, 216
Proto-industrialization 37
Pulp Methodism 7, 11, 14, 17, 18, 20, 32, 66, 97, 104, 116, 119, 130, 136, 158, 163, 184, 187, 198, 199, 200, 211, 212, 213, 214, 215, 216, 217

Q

Quakers 78, 86, 102
Quethiock, Quintrell 11, 12, 23, 25
Quiller Couch, Arthur 70, 78, 94, 116, 164, 190, 202, 204, 212, 213, 218

R

Rack, Henry D. 17
Rationalism 214, 217
Reedyford or Creed and Character 68
Reformation, The 17, 18, 21, 151, 162, 165, 215
Religious merger in Cornwall 21
Rescrowsa 35
Resugga Castle 35, 36
Rhodes, Cecil 78
Richard, Earl of Cornwall 33
Riddel, Betty 86
Ritzoom, Father Anthony 106
Roche Rock, 165
Roger Trevanion 164
Rolph, C. H. 16
Romance 16, 23, 130
Romance of Michael Trevail, The 163
Romanticism 111
Rome 8, 107, 169
Rosaleen O'Hara 167
Rosogan family 34
Rowe, John 19, 37
Rowse, A.L. 154, 155
Royal Literary Society 75
Rugby 24
Russia 57, 132, 133, 187

S

St Agnes 37, 47
St Austell 41, 60, 61, 98, 99, 139, 184
St Columb Major 61
St Dennis 33
St Erme 34
St Gwynifer 157
St Ive 78
St Ives [St Ia] 112, 158, 171, 176, 188
St Mawes 37, 47, 48, 204
St Stephen-in-Brannel 9, 12, 31, 32, 33, 34, 35, 36, 37, 38, 39, 40, 41, 42, 43, 44, 45, 46, 47, 48, 49, 50, 58, 60, 80, 97, 98, 114, 119, 130, 131, 136, 139, 149, 178, 182, 183, 184, 185, 186, 196, 197, 213
- church 31, 34, 35, 36
- Dabryn Way 139
- Fifield House 139
- Methodist church 35, 39, 98, 130, 196
- Parish 33, 34, 58
- place-name 33, 34
Saltash 33
Sandford, Christopher G. 10
Scarlet Woman, The 105, 106, 164, 169
Scott, Walter 60, 91, 99, 121
Sea 16, 59, 67, 129, 130, 147, 149, 185
Sea-Waif: A Tale of the Cornish Cliffs 68, 148, 149
Second Lord Camelford, The 33
Second World War 45, 85, 120, 204
Secret of Trescobell, The 206
Secret of Upland Farm, The 83, 98
Secularization 18, 22, 97, 120, 151
Seekers, The 111
Segregation camps 83, 170
Semmel, Bernard 19, 143
Shakespeare, William 28, 60, 148
Shall Rome Reconquer England? 169
Shaw, George Bernard 75, 118, 131
Shaw, Thomas 18, 19, 39
Sign of the Triangle, The 107, 176
Sir John Constantine 164, 212

Smale, Courtney V. 38, 44, 45
Smith, George 21
Smuggling 16, 24, 59, 159
Socialism 21, 127, 131, 136, 178, 186
Some Old Cornish Folk 48, 136, 183, 184, 185, 186, 211
Soul of Dominic Wildthorne, The 108, 168
South Africa 77, 78, 79, 83, 148, 177, 186, 204
Southport 12, 72, 73, 74, 76, 82, 88, 130
- Duke Street Methodist Church 72
Spalding 64, 80, 88
Spirit of the West, The 107
Spiritualism 115
Squire, John 46
Stannary Courts 34
Story of Andrew Fairfax, The 116, 163
Stowe, Harriet Beecher 99, 118, 121
Strange Adventures of Israel Pendray, The 158,159
Sunday School 12, 21, 50, 71, 98, 99, 102
Switzerland 73, 74
Sword and Cross 79
Sword of the Lord, The 165
Symons, Andrew C. 98, 208
Symons, Brenton 43

T

Tales of a Tin Mine 151
Tanner family 33
Taylor, Thomas 216
Telford, Rev. S. 136
Temperance 21, 60, 61, 129, 178, 182
Temple magazine 74, 86
Tenant of Cromlech Cottage, The 171, 172
Terras 7, 31, 32, 33, 34, 35, 36, 37, 38, 39, 40, 41, 42, 43, 44, 45, 46, 47, 48, 49, 50, 58, 60, 97, 99, 130, 178, 195, 217
- New Terras Tin Mining Company Ltd 43, 44
- South Terras Mine 39, 44, 45, 217
- Terras Open Workings Tin Company Ltd 41
- Terras Tin Mining Company 39, 43, 177
Testament 195, 200, 201
Thacker, Joy 133
Theatre-going 31
Theosophy 115
Thomas, Charles 18, 19, 123, 192
Thomas, D.M. 212
Thorne, Michael E. 4, 13
Thorne, Roger 13, 168
'Three-life' system 37, 38, 39, 50, 68
Thurlow, Charles 36
Tolstoyan Land Schemes 38, 127, 133, 134, 135, 186, 187
Tolstoy, Lev Nikoaevich 132, 133
Tommy: A War Story 170
Too Many Cousins 57
Transvaal 77, 78
Tregarthan family 33
Tregeagle's Head: A Romance of the Cornish Cliffs 150
Tregellas, John Tabois 16, 69
Tregony 37, 39
Trelion 31, 32, 33, 34, 35, 36, 37, 38, 39, 40, 41, 42, 43, 44, 45, 46, 47, 48, 49,

50, 58, 60, 130, 178, 217
Treneague, Little 37
Trenowth Collar 35, 38
Trenowth Woods 35, 36, 38, 136
Trevanion, William 33
Trudgian, Esther Ann 196, 199
Truscott, Norman 97, 99, 112
Twain, Mark 75

U

Uitlanders 77, 78
Ulster 24, 29
Unwin, T. Fisher 79
Up the Rhine and over the Alps 73
Utopian Communities 133, 134, 135

V

Vanity Fair 80, 81, 82, 83, 87, 169, 196
Veganism 186, 187
Vestamis, M.F. 135
Vickers, John A. 12
Victoria, Queen 65, 133, 175
Von Tirpitz, Admiral 83
Vyvyan, Charles 204

W

Wales 62, 64, 65, 116, 169, 176
Walke, Bernard 27
War of Five Peoples [English Civil War] 34, 162, 164, 166
Warne and Company, Frederick 68, 79
Watchers of the Dawn 85
Weapons of Mystery, The 163
Weatherhill, Craig 33, 35
Wesley, Charles 17, 21, 117
Wesley, John 17, 20, 21, 39, 40, 41, 158, 159, 163, 171, 195
- Journal 40
- travel 17, 39, 40, 41
What Shall it Profit a Man? 44, 177, 178
Wheal Martyn China Clay Museum 26
Where Duty Lies 151
Whitefield, George 17
Whiteway Community 133, 134, 136, 186, 187
Who Shall Judge? 157
Wilding Graft 180
William I 35
Williams, Raymond 144, 145
Wilson, Woodrow 85
Withington, Revered J.S. 68
Woman of Babylon, The 167
Women's Rights 71, 72, 78, 127, 129, 131, 132, 133, 134, 137, 181
Woodford Green Chapel, Essex 103, 104, 105, 109, 116
Woolf, Virginia 118, 187
Working Classes 16, 17, 24, 151
Wrecking 16, 24, 98, 217
Wrestling 24, 164

Y

Yelland, Richard 35
Young Man's Christian Association 48, 83

Z

Zennor 114, 164,
Zillah 169